IMAGINE THIS

Julia Baird

IMAGINE THIS

growing up with my brother
JOHN LENNON

HODDER &
STOUGHTON

Copyright © 2007 by Julia Baird

First published in Great Britain in 2007 by Hodder & Stoughton
A division of Hodder Headline

This paperback edition published in 2007

The right of Julia Baird to be identified as the Author
of the Work has been asserted by her in accordance with the
Copyright, Designs and Patents Act 1988.

A Hodder paperback

8

A CIP catalogue record for this title is
available from the British Library

ISBN 978 0 340 83925 6

Typeset in Monotype Sabon by Hewer Text UK Ltd, Edinburgh
Printed and bound in the UK by CPI Group (UK) Ltd, Croydon, CR0 4YY

Hodder Headline's policy is to use papers that are natural,
renewable and recyclable products and made from wood grown in
sustainable forests. The logging and manufacturing processes are expected
to conform to the environmental regulations of the country of origin.

Hodder & Stoughton Ltd
A division of Hodder Headline
338 Euston Road
London NW1 3BH

A healer is called to a woman who is considered 'off her head, out of her mind'. 'So I say, "Sweetheart, what's the matter?" and she says, "my mama died and I feel so bad. I can't go on – dah, dah, dah."

'Her mama died – she's SUPPOSED to feel bad . . . expect to feel good when ya mama's gone? Climbed right into my lap, two hundred pounds of grief.'

From *The Salt Eaters* by Toni Bambara

John was still climbing. I am still climbing. My sister is still climbing.

'I lost my mother twice. Once as a child of five and then again at seventeen. It made me very, very bitter inside. I had just begun to establish a relationship with her when she was killed. We'd caught up on so much in just a few short years. We could communicate. We got on.'

John Lennon

To my wonderful Mother, who instilled in me the deep love and spiritual strength in the short time I had with her, which have let me go on.

Acknowledgements

Many thanks to Rowena Webb and to all at Hodder, for their ready acknowledgement of my story – following on from Cynthia's story – enabling us to recall as full a history of John as we could. To Helen Coyle for fielding my constant final amendments with such good grace and to Celia Quantrill for a final read through, checking for dates and times. But most especially, I wish to thank Caro Handley for her sound advice, and her excellent organisation and overview, which I could never have managed on my own.

Thank you to Paul Wane of Tracks, for allowing me to use the four photographs depicting John on his Isle of Man school trip.

I am extremely grateful to John's fellow Quarry Men, who were happy to talk to me about their time with John: Rod Davis, Colin Hanton, Nigel (Chris) Walley, Len Garry. Sadly, I missed speaking to Eric Griffiths, who has recently passed away. Also to the wider diaspora, tracked down in the early stages of writing the book, who were absolutely vital in tracing John's childhood, adolescence and young adulthood. I wish to express my profound gratitude to David Ashton, Michael Hill and Tim Holmes.

Thank you to Michael Fishwick, for his courageous decision to confess his four-year secret affair with Mimi, during the time John was living at Mendips. This has given me an insight into Mimi and opened up an understanding I had thought no longer possible. I am extremely grateful to him for his disclosure, which explained so much, including my troubled relationship with Mimi.

A warm and loving thank you to the Starkey family from across the road in Springwood. To Hannah, who died some years ago and who had become a lifeline to my mother. And to Hannah's daughters, Pat, Rita, Ann and Clare, who reinforced what I already knew: that John had been torn away, not given away. Thank you all.

I wish to convey warm thanks to Arthur Pemberton, who taught John the basics of the harmonica, and to his wife Mary, for talking with me about our lives as near-neighbours and their friendship with my parents.

Thank you to my friends Ray, Shirley, Margaret, Geoff, Martine, and Dick and Wendy in Ireland, for listening to me throughout. Don't stop now, please!

Thank you to Cynthia and Julian for your ongoing support and encouragement.

Many thanks to Stan and Jan for all their encouragement and support, including photographs from Stan's portfolio, most of which he took himself.

I want to thank Roger for all his home support, whilst I have been in the throes of agonising and writing.

My love and thanks to Jackie for being Jackie.

And last, but top of my list, I wish to thank my lovely children – Nicolas, Sara and David – for tolerating yet another book about the Uncle they never met, but who has always been in their lives. Thank you, my loves. Bear with me. I had to do this.

Picture Acknowledgements

Most of the photographs reproduced on the insert pages 1-16, are from the author's collection. Additional sources: Courtesy of Paul Wane of www.tracks.co.uk, pages 4, 5. With thanks to Tim Holmes, 6 bottom. Charles Roberts, 12 top.

Every reasonable effort has been made to contact the copyright holders, but if there are any errors or omissions, Hodder & Stoughton will be pleased to insert the appropriate acknowledgement in any subsequent printing of this publication.

Contents

Contents

Contents

Foreword

Writing a story is a well-tried way of making sense of your life, attempting to give it shape and meaning. The putting of pen to paper, the committing of invisible thoughts to readable words, allows us both to perceive our world boldly and to give form to our place in that world. This book is my attempt to make sense of my own life and that of my half-brother, John.

All families have secret stories and most spend their lives trying to keep them hidden, even from each other. In our family, however, our hidden histories have been hung up across the giant screen of the sky, inviting inspection and criticism from all and sundry and dissection from the Beatle experts and the John experts. We just had to let them get on with it, knowing that much of it was wrong. In fact so much that is inaccurate has been written about John and our family that sometimes I have to remind myself of the basic truths.

First among these is that there were four of us who shared the same mother: John, me, our sister Jackie and our other sister, Victoria, the baby our mother was forced to give up and who grew up as Ingrid, unknown to us for many years. Our mother was an extraordinary, vibrant and loving woman who adored all her children. Yet over the years she has been vilified, portrayed as a feckless woman who gave one child up for adoption and then handed her son to her older sister to raise, rather than care for him herself.

These myths were accepted and confirmed, first by some members of our family (even if only by not denouncing them as they began to spread), and then by the world at large.

Our mother never had a chance to speak for herself. She went, one evening in 1958, to visit John at her sister Mimi's house. She left a few hours later to catch the bus home. As she was crossing the road, she was knocked down by a car. A very short distance away, Jackie and I were in bed, asleep. John, who had left Mimi's ahead of our mother to come to our house, was downstairs talking to my father, waiting for Mummy to come home. That ordinary group of people, doing ordinary things, were unaware that Mummy had died. That the world as they knew it had been hurled into a black night.

John was seventeen, I was eleven and Jackie was eight years old. All three of us were devastated. The impact on our lives is endless. It went on for John until he died, and for me and Jackie it still continues. For some reason, we girls were sent away, away from the truth. The lack of a funeral has meant a life of grief-in-waiting; a life that wears you out, where only a part of you is awake as you drag the past into your present, seeing everything through searching eyes, whether you are conscious of it or not.

While John threw himself into alcohol, music and cynicism, Jackie and I became a 'problem' to the family. What to do with two small vulnerable, needy girls who had lost their mother? Where were we going to live? Who would pay for us? Our mother's sisters didn't want us, they took us in reluctantly, making us wards of court, virtually excluding our father from our lives and continually reminding us that we did 'not belong in this family'.

But my family couldn't wipe my mother from my existence, though her sisters gave it their best shot. Despite what happened I still have a relationship with my mother, and I always will have. This is how I make sense of my world. For John, too, I know this was the truth. The last conversations I had with him were about Mummy, our memories of her, our love for her.

So, here I am, trying to make sense of it all, make sense of John's life and of my own. I am still readjusting the picture, laying ghosts and making a pathway along which to move on.

In this I was helped greatly by my mother's older sister Anne – known to the family as Nanny. She was the last of the five sisters to die, in 1997, and in her last years I spent a lot of time with her.

In her final months, after years of stonewalling from all the sisters, Nanny suddenly wanted to talk. In fact, I couldn't stop her. She had always been the family chronicler, never forgetting birthdays, and in the closing days of her life she was a river in full spate. I sat by her side, or at her feet, as she relived her childhood, her adolescence, her young adulthood, her marriage, her life, with and without her sisters. She talked of my mother, Julia, of the secret baby, given up for adoption, and of Mimi, the older sister who took John away from Julia so that she could bring him up as her own child, the child she never had.

I listened with my whole being, scared of missing some morsel. Over the years I had heard snippets of most of what she was saying, but this was the book, being read to me, as she gazed out through the big bay window towards the weeping willow in her garden. Often oblivious to my presence, Nanny talked on, and I was finally able to unravel the bits of information I knew and weave them back together to make sense of the story that gave birth to Jackie and me and to our brother.

This memoir of our childhood is the result. I have worked from conversations with people who were there at the time, from memories, from painstaking research and from emotion.

1: *Reflecting Mummy*

I must be about seven years old. I am sitting astride my mother's bony hips, with my arms wrapped tightly around her neck, and her arms clench my waist, wrapping me tight, tight. Our faces are pressed together, cheek to cheek. We are smiling at one another in the mirror. Every now and then, my mother has to tug me up, to stop me sliding to the floor. We are holding our faces together. I can feel the warmth, skin on skin, and a tingling sensation. She is singing to me. I must have heard words then, but no matter how hard I try, they evade me now. I can feel the sound as la-la and hmm, hmm. I can feel my mother, I can smell her. She is mine, for this time. For too short a time. Mine.

I am so happy. It is one of those special spaces in your life when you know and understand reality, while knowing and understanding nothing. I want to stay in that place. I want it to be a bottomless chasm, where I can go on and on falling but not falling apart.

I can still call my mother to me. Sometimes, I dream her. When I do, I don't want to miss anything, not a nuance, not a smile, not a squeeze. I try not to rush it, although I am in a hurry to be there, in the kitchen, looking into the mirror which hangs on a nail, over the sink, in the middle of the long window with the small panes. A window with blue frames and with blue gingham curtains on a wire. We can see the garden, trees blowing in the wind, and sometimes a bird will fly past, which makes us smile. The gas rings are burning on the cooker, keeping the kitchen warm. The sights, smells and sounds mingle with Mummy's. I am breathing my Mummy. It is hauntingly, almost painfully beautiful and then unfailingly, heartbreakingly sad. She fades away, she just fades away. I can't feel the bones in her hips. My arms are holding air. I look and look into the magic mirror with intensity and despair as her cheeks melt away from mine. My lovely Mummy leaves me. My sanity and my insanity. Having her. Not having her. Loving her. Losing her.

Having my mother, loving her so deeply and then losing her has given me my most intense happiness and my most bereft sadness. Like any child who has lost a beloved parent while still very young, the happiness and sadness of her memory are inextricably linked.

When I had her, I wasn't aware that things could change. Like any child I was simply living life, as I had always known it. You don't know that life can be snuffed out in the blink of an eye, until it happens.

I was eleven years old when my world turned inside out; when my mother, after whom I was named, was killed when she was hit by a car on a July evening in 1958. From that moment on my sister and I became problems to be solved in a family that had little room or time for us. In a world empty of the one person we longed for most, we learned that we had little worth; once loved children, we became nuisances to be tolerated by aunts who saw it as a duty to look after us.

I am a middle child. My brother John was seventeen when our mother died, and my sister Jackie was eight. Even when I discovered the existence of another sister I was still a middle child because she was younger than John but older than me. Our mother called her Victoria Elizabeth for the six weeks that she had her, but she was taken away for adoption and grew up as Ingrid. She became one of our family's secrets. Discovering the secret of the other child, the child apart, triggers instability, no matter which child you are and no matter what your age and maturity. It raises feelings hitherto unknown – raw feelings – and leaves you dangling there. It challenges your ideas of who you are and even who you thought you were and who you might be tomorrow and why . . . just as the paint is drying on your self-image, again, a careless brush sweeps across it and makes a mess.

But all that was to come much later. I grew up knowing only that Jackie and I lived with our parents and that my older brother came to see us often and stayed as much as he could. John lived with my mother's older sister Mimi, and we lived in Springwood, Allerton, a suburb of Liverpool, in a three-bedroom house, on a council estate. When John stayed the night, Jackie slept with me in the double bed in my room. That's probably why I had it . . . I spent a lot of time sharing that bed.

We went to live in the Springwood house in 1949, when I was two and a half and not long before Jackie's birth. The story of how we ended up there, and how my mother ended up with two children who lived with her, one who lived there part-time and another who lived in another place completely, secretly, is the story of my mother's struggle against society and family. A tale full of anguish and fear, desperation and helplessness, but also great courage.

My mother's story, and ours, is also the story of the early life and background of the genius who was John Winston Lennon, who became John Ono Lennon, but who never stopped being just John, my big brother.

2: *Family Roots*

My mother was the fourth of five sisters born to a prosperous, middle-class couple, George and Annie Stanley. All five girls were born at the beginning of the twentieth century, in the shadow of Liverpool's Anglican Cathedral, which was then still under construction. My mother must have watched it grow.

In those days Liverpool was a thriving city. It boasted seven miles of dockland and was one of the busiest ports in the world, with a constant flow of cargo ships carrying grain and cotton from America and sugar from the West Indies. It was also home to the Cunard Steamship Company, with its shipyards just over the Mersey in Birkenhead at Cammell Laird, where the world's first ocean-going liners were built.

George Stanley, like so many other Liverpool men, went to sea. Born in 1874, he sailed around the world as a sail-maker on the tall ships. Eventually, when his daughters were still growing up, he tired of travelling and took a job as a crewman on a salvage tug, working for the London-Liverpool-Glasgow Tug Salvage Company and he settled his family in a flat in Berkeley Street.

My mother's family was Welsh. My great, great grandmother, Anne Roberts, who married William Morris, was from a Welsh-speaking, land-owning farming family in North Wales, and it was their daughter, Mary Elizabeth Morris, who first moved with her family, including George Stanley's future wife Annie, to Liverpool.

I am very proud to have Welsh ancestry and John felt the same. One of his ambitions was to have a farm in North Wales, and in 1975 he asked me to find him one, suggesting that Jackie and

4

I live there, while he would visit and use it as a bolt-hole. The plan never came to fruition, but John was very much aware of our Welsh roots. And as John's father, Alfred Lennon, was a full-blooded Irishman, John was a Celt through and through.

Our grandmother, Annie Jane Millward, was born in Chester and moved with her parents to Liverpool as a small girl in the late 19th century. A rich uncle had died, leaving a large sum of money to Mary Elizabeth, which she invested in several flats. These flats – there were at least five of them and probably as many as seven – were in the fine Georgian houses which surrounded the Anglican Cathedral, in the town centre. They were rented out, and the family lived in all of them periodically, as they became vacant.

After Annie grew up and married George Stanley they continued living in the various houses and flats. Each of her children – my mother and her sisters – was born in a different one. Today some of the houses have been demolished to make way for modern housing and some have been restored as part of Liverpool Housing Development.

George and Annie's first two children, Henry and Charlotte, both died in infancy and are buried in the original burial grounds at the side of the Anglican Cathedral. So it must have been a great comfort to them to produce five sturdy, healthy girls over the next ten years.

The first, Mary Elizabeth, known to her sisters as Mary but to all the subsequent children in the family as Mimi, was born in 1906. Next came Elizabeth Jane in 1908, known as Betty or Liz to her sisters and Mater to us. She was followed by Anne Georgina in 1911, Anne to her sisters and Nanny to us. Then there was my mother, Julia, born in 1914 and known sometimes as Judy to the children. Like me, my mother had no middle name. My father used to tell me that it was because the name Julia was unmatchable, and that was always good enough for me. My mother's younger sister, Harriet, was born in 1916 and also had only one name. She was the spoiled baby of the family and was called Har or Harriet by her sisters and Harrie by us.

Our grandfather, George Stanley, was known as Dada, the Welsh form of address, to his children when they were young, which changed to Pop when they grew up. Our grandmother, Annie Stanley, was known as Mama to her children and grandchildren. Pop was a straight-laced man, who demanded his own way. He had been brought up strictly and he continued in this Victorian tradition with his own family. He believed in hard work, good manners, best frocks on Sunday and church in the morning followed by Sunday school in the afternoon. When he left the sea, he expected shipshape order on dry land. It may have been fortunate that the children were born during his seafaring years, and it must have rocked the all-girl establishment when he returned home.

I never met Mama, who died before I was born, but all the sisters spoke of her with absolute adoration. When we were younger, Mama was the one we heard about. Pop was merely a gruff, background figure who was away at sea and who changed things for the worse when he came ashore for good.

When I asked my cousin Stanley, Mater's son, about Pop, however, he had an altogether kinder story to tell. He remembers being taken, with John, on tours of the docks and long walks on the promenades. Pop may have been a distant and rather harsh father, but he had good relationships with his grandsons, who both called him Dada.

My parents lived with Pop until he died, when I was two and a half, so we knew one another a little. My clearest memory of him is when he swung me upside down over the kitchen sink while my mother hit the back of my neck to dislodge a fishbone.

Our great-grandmother, Mary Elizabeth Millward, née Morris, was by all accounts a determined woman. When one of her daughters married a Roman Catholic, Mary Elizabeth disowned her and her children, sticking a black band on her front door, as if to mourn her death. This daughter and her family emigrated to New Zealand and eventually her brother, George Millward, who was in the Navy, took a commission that would take him to New Zealand so that he could see his long-lost sister. He loved the place so much that he bought property and settled down there himself. George was never to marry, but years later he struck up a relationship, by letter, with his niece, my aunt Mimi, that continued until he died. This was how a New Zealand branch of the family came to be established, and years later we met some of the younger ones when they visited us in Liverpool.

3: *The Stanley Girls*

Despite, or perhaps because of, their strict conservative upbringing, all five of the Stanley girls were in some ways well ahead of most women of their generation. Determined, feisty and unconventional, they spoke their minds, and each one of them, in her own way, defied convention.

The first shock was Mimi (Mary). In those days girls were expected to marry and have children – that was what marriage was for. But Mimi had other ideas. Her position as the first (surviving) daughter of five girls does much to explain the Mimi we grew up with and saw into feeble old age. In her case, being the eldest daughter was more a curse than a privilege. Maybe, if she'd been born a boy, back in 1906, her life would have taken a different course. Undoubtedly it wouldn't have fallen to her to look after her sisters quite so much. As it was, as each new baby came along, Mimi was expected to pull her weight, and more and more as she grew older. I heard many times, from both Mimi herself and Nanny, the middle sister, that by the time she had left home, she had already made a firm decision that she was not to renege on: no children. It was quite amazing, for the time, to make such a momentous decision, and particularly unusual to carry it through.

Mimi and her father were always at odds with one another and had loud shouting matches, mostly about what Pop thought she should and shouldn't be doing. Nanny told me many stories in her latter years and remembered rows between Pop and Mimi and Mater and Mimi, with our grandmother arbitrating.

Sometime in the early 1930s, Mimi became engaged to the

love of her life, a young doctor she met in Liverpool. Desperately sadly, he caught an infection on the ward where he was working and died soon afterwards, leaving Mimi distraught.

She had known George Smith of Woolton Dairy Farm for at least ten years before she married him, in September 1939. He was ten years her senior, and by the time of their marriage Mimi was 33 and George 43. They had courted in the front room of Pop and Mama's home in Penny Lane over the previous couple of years. My cousin Stanley remembers our grandmother forbidding him to enter the room, as 'Mary has her friend in there and you mustn't disturb them.' George had to work extremely hard to convince Mimi to marry him, but eventually she accepted his proposal. And George, for his part, accepted Mimi's condition that there were to be no children.

Once Mimi was married and had her own home, she assumed complete authority over her own life and everyone else's. No one was to gainsay Mimi, whose almost obsessive need to control the lives and actions of all those around her affected all of us in the family. Our lives were shaped according to the laws of Mimi.

The next daughter, Mater (Betty), was a stunning beauty who had many admirers. She could have picked from any number of eligible suitors, when she chose a retired sea captain, Charles Parkes. Their son, Charles Stanley, known for ever after as Stanley or Stan, was born prematurely in 1933 and not expected to live. He was baptised within hours, as our grandmother sat through the night with Mater and the one and a half pounds of baby, feeding him with a pen filler. He survived the night, and for the next few weeks they fed him drop by drop, determined that he would live. Mater stayed with Mama until she and Charles bought a bungalow in Halewood, on the outskirts of Liverpool.

Then came Anne Georgina, known to the family as Nanny. Soon after she was born Pop came home from sea to meet this latest daughter and promptly disowned her. Nanny had golden-red hair, and for him this was reason enough. He could never have fathered a child with such colouring, he stormed. He, with the red-gold moustache. This upset my grandmother terribly, but despite the fact that Nanny was only weeks old, the father-daughter relationship was set.

As Nanny grew up, Pop hardly acknowledged her. He avoided speaking to her, and when he did he told her that she didn't belong in the family, that she was a changeling. He called her Plain Jane.

Under the weight of this rejection Nanny became a silent, withdrawn child who watched and listened. She lacked Mimi's strength of character and resilience when it came to challenging their domineering father, preferring to avoid him if she could. When she was about twelve years old she developed severe asthma which was to blight the rest of her life.

When she grew up Nanny found a good job as a civil servant. But as the years advanced without marriage, Pop re-christened her the Old Maid. It seemed that the daughter Pop didn't want was the one destined to stay at home with her parents, left behind as the others married and acquired their own homes and families.

Then, in her mid-thirties, Nanny surprised everyone by marrying a fellow civil servant, Sidney Cadwallader, and having a son, Michael, after which she declared there would be no more children. And once she had established her own home she finally found the courage to stand up to her father, refusing to give in to his demand to live with her five years after Mama died.

This rejection and confrontation was to have its repercussions for me and my sister, as was the acerbic tongue Nanny developed as a barrier to the pain she had suffered.

My mother Julia came next. Another redhead, just like Pop's red moustache. But this time, three years after Nanny, he was at the birth and he fell in love with her. So Julia was the fortunate one, the well-loved one. How a father could treat his daughters so very differently is baffling. There seems to be no explanation as to why this happens. It just does.

Julia was unusual, unpredictable and talented, and as far as Pop was concerned, she could do no wrong. She grew up to be beautiful: five foot two, with shoulder-length Titian hair and the kind of carefree confidence that melted hearts. Always musical, as a little girl she was taught to play the banjo and piano by her grandfather, William Stanley. She was always laughing and joking, she could sing and dance and she turned heads wherever she went. She was also determined, headstrong and wilful. So it was perhaps not surprising that, at the age of fourteen, she began seeing a young hotel bellboy she had met in a local park. Although Mama was tolerant and extended to him an open invitation to visit the family home, Pop was horrified. Alf Lennon was not good enough for Julia, and that was that. He didn't come from the right sort of background, he didn't live in a decent home and he didn't speak with the right accent. But Julia adored Alf and refused to stop seeing him.

Harriet, the youngest in the family, was born two years after Julia and was just as favoured. She was very beautiful and was spoiled by her grandmother. In her late teens Harrie created a scandal by marrying Ali, a young engineering student who had been brought up in Egypt and who had an Egyptian father and a Turkish mother. Their daughter Liela was born, in 1937, when Harrie was 21, and soon afterwards they went to live in Cairo with Ali's family. Heartbreakingly, Ali died after a tooth extraction just a few years later. In 1941 Stanley's father, Charles, sent Harrie the money to return to Liverpool with Liela, but while they were still on the ship which was bringing them home, Mama died, at the age of 76.

It was a desolate homecoming. Liverpool was being torn apart by bombs and Harrie and her sisters were grief-stricken over their mother's death. Also, as the widow of a foreign national, Harrie was pronounced an alien on arrival and had to report to the police station daily until she married again. Soon after the war she married an army officer, Norman Birch, with whom she had a son, David, in 1948, after which Norman was posted to Burma.

Between them Mimi, Mater, Nanny and Harrie broke just about every convention of the time. Heaven knows what Pop made of his daughters' choices, what with the one who refused to have children, the one who married a much older man, the one who became a career woman and married late and the one who married a foreigner and emigrated to a strange, far-away land. And what did he make of Julia, who was to become a mother four times over? She broke more taboos than the rest of them put together, when she had a baby after an extra-marital affair and then went on to live for many years, and have two more children, with a man whom she never married.

But before any of that happened, Julia married and had a son, a little boy whose extraordinary musical talent was in the genes he inherited from both his mother and his father.

4: *The Sins of the Fathers*

With the war imminent, a friend of the family offered my grand-parents the use of a house in a suburb called Penny Lane, five miles out of town. Pop, Mama, Mimi, Nanny and Julia moved into a terraced house at 9 Newcastle Road, which was eventually to become the first home to John and then to me. Harrie was in Egypt with her husband and baby daughter, and Mater was living with her first husband and her young son, Stanley.

Mimi was now 32 and contemplating marriage to George, who regularly called at the family home to woo her in the front room. Nanny, who at 26 was beginning to think that she would never marry, was forging ahead with her Civil Service career.

Julia was 24 and was still seeing Alf Lennon. Theirs was an unusual romance. Despite the fervent opposition of her father and Alf's long absences at sea as a ship's steward, it had endured for ten years. They can't have seen one another for more than a few weeks a year, when Alf was home on leave, yet it seems that Julia waited patiently, and never dated anyone else.

The two of them had met in the city's Sefton Park, when she was fourteen and he was fifteen. He had flirted with her and she had told him to take off his 'silly hat'. He obliged by promptly removing it and throwing it into the lake, which made her laugh and won her heart. At that time Alf had only just left the Bluecoat Orphanage in Penny Lane to take up his first job, as a bellboy at the Adelphi Hotel. He was a good-looking boy, but the family considered him unsuitable for Julia, not least because his family were poor and Irish.

Alf's father, John's grandfather, was a Dubliner, also called John Lennon, whose parents had emigrated to Liverpool while he was still very young. He grew up loving music, but after leaving school he decided – perhaps under pressure from his family – to become a priest. Some years later, unhappy with the priesthood, he left for a new life in the United States, where he married and became a founder member of a minstrel group. They played vaudeville music in the southern states of America and became extremely successful. When his wife died very young, John came back to Liverpool. After a few years he married a Liverpool-born Irish girl, Mary Maguire, who was always known as Polly. John continued to earn a living as a musician and entertainer until 1917, when he died, aged 62, leaving Polly and the couple's six young children almost destitute.

Unable to provide for all her children, Polly was forced to send the two youngest, Alfred and baby Edith, to the orphanage. But she kept in touch, and Alf and Edith were allowed to visit the family during the holidays. This meant that although Alf had grown up in care, he knew his family and was loved by his mother. He was five years old when his father died.

Despite the longevity of the romance and their daughter's headstrong determination, Julia's parents still hoped she would tire of Alf and find someone suitable to settle down with. After all, she could have had her pick of young men. Julia was the most obviously pretty of all the Stanley girls and the most charismatic. My cousin Liela describes her as 'pretty as a picture, five foot two tall, her tiny feet on six-inch heels, with shoulder-length auburn hair. A petite doll walking down the street. People used to turn back for another look at her. When some cheeky boy gave her a wolf-whistle she would say, "Hmm, not bad yourself." It was all light-hearted fun. She had heaps of personality and a great gift for words which made her very, very witty. No one had a bad word to say about her, she was lovely to everyone. If you ever went to Julia in a bad mood she would have you laughing in no time. She was a thoroughly charming person who could capture anyone's heart.'

Little wonder, perhaps, that her parents hoped she would capture the heart of a far more successful and wealthy man than Alf Lennon. But that hope ended when, one winter's day, Julia and Alf decided to get married. If Pop and Mama were horrified by the romance, they must have been doubly horrified by the marriage. There may well have been rows – certainly they had nothing to do with the wedding.

Alf later claimed that it had been Julia's suggestion and that they'd both treated it as a bit of a joke. Certainly it all happened at short notice and without any fuss or frills. They married at Liverpool's Mount Pleasant Register Office on 3 December 1938, without a single member of Julia's family present. No one knows who their witnesses were – they must have been passers-by, asked to stand in as a favour.

Their son John's wedding to his sweetheart Cynthia, 24 years later, was to be almost identical, taking place in the same register office in similar style, without any of John's family present. Their witnesses, however, are known. Brian Epstein, Paul McCartney and George Harrison were there, along with Cynthia's brother and sister-in-law.

Julia and Alf celebrated their wedding by going to the cinema (John and Cyn would celebrate theirs with a meal in a local café and toast their union with water). Julia had always loved films and had even put 'cinema usherette' on her marriage certificate as a joke. Afterwards she went back to her parents' house and Alf went back to his rented room; even as a married couple they had nowhere they could go to be alone together, let alone set up home. Their son and his bride would also marry with no home of their own, but Brian Epstein would save the day by lending them a flat in which to start married life together.

For Julia and Alf there was no such saviour. Far from living together as man and wife, they were to be parted for the next few months. The day after he married Julia, Alf signed up as a steward on board a luxury liner going to the West Indies and sailed away for three months. It seems that Pop, busy directing from behind the scenes, had organised this rapid departure. He asked Mater's husband, Charles, the former sea captain, to use his contacts and influence to get Alf a job on a liner. There is no way of knowing whether his intention was to provide Alf with a decent job, or simply to get him as far as possible from Julia, but the latter motive seems in keeping with Pop's style.

Within nine months of the marriage, war was declared. The blitzing of Liverpool began soon afterwards, with the bombing directed at the huge Cammell Laird shipyards but inevitably hitting most of the city. The beautiful Georgian houses which gave the city great architectural status were being bombarded, night after night. Fortunately, in their new home in Penny Lane outside the city centre, the family escaped the most immediate effects of the bombing. Mimi had married George in September 1939, just as war broke out, and he had been called up to fight in France shortly afterwards. So Mimi, like Julia, stayed at home at the start of her marriage.

Both husbands, Alf and George, came home on leave from time to time and stayed in the Penny Lane house. In Alf's case he was only just tolerated by Pop, who accepted, grudgingly, that he was their daughter's husband and therefore part of the family.

It was on Alf's shore leave in January 1940 that Julia became pregnant. By the time she realised she was expecting a child Alf had already gone back to sea, this time as a merchant seaman, crossing the Atlantic. Perhaps Julia wrote to tell him he was to become a father, but he was still away when their son was born at Oxford Street Maternity Hospital at seven a.m. on 9 October 1940. He was immediately placed in a cot underneath the iron bedstead, as a safety measure against possible debris or flying glass from windows shattered by bomb blast. My mother named him John after his paternal grandfather and Winston as a patriotic gesture. There must be many other baby boys who received that same distinction during the war years.

In the absence of John's father, Mimi was the first family member to see him. She walked to the hospital from Penny Lane, and held her new nephew soon after the birth. After a few days Julia and John were discharged from hospital and went home to Penny Lane and to Pop and Mama.

For the next year Julia heard almost nothing from Alf, apart from a message from Southampton, where his ship had docked briefly before departing again. It must have been hard for her, living with her parents and a new baby, with no possibility of family life with her husband.

Once a fortnight Julia went to the Seaman's Mission in the city to collect the eight shillings Alf sent her from his wages. Most of this money was handed to Pop for her keep, there certainly wasn't enough to set up a home for her and Alf and their son, but at least there was something coming in.

However, one day when John was about a year old Julia went to the Seaman's Mission as usual, to be told that Alf had jumped ship in the States and gone AWOL – absent without leave. This meant there were no wages – and no money for Julia. Worried, puzzled and frustrated, Julia was left to break the bad news to Pop. There was no word from Alf for another eighteen months.

By this time Harrie had come home from Egypt after the untimely death of her husband, and Mama had died, leaving Pop a widower. George Smith had also returned home, and he and Mimi moved into a rented three-bedroomed semi-detached house in Vale Road, Woolton.

In Alf's absence Julia moved with John into a small house

owned by Mimi's husband George and known as The Cottage. It was the first opportunity she'd had to live in a home of her own.

George's family had owned the Woolton Dairy, but while George was away at war, the Dairy Farm and its lands had been requisitioned by the government in order to help the war effort. On the land at the back of the farmhouse, a factory was built which made barrage balloons. As recompense, Frank, George's older brother, had benefited from the sale of the main farmhouse and George was presented with The Cottage, which was attached to the farmhouse. This was definitely the smaller portion, and both he and Mimi were bitter about this for many years afterwards.

After the war, Bear Brand bought the factory buildings and the main farmhouse from the company that had made the barrage balloons. From silk balloons to silk stockings . . .

Julia was still living in The Cottage when Alf finally reappeared in 1943, by which time John was two and a half years old. Alf explained to Julia that he had not gone AWOL but had been jailed for three months for theft – a charge he vigorously denied – after which he had resumed his job.

Alf stayed with them at The Cottage and to my knowledge this was the only time that Julia, Alf and John shared a family home together.

Julia's family life in The Cottage didn't last long, as Alf soon went back to sea. Although Julia desperately wanted him to stay at home and find a shore job, he insisted that it was wartime, he was a sailor and that was his duty. He left Julia to face a future in which she and her son would spend most of their time alone. It was a life she knew all about. She had grown up with a father who was absent for most of her childhood, coming ashore only to leave Mama with the next baby. It was not a future Julia wanted for herself or her son.

Alf knew how much Julia wanted him to stay with her and

John and create a family life, and no doubt his inability to commit was linked to his traumatic childhood. Alf had, effectively, lost his entire family when he was five. So often those who are abandoned will, in turn, abandon those they love. For John, still a toddler, it was desperately sad that his father was barely in his life. His father's choices were already shaping him.

When Alf returned to sea, Julia and John returned to Penny Lane to live with her beloved Pop. There was little money coming in to the Penny Lane house. Pop was on a pension, Alf wasn't sending any money home and Julia had to take on a series of part-time jobs. She didn't have to go far to find work. She asked at the local picture house for a job as an usherette – the employment she'd jokingly entered on her marriage certificate – and got the job. It was in the cinema that, towards the end of 1944, Julia met a young Welsh soldier who was home on leave and they had an affair.

Like so many wartime affairs, this one would probably have melted away with time, a secret known only to the two people involved, had Julia not become pregnant. This changed everything. It was a catastrophe – for Julia, for the unborn child and for John – and its repercussions would affect the whole family, including those of us yet to be born, as the sins of the fathers and mothers began to cast their long shadows.

Julia was condemned, outright and relentlessly, by her family and by society. She was a married woman who'd had an affair and become pregnant. Never mind that she had seen her husband two or three times in almost five years. There was no excuse and no compassion.

The pregnancy set in motion a sequence of events, all of which seemed unstoppable, and which wrapped a chain around my mother's heart. At first it seemed there might be a chance that she could keep her baby. The father of her unborn child wanted to stay with her and their child but wanted nothing to do with John. Julia was outraged and refused to consider such an option, and the young Welshman was put out of the house by her Pop.

Ironically this pregnancy coincided with Alf's second visit home. Shocked to find his wife pregnant by another man, he made an extraordinary proposition. He offered to adopt the new baby. This might have given Julia real hope, both of keeping her baby and of a family life with Alf, had he backed his offer with any serious sign of intent or care. Or money. But he did not – he went straight back to sea, leaving Julia totally dependent on her family. Pop made his decision clear: the baby would be born in a Salvation Army mother and baby home and surrendered for adoption at birth.

In today's more enlightened times, this seems barbaric. Nowadays mothers, whatever their marital state, are offered support and can keep their babies. But back then times were far harsher. I can only imagine the anguish and heartbreak my mother went through at the prospect of giving up her baby. Certainly she endured a debilitating pregnancy, throughout which she was suffering from sickness and depression.

Her daughter, Victoria Elizabeth, was born in June 1945. Julia was allowed to keep her for the required six weeks before handing her over to her adoptive parents, a Norwegian man and his Liverpool-born wife who took her away as Ingrid.

Julia believed – I'm not sure why – that they had taken the baby to Norway. It was only many years later, when I met Ingrid, that she told me she had grown up, initially, just a few miles from where we lived in Liverpool and later in Hampshire.

Bereft, Julia returned to John and her father, with a cloud, which would never fully lift, hanging over her head.

She was now carrying the secret shame. She had stained the family honour, and the price exacted was denial.

Silence.

As far as the family was concerned, from that moment on, there was no baby. Doubtless, it didn't occur to any of them that the shame belonged to them too, for the pain they caused Julia, and for abandoning a child of the family. Julia may not have even allowed such disloyal thinking to penetrate her guilt. But the rest of her life was dictated by the no-baby.

5: *My Father Appears*

During Julia's pregnancy John had begun to stay over with Mimi. Julia was constantly unwell, so it gave her a much-needed break, and a stay at Mimi's home, with plenty of cuddles and tickles from Uncle George, would have been a treat for four-year-old John and a diversion from his mother's condition.

By this time Mimi and George had moved into a new home. The house she and George rented in Vale Road, backed on to an identical one, called Mendips, in Menlove Avenue. The two back gardens were separated only by a fence, so Mimi had a clear view of what was going on in the other house.

One day she noticed that the tenants were moving out of Mendips. Mimi wasted no time. She immediately started to pile up the Vale Road furniture beside the fence at the bottom of the garden. She then manhandled it over the fence into the other back garden. Within the day, Mimi and George were the new occupants of 251 Menlove Avenue, fronting on to the main thoroughfare into town. The owner of the house only found out when it was a 'fait accompli'. Which meant that Mimi was a squatter!

The law was strongly weighted in favour of tenants during those dark war days. The woman who owned the house had been waiting to sell it when the previous tenants left. Now, she had no choice but to sell to the new incumbents, Mimi and George, if she wanted to realise the money from the house.

Mimi was very pleased with herself. As the occupant she was able to drive a hard bargain, relying on possession being nine-tenths of the law.

Not long after they settled into their new home Mimi began

to take in students to bring in some extra income. The first batch came from a domestic science college about half a mile away. They were girls, of course, in that era; the majority of the students would have become cookery teachers in schools. Mimi soon decided that they were not for her. If she had to share her home then young men would be better, less mess and distraction.

Mendips was to be Mimi's home for the next twenty years, and was to become a pivotal force in all our lives, most of all in John's. After the birth of the sister he never knew, John continued to visit Mimi and George regularly.

It was a help to Julia who, still recovering from the birth, had to look after John and her ageing father. Nanny told me how, when she returned home after Victoria's birth, our mother was depressed, often weighed down with despair and crying in her room. In those days traumatised people just had to deal with their pain and grief within the deepest recesses of their hearts and minds, while carrying on as normal on the surface. And for Julia carrying on meant getting a job, because Pop's pension wasn't enough to keep all three of them.

In Autumn 1945 John joined the infant class at Mosspits Lane Primary School. Soon afterwards Julia found a part-time job as a waitress in a café at the top of the road, close to the school, which meant she was able to work the lunchtime shift in the café and still collect John.

Life for Julia and John seemed settled then. They lived quietly with Pop, John loved school and Julia enjoyed getting out of the house to her job before collecting John from school. But the prospects for the future must have seemed grim, with Alf nowhere to be seen and the family's disapproval still weighing heavily on her.

One of the customers in the café was a man named John Albert Dykins. My mother had known him for some time already, but he had started to come in most lunchtimes, and he and Julia often talked in her tea-breaks. Towards Christmas, he suggested that they meet after work, she said yes.

John Albert was a couple of years younger than Julia – she was 31 and he was 29. He worked as a demonstrator of invisible repairs, showing housewives how torn fabric could be almost seamlessly mended using the latest sewing gadget. Like Julia he still lived with his parents. He was a man of medium height and of very dark complexion, with black hair and deep brown eyes. He often had a moustache, although I don't know whether he had one when they met. After he had been seeing Julia for a few weeks John Albert went to introduce himself to Pop and was promptly shown the door. As far as Pop was concerned that was that. Order restored.

The rest of the family's attitude was the same. As a married woman with a child, not to mention an illegitimate pregnancy in the closet, Julia was expected to pay the price for her failure, toe the family line and forget about men. Alf may have been gone for months, with no word or money sent home, but his ghost still tied her with invisible, seemingly indestructible fetters. The idea of her father accepting a new relationship was out of the question.

In addition, John Albert was, in the eyes of the family, barely more suitable as a partner than Alf had been. They felt he was of a lower class and in no way good enough for their Julia.

But Julia was young, beautiful and longing for a life of her own. And she had found a man who adored her and made her feel alive again. She wanted to be with him and she wasn't going to let her father, or her disapproving sisters, deny her the chance of happiness.

John Albert, who was to become my father, was nothing if not persistent in his pursuit of my mother. Having been turned away without much ado on the first occasion, he decided to adopt a different approach. He set about trying to relate to Pop and wouldn't accept being rebuffed. It was wartime, a time of shortage. John Albert had contacts and was able to supply various items that would otherwise have been unobtainable, or too expensive to consider. I can only guess that these items might have included cigarettes or tobacco.

His dogged persistence paid off. How it came to be, exactly, I don't know, but by the spring of 1946, Pop had relented and John Albert was able to call at the house for my mother without being turned away.

Pop could certainly see that his daughter was determined to move on with her life. He could also see that she had met a man who was determined to be with her and who saw little John as part of the package. Nanny told me that John Albert knew all the circumstances of Victoria/Ingrid's birth and adoption and I believe this only served to inflame his passion. He was a knight to the rescue. Sir Galahad.

The deference that Julia had had to show when she was pregnant was lessening. Destitution was no longer staring her in the face. Now she had a choice. Here was someone wanting to look after her, who would take her away, if that's what it took. If Pop wanted Julia to stay he had to reconsider.

Julia started to call John Albert 'Bobby', and he became known as Bobby to all the family. I think my mother wanted her son John to know that he was the number one John. Her John.

It was Mimi's turn to be outraged. She poured a tirade upon her father for allowing Julia and Bobby to openly parade their relationship. She pronounced loudly that the situation would not have been allowed to develop if she had still been at home. Julia and Bobby were having a sinful relationship. My mother was no longer a fit mother for John. She was a married woman, who had already disgraced them all by having a baby out of wedlock. She was not to have a man in her life. And that was that. This was no longer a fit home for John.

Even though he had relented, rather than face living alone,

Pop still disapproved of Julia and Bobby being together and he encouraged Mimi to remonstrate with my mother. And when she demanded that John be allowed to stay with her at Mendips, while this immoral situation was sorted out, Pop backed Mimi. John was taken to Mendips, I suspect, to make my mother come to her senses. When she realised that she must give up her sinful relationship, then talks could begin. For my mother this must have been terrible. Always passionate, with her emotions close to the surface, Julia would have grieved openly, distraught about the removal of her beloved son. She had now lost not one child, but two.

6: *Blackpool*

About two weeks later, Julia had a visit from the elusive Alf Lennon. He had decided to come and check out the state of his wife and child and he turned up at Pop's house. Julia gave him short shrift, demanding to know where he had been all these years and how he thought they were coping without him as a husband, father and provider. The response was that he knew they had Pop and would be all right. Pop the pensioner, with no Welfare State! John was five and a half years old and barely knew Alf. He had simply been told his father was in the merchant navy and at war, which was true.

Alf had been through his own childhood traumas, with the dreadful and desperate loss of his father at the tender age of five and then the abandonment and the orphanage. Yet it is still almost impossible to comprehend that he could neglect his own son as he did. Maybe he really thought that my mother would be waiting, with John, without complaint and that they could all carry on together as a happy, reunited post-war family. As such a damaged soul himself, perhaps he had lived out this fantasy many times before he arrived back in Liverpool. In that case, the rebuff would have been astounding to him. It must have been a shock for Alf to realise that, just as he had changed over the five years, my mother had also altered and the space was no longer there in her life for him.

The biggest shock, by far, must have been Bobby. Not only that he was in Julia's life, but that he was actually allowed in the house. That Pop, the stiff old seafarer had let him in. Perhaps as well as seeing Pop, from afar, as the crusty old seadog who could be relied upon to support his daughter and grandson and keep them safe, Alf had also been relying on him to keep them waiting for him. Again, I can step in his shoes. No matter what had gone on during the harsh and desperate war years, Alf had probably been carrying the dream. The reuniting dream. Maybe at this point he felt just as abandoned as Julia did.

Nevertheless, a row ensued. Julia said she wanted nothing more to do with him. Pop reinforced this, on the grounds of Alf's failure even to write and let them know what was happening. He felt that he had borne the brunt.

Whatever had happened with Julia, Alf wanted to see John, and John was no longer with his mother. Mimi had him at Mendips. It was early 1946, and John was still attending the local primary school, a short walk from where Julia and Pop lived, but a bus journey from Mendips, which Mimi had to take with him each day.

Alf knew Mimi well enough not to turn up out of the blue. He telephoned. Mimi put John on the phone to talk to Alf. She knew that they had never talked much before – last time Alf had been home John was a toddler. I wonder how she introduced the almost stranger who wanted to talk with him? And how did John feel?

Did anyone ever think about how John was feeling? Or that he had any feelings at all? He had just been taken from his mother. Now he was being collected from school by Mimi and taken to her house, instead of going home with Mummy. He wouldn't have been able to explain this to himself, much less to teachers and friends at school. The same thing happened to my sister and me after Mummy died, and I know my family well enough to be sure that nothing was said to him. Did they just hope that he didn't think about it? About his Mummy, and why he wasn't with her, safe at home, where he belonged?

Alf went to Mendips and spent the afternoon with John, Mimi and Harrie's daughter Liela, who was staying with them.

John was excited to see his Daddy and wanted him to stay, and Mimi agreed that he could stay the night. Mimi complained to Alf of the costs involved in looking after John. Alf gave her twenty pounds, a grand sum for the few weeks she'd had his son.

That night Alf went to bed and pondered the whole situation. He decided that John was not to stay with Mimi, who had spent the afternoon complaining about him. Nor to return to his mother and her new relationship. Alf was beginning to formulate another plan.

The next morning, he was woken by a happy John and Liela, bouncing on him, pulling the bedclothes, wanting him to get up. John had been promised a day out with Daddy and was excited. Mimi had wanted to accompany them, to go shopping for new clothes for John, but she had already promised to take Liela home that day. Mimi didn't trust Alf, so he must have worked hard to reassure her that a day with his son was what they both wanted and needed, and that John would be fine with him. So Mimi set off with Liela while Alf set off with John. The two of them got on the train to Blackpool. Only this was not to be a day trip. That was never the intention. Alf had decided the previous night that John was to leave Mendips and Mimi and his mother and start again. With his father.

In Blackpool they stayed with Alf's eldest brother Sidney and his wife, and Alf gave John a little boy's seaside holiday. The funfair, the beach and the donkey rides. Meanwhile, he was making plans to emigrate, with John, to New Zealand. Back in Liverpool, Julia went to see Mimi, to find out about the meeting between Alf and John. She was astounded and distressed to find that they had disappeared, without her knowledge or consent. Mimi had assumed control over John and let Alf take him without even telling Julia. She was doing her utmost to distance John and his mother from each other.

Was Mimi on a power trip? If she had borne a child of her

own, would she have behaved like this? She had taken John, almost forcibly, to stay with her and now she had lost him.

Julia went back to see Bobby and they made a decision. This had to stop. Julia went in search of an address for Alf, so that she could find her son, and Bobby went in search of a place of their own. They wanted the three of them to live a family life, free from this relentless interference.

While Julia tried to find out where Alf had taken John, Bobby went straight out and found a flat. It was a tiny place, with one bedroom, but it was as much as he could afford. Apart from her brief stay in The Cottage three years earlier, Julia had never left home before, despite having a five-year-old son, and Bobby was still living in his family home, with his parents, two miles away in Wavertree. They had only had a close relationship for three months, but the challenging situation was propelling things forward at a rapid rate. In order to keep John, they set up home in a weekend.

Meanwhile Julia went to Alf's friends. They didn't know his whereabouts, but they directed her to the Seaman's Mission in Liverpool City Centre, where she had collected her money from Alf years before. She told them how Alf Lennon had come to see their son, in good faith, after a long absence and disappeared with him, leaving no note, no address and no explanation. She was desperate. They had to have an address for him. They gave her the forwarding address they had, which was his brother's house in Blackpool.

There are various accounts of the episode in Blackpool, but without Alf, John, or even Alf's brother Sidney here to recall it, maybe the whole truth will never be known.

What is certain is that Bobby and Julia went together to Blackpool. Bobby hadn't passed his driving test at that time, so I am assuming that they went by train, as Alf and John had done. They found Sidney's house and Bobby waited at the gate while my mother knocked at the door. She was invited in. I have knitted together what happened next, from family accounts. Alf proposed to Julia that they give it another chance. That they fulfil his dream of a fresh family start in New Zealand. He told her that he intended to send John there with his brother to wait for him, as he was going back to sea. He would join them over there as soon as he could. He wanted Julia to go too.

John was five. Alf had lost his father at five and had been sent to the Bluecoat Orphanage, with his two brothers. I feel sure that he wanted John to have some sort of normal family life and thought that this was the time to forge a new beginning. But it was too late. Julia refused. John had been out of the room, in the kitchen, during this discussion and now he was brought back in. Alf had obviously talked to John about going to New Zealand, so he asked him if he wanted to go there or if he wanted to stay with his mother. John climbed on Alf's knee and said that he wanted to stay with his Daddy. Julia got up to go, weeping.

As she went out of the door John panicked and ran after her. It was his Mummy he wanted, after all.

Alf accepted that John wanted to stay with Julia, but said that his son was not to go back to Mimi. Julia said there would be no need for that, as they now had a flat of their own. She left, with John. Bobby was waiting at the end of the road and the three of them went back to Liverpool.

The next John saw of Alf was a newspaper picture of him washing up in a hotel, twenty years later.

7: *The Too-Small Flat*

The flat Bobby had found was in a large house in Gateacre village, right next to Woolton, where Mendips was situated, and about three miles from Penny Lane. Even though the war was over, people were still trying to escape the city centre, rather than relocate within it. Liverpool had been bombed mercilessly, many of the blitzed buildings were merely shells, and it was still regarded as a dangerous place to live. The legacy of the war for our once proud city was poverty and struggle, and it was to be many years before it even began to be restored.

So the flat, on the outskirts of Liverpool, was a safer place to be. Their living accommodation was a tiny part of a large house, comprising a small kitchen, a bathroom, one small living-room and a small bedroom. Small is the word. But they didn't mind, they knew it was a temporary measure, until they could save some money and find somewhere bigger. They had rushed into it for the purpose of reclaiming John. It was a stepping-stone.

Julia, Bobby and John came hot-foot from Blackpool to Gateacre. Bobby went back to work and Julia stayed in the flat with John. They visited Pop to reassure him that John was all right after his ordeal in Blackpool, and as John was still at Mosspits Lane School, at the top of the road, they would have been travelling back to Penny Lane most days.

Apart from school, there was another very important reason why my mother regularly had to go back to Penny Lane. This was early 1946, the year following the end of the war. Ration books were registered with certain shops in your locality, and Julia's allocations, firstly for herself and John and later to include me and my sister, were all in Penny Lane, in the shops on the round-about, since she had been living there when they were given out. These trips were to remain very clear in John's memory, as in my own, because post-war rationing was to continue, throughout the country, until 1953. John was also eligible for the concentrated orange juice in the clear glass bottle with the bright blue, screw-cap top. We all three of us loved that orange juice and would drink it, undiluted, straight from the bottle.

Despite the fact that he was now in his seventies, this was the first time that Pop had lived on his own. Mama had died in 1941 and his daughters had left home one by one. My mother was the last to leave, as Nanny was spending most of her time with Mater, Charles and young Stanley in the large house they had bought over the water, in Birkenhead. Pop was outraged that Julia had left and was living openly with Bobby and John. He had fought against this for several months now. Even when he had succumbed and let Bobby into his home, he had been instrumental in helping Mimi to remove John from his mother in Penny Lane to Mendips in Woolton. Now all his attempts to hold on to Julia seemed to have failed and he was living by himself. He felt thwarted, and he was angry.

Pop now had two missions. One was to remove John back to Mendips, as long as my mother had a man in her life. To teach her a lesson. The other was to arrange his own future. He was becoming more frail and had thought that Julia was going to be there to look after him. He had thought that the matter of his care had been organised.

He instructed Mimi to go to Gateacre to inspect the flat and report back. I have no idea how long they had been there, certainly no more than days or weeks, but I do know that the intention was not to help them set up home. Mimi arrived and promptly demanded that John return to Mendips with her, as Julia was an unfit mother, living in sin.

When I think of this scene – Mimi demanding John, and Julia, horrified, refusing to hand him over – I always hope that John was at school when it took place. It's hard to think of him hearing it, a small boy between angry adults, listening, confused and anxious, as they fought over him.

The dispute ended when Bobby stepped in. He was decidedly firm with Mimi. John was Julia's son and should be with his mother. End of story. Go away Mimi. John Albert was a brave man. I'm sorry I missed that show.

Thwarted in her attempts to remove John, Mimi had the bit between her teeth. Days after her last visit she returned to the flat with a young social worker. She announced, on arrival, that her sister and this man were not married and that she wanted to take John back to her own home, until 'matters were sorted out'. Mimi knew well that the chances of Alf staying in one place for long enough to go through a divorce were next to none, and that Bobby had made Julia happy and was supporting her and John. But all this was brushed aside. It was as if she had already decided that she was going to have John at any cost, no matter how devious or dishonest the route and no matter what price my mother would have to pay.

Mimi lost again. The social worker said she couldn't see a problem and that John was clearly well looked after by his mother and Bobby.

Then there was yet another visit. Mimi was on her relentless, righteous war-path and she wasn't to be deflected. This time she was accompanied by an inspector from Liverpool Social Services and by Pop. Mimi pressed the point that John didn't have his own room. He was sharing the one small bedroom with his mother and Bobby, a man who was not his father and was not married to his mother. The inspector agreed with Mimi and decreed that the flat was an unsuitable home for him. He was handed over to Mimi until Julia and Bobby could provide him with a room of his own.

The damage done to John cannot be overestimated. What did

he harbour in his head and in his heart? How did he punish himself for the madness of these adults? How did he face yet another new life?

Mimi immediately changed John's school, taking him out of Mosspits Lane near Penny Lane and sending him to Dovedale Primary, closer to her house. His first day at Dovedale was 15 May 1946, half-way into the summer term. This of course was while she was waiting for 'matters to be sorted out'.

It seemed that Mimi had won her case. The case which she and Pop had brought about between them, in which they acted out all the parts; judge, jury and chief witnesses for the prosecution. I would like to say that my mother was the defendant, but this was a kangaroo session and her attempts at defence were laughed out of court.

There are still times when I feel desperately sad and forlorn about this whole fiasco, this morbid theatre which was being played out over a small boy's head. A production in which the main protagonists were reduced to bit-part players. And there are times when I feel angry.

I could never talk about it with my mother, of course, as she died when I was eleven. I did, however, talk about it with Nanny, who filled in many of the pieces of the story in her final few years. And with John, in the mid-1970s. When John and I talked about the situation of his living with Mimi and not with us I didn't yet know many of the stories that Nanny was to tell me in those last talkative years. John said that at the time he 'didn't have a bloody clue' why he had been sent to live at Mendips. Of course he would rather have stayed with his mother, he said. I told him how Mummy had cried for him. He knew about the record, of course. Mummy played the song, 'My Son John, To Me You Are So Wonderful' incessantly and John had heard it himself in the house. He said that he was just about to make the move back to live with us in Springwood, when our mother died. He was coming in the summer. When we talked about our memories of her he suddenly said, 'It's not fair. You had her and I didn't.' I didn't know what to say and we both cried.

My grandfather must have suffered the shock of shocks when Julia defied him and left the family home with Bobby and John. He needed my mother there. And now he got her. Julia realised that her only hope of a home with a separate room for John was back in Penny Lane. Without John, there was no point in being in the flat. So my parents returned to live with Pop who, quite astonishingly, allowed Julia and Bobby to move in together.

As soon as they had moved back, Julia went straight to Mendips and remonstrated with Mimi. Now they were back in the Penny Lane house there was room for John. His own room. But if she believed that Mimi would hand him over, she was horribly, painfully wrong. Mimi shouted at her, 'Go home. You're not having him!' She flung John behind her chair in the morning room, where the exchange took place.

My cousin Liela, then aged eight, was there watching it all and has told me about it several times.

Julia was drained. She had no powers in the face of Mimi's anger, determination and her endlessly judgemental attitude. She was coming to the end of her strengths, both spiritual and physical. She had lost Victoria nine months previously, and I believe, from what Nanny later told me, that she had sunk into a form of post-natal depression.

Shocked, chastised and beaten, she turned and left. The pain must have been all-consuming. Her sister had won. In future she would have to visit Mimi in order to see her own child. She must have wept bitter, angry, hopeless tears.

8: *Time Together*

Although Mimi had taken John from Mummy, she was not able to ring-fence John as she would have liked. Pop, her partner in removing John from a permanent home with his mother, now became, ironically, her stumbling block. Pop and Mimi, who had always been at odds with one another, had been strangely united in their determination to wrest John from his unsuitable mother. Pop, however, was a brake on Mimi's narrowing focus. It wasn't only his mother who wanted to see John. His grandfather wanted to see him too. He must be brought to the house. Pop couldn't see the contradiction.

So, for the next three years, from 1946 to 1949, while Pop, Julia and Bobby remained at Penny Lane, Mimi brought John on regular visits and Julia was able to collect John, bring him to Penny Lane for visits and then take him back. He came to spend time with Mummy at the weekends and, of course, in the holidays. Pop insisted on that. At other times Nanny, who had helped Julia to care for John as a baby, would pick him up and bring him over for the day. And in the holidays Mater's son Stanley came to stay and brought John over for extra visits, which was a joy for both Mummy and John.

By the summer of 1946, Julia was pregnant, with me. The news was kept from Pop for as long as possible, but inevitably he had to know, and when he did he was incensed. He wasn't going to stay in the same house another day. He went straight to Birkenhead to see his least favourite daughter, Nanny.

This was Anne, the reject child. The one who couldn't possibly have been his. The one whose presence he had chosen to ignore from the start, causing Mama so much pain. Plain Jane, the Troublesome Asthmatic, the Old Maid.

Well, the Old Maid had found herself a husband and an excellent one at that. Sidney Cadwallader had bought her the big house she wanted, the house where she had already spent a lot of time with her sister, her brother-in-law and their young son Stanley. She had escaped and she was happy, at last. But the oppressor was in hot pursuit. He told her he was moving in. He even chose his room. There were plenty to spare. Pop was doing what Pop did. Making decisions to suit himself.

Amazingly, at the age of 36, Nanny finally found the courage to face her father. She turned him down and sent him home. One can only imagine his fury. He had no choice but to stay where he was.

The winter of 1947 was the worst that England had suffered in years. It became known as 'the Big Freeze'. I have always loved snow. On 5 March my mother was taken by ambulance through a snowdrift to have me, in Sefton General Hospital. My sister Jackie would also be born there two years and eight months later.

I returned with my mother to live at Penny Lane. My memory is long and good and I remember some things from the two and a half years we lived in that house. I remember Pop, with collarless, striped shirts, reading, listening to the radio, talking with my mother. He didn't go out much. I wonder how similar grandfathers are? When I met my husband's grandfather in Ireland years later it was like Act one Scene two. My own Pop had died in 1949, and in 1966 I met him again!

I have to think hard to visualise my father in those early years. He was on lengthy shift work as a waiter, so was often absent. He had decided that bar and hotel work suited him and, as an unprofessional, unskilled man with a family to support, it paid. My mother never had an outside job again; she was at home, looking after my father, John, when he was there, and me and Jackie.

I was born in March, and my cousin Stanley remembers meeting me for the first time in the Easter holidays. He brought John to Penny Lane, so that will have been the first time John saw me too, as I can't imagine Mimi rushing to the hospital, or even to the house, to congratulate my mother.

I remember John in the Penny Lane house. Sometimes I slept with my parents, so maybe he was staying then, sleeping in the small back bedroom with the same furniture that was later to be transported to Springwood.

Mummy had friends in the neighbourhood. They visited, we visited, we went for days out and played with other small people on days in. One of my earliest friends had a swing suspended on her back gate, opposite our back garden, where we spent many happy hours. John also played on that swing, as did all the neighbourhood children. It was a party-time back gate.

I have a memory of the inside of the house, particularly down-stairs. The front room was not in daily use, or not for the children, at least. I remember sleeping on a sofa in there, probably my afternoon nap. The main living area was the back room, with the big table, leading into the kitchen. The radio, or rather the wireless, was always on, near the chair where Pop installed himself, by the fire. I can see Mummy in and out, between these two rear rooms, the hub of the house. Then, unexpectedly, Pop became sick and had to go into hospital, where, after a short illness, he died. He was 77 years old. His death must have been a sad loss to his daughters and his grandchildren, particularly as it was so sudden. Stanley says he died of old age, although 77 doesn't seem so old now.

I do wonder, however, how my mother felt. She had undoubt-edly remained his favourite daughter and had looked after him more than her sisters, living with him until the end. I know that when Mama died, in 1941, aged 71, she had exhorted her daught-ers to 'look after Pop'. But, if he had been indulgent with Julia during her early years, that was not the case in adulthood. He had proven a stern and unbending father when my mother had a wartime baby out of wedlock and self-righteous and domineering concerning John's welfare. Mimi could never have taken John without his explicit encouragement and approval. As it was, his death promoted the next sea change.

My parents had to move house quickly and, in Pop's absence, Mimi was soon to assume complete authority over John.

9: *The New-Start House*

Pop had been the tenant of the house and shortly after his death the owner declared his intention of selling the property. My parents were given the first option to buy, but they had no money. They needed, therefore, to find another house to rent quickly. They had already made one devastating mistake, three years earlier when they rented a flat that was too small. And by this time they not only had me but Mummy was pregnant again with my sister. They needed room for John, too, so they were looking for a three-bedroom house, like the one they were leaving.

My father went to Liverpool Corporation and somehow secured a roomy, semi-detached, pre-war council house on the Springwood Estate in Allerton, just a short tram journey further out than Penny Lane.

It was a hot summer day when we made the move to Springwood, sometime in August 1949. My parents arrived as Mr and Mrs Dykins; it was a fresh start for them, in their own home, with their family. I remember being in the garden as the big kitchen table was carried in, my father huffing and puffing, turning it this way and that, in order to manoeuvre it through the front door, and my mother at the other end, pulling it into the hall. Other bits of furniture already littered the garden path at the side of the house, which is probably why they didn't take the table through the back garden gate and directly into the kitchen. I don't know if it was the table from Penny Lane, but I imagine that a lot of the furniture was imported from there. I can't see that my parents would have had spare cash to go bargain hunting.

The house had a sunny aspect, with garden on three sides and allotments at the back, so that you felt space and light. The long back kitchen window, where the magic mirror would later be placed, faced the allotment sky.

The previous occupants, Mr and Mrs Salt, liked privet hedges. They had surrounded the front garden with them, so that you couldn't see in unless you looked over the gate, although the back garden had a low hedge with a gate leading into the allotments. There was an air-raid shelter at the side of the kitchen window, which made a good den as we grew up. There was also a coal shed, with a wooden latched door, that echoed wonderfully when we played a favourite ball game Mummy taught us.

Inside, there was the kitchen with a separate pantry and two living-rooms. Upstairs there was a bathroom, separate loo and three bedrooms. The small room facing the top of the stairs and looking out over the allotments had a single bed. This was to become my sister's room and also John's room; when he stayed, Jackie came in with me. My parents had the room next to it, facing the road at the front of the house, and I had the room next to theirs, also at the front. I had a double bed in my room, which probably came from Pop's house, like most of the furniture. I shared my bed on many occasions; with my sister, when John was there, with my paternal grandmother, Nana, when she came to stay, and with my cousin Liela, too.

My next clear memory, after the moving day, was the arrival of my baby sister, Jacqueline, known as Jackie. My mother had been due to give birth around Christmas 1949. She decided to be born, however, on 26 October. My Aunt Harrie had been visiting my mother on that day, with my cousin David, who is eleven months younger than me. My mother had said that she was feeling tired and was going to have a warm bath and an early night. Harrie bathed me and put me to bed and took David home. Shortly after she arrived home, she had a phone call from my father. My mother was in Sefton General Hospital and had already had a tiny baby girl. Harrie went to see her straight away. Jackie weighed only two and a half pounds – just over a kilo. She was two months premature and was in an incubator.

I remember missing Mummy then. I don't know how long she was in hospital, but I do know that it had been a difficult pregnancy and that following the birth she was quite ill. It was a couple of weeks, maybe even three, before she came home. Although I must have been told about the new baby, it wasn't something I could grasp as I wasn't allowed to go to the hospital to see the evidence! I know that Nana came to stay to look after me and Daddy, and that she stayed for a while even after Mummy came home, as she was disappearing all the time. I later realised that Mummy was going to the hospital to feed and care for Jackie as much as she could.

Jackie finally came home in the New Year. I do have a memory of that day. My large, white pram had been passed to my cousin David and now it had come back. In fact it had arrived some weeks before, in preparation for the homecoming, and on this day was parked in the kitchen. My father carried the new baby up the garden path, a lot more carefully than he had carried the table the day that we moved in. He walked slowly and gingerly into the kitchen, where Mummy pulled back the covers of the pram and he lowered Jackie in. Then I climbed on to the wheel, supported by my parents, and peered in. I could hardly see her. She was still very, very tiny. In fact, I had bigger teddy bears! I inspected her head with my hands, looking at her with my fingers. I was helped to kiss her. I am sure I approved.

I have no specific memories of other times, between our moving into that house and Jackie's joining us there, but there are photographs which tell me that we visited Nanny. There exists a group of snaps, taken on a summer's day, with Mummy, who is visibly pregnant with Jackie, John, me, my cousins Liela, David and Michael. I was two and a half, Liela was ten, David three

43

and Michael not yet two. John was eight. We all spent a lot of time together but it wasn't often recorded on film, so these pictures, which Stanley copied for all of us, have become very precious.

Although there are no family photographs of visits to Springwood, as far as I know, Nanny came visiting with Michael, and Harrie came with David. Stanley visited during the school holidays and Liela was a regular and most welcome family member, staying nights, weekends and longer during the school holidays. She and Mummy adored each other and spent many hours talking together. I can hear her saying 'Judy' (her name for Julia) this and 'Judy' that, as she followed Mummy round the house and garden, intent on having her attention. Liela was like an older sister to us. The only ones who didn't come were Mimi and John.

He was eight years old, almost nine, when we moved into that house. Mimi was still insistent that my parents' relationship was unsuitable for the young John, and now that they were no longer in the family home in Penny Lane it was even easier for Mimi to lay down the law.

My mother had been hoping for a different attitude from her eldest sister, a softening that might allow her to see more of John. But with Pop no longer there to contain Mimi's worst excesses, her attitude hardened, and the move from Penny Lane gave her the perfect opportunity to make a total break. To her my parents were officially sinners, living in the house of sin. Jackie and I were illegitimate, and therefore we did not belong in this family and never would belong in this family. This was to be Mimi's attitude for the rest of her life. We were to hear it, many times, from her and from Nanny and Harrie too, in later years.

Mimi decreed that John would not go to our house to witness his mother's sinful union or see us, the illegitimate children. She said that seeing his mother unsettled John. He was unhappy when she left, so she wasn't to come. She had to stop trying to see him. Mimi would not set foot in our house and my mother was not to go to Mendips. John must be left alone to live a proper life. But Mimi should have known that rules are made to be broken and that the more unjust the rule, the more certain it is that it will break.

We had a room for John, furnished with his own bed from Penny Lane. My parents had settled into a stable relationship with their two daughters. And they wanted John. My mother was not going to give up on her son. She would see him, with or without Mimi's permission. And nine-year-old John felt the same way. No one was going to keep him from his mother.

10: *Stanley the Hero*

So, here we are in the new-start house with the new-start rules. Rules made by Mimi. My mother opens the house, where everyone is welcome. Harrie comes with Liela and David, Nanny comes with Michael.

Only Mimi will not come, and John cannot come.

Our mother must have been absolutely exhausted, both physically and mentally, with the house move, the difficult pregnancy, the premature birth, living for months between the hospital and home and looking after me. But she never gave up on John.

Despite Mimi's decree, Mummy went uninvited and unwelcome to see her son. Sometimes Mimi let her knock on the door but wouldn't let her in, and she cried when she returned home.

She had her record, which went, 'My son John, to me you are so wonderful/My son John, to me you are the world'. She wore it out.

Between August 1949 and April 1950 I don't think John came to our new house at all. In all those months he had only been able to see Mummy if Mimi let her in, which was rarely, or if they were all at Nanny's house. The fence was being erected. John knew that his mother had left Penny Lane, but he didn't know where she was living. Mimi told John that his mother had gone away to live with Bobby. She didn't know where. In those days nobody ever told us children anything, even if it was important. Or even if it was going to change your whole life.

But John found his mother. Stanley, his hero, led the way.

Mater had met the man who was to become her second husband, Robert Sutherland, or Bert. He was an army dentist and they had first met in Preston four years earlier and then again in Fleetwood. They married in November 1949 and moved up to Edinburgh, with Stanley. He was sixteen. His holiday habits hadn't changed, however, and he started to get the bus down to Liverpool. His first journey from Edinburgh bus station to Liverpool's Ribble bus station was the following Easter.

He knew that his Aunt Judy, as he called her, was in a new house. His mother had written down the address and told him how to get there. He went to Nanny's, as usual, and the next day he crossed the water to start his holiday round of visits. He arrived at Mendips and said he wanted to take John to see his mother.

Mimi told Stan that he was not to take John to see his mother. She said my parents were living in sin, that their children were illegitimate and that John was never to see them and Stan was never to see them. They were not part of the family and never would be.

Stan said that he would take John round to see Harrie, Liela and David, who were how living at The Cottage. That was allowed: he couldn't see his mother, but he could see his aunt. So Stanley and John went adventuring. Stanley remembers it well. They had an address and they found it. They came to see Mummy and the new baby and me. When Mummy saw them she shouted what she always shouted when she was really happy. 'Oh! My dream's out!'

When Stanley took John back to Mendips he had to tell him what to say.

Don't tell Mimi. John was to repeat this refrain until he died, because he died long before Mimi. John always called Stanley the prodigal son for bringing him back to his mother. He might have got his terms a bit mixed up, since really, it was he who was the prodigal son, but I knew what he meant – coming back to Mummy was the most joyous thing.

Stanley had spent much of his early childhood with my mother. First in Berkeley Street, with Mama and Pop, and all his aunts. Then, following the move to Penny Lane, he stayed with our grandparents again, as his parents went backwards and forwards to Germany, on business. Nanny and my mother looked after him throughout and they forged a close relationship. When Mimi laid down the new no-Springwood law, on Stanley's arrival from Scotland, he simply ignored it. John asked where his mother was as soon as they were out of Mendips, and Stan, believing Mimi to be wrong, took him to her straight away.

I was three years old then and I remember John. My own short life had, by then, been shaken up when Mummy disappeared to have my sister and then spent as much time in the hospital as at home from late October to January.

I didn't know then, of course, that John's visit was the Big Secret. My brother came, he ate, he played, he hugged Mummy and laughed and cried with her. Now John knew where she was. But after Stan went home, he could only come rarely, except during Stan's holiday visits. On one occasion, ten-year-old John came, when he was supposed to be working as a Cub Scout for 'Bob-a-Job' week. But apart from snatched visits like this one he had to wait for Mimi to let Mummy in, or to meet him at Nanny's.

That summer he was sent to Edinburgh on the bus, for the first time. The driver looked after him, and Stan was waiting at the bus station at the other end. Mimi wasn't taking any chances; she wanted to put a long distance between Mummy and John.

Stan's stepfather, Bert, had been raised on a croft on the northern coast of Scotland, in a small village called Durness, in Sutherland. The croft remained in the family for many years and was used as a holiday retreat. Stan and his wife later went to live there.

After a few days in Edinburgh, John went north with Stan.

This was to set the pattern for John's summer holidays for a few years to come.

He was taken by his aunt and sent to another aunt, to keep him away from the sins of his mother.

I am forever trying to understand.

11: *Growing Up*

My mother found a treasure trove in the amazing family who lived directly opposite. We all did. In Hannah Starkey, Mrs Starkey to us, right until she died a few years ago, my mother met her mentor. Julia was hiding with and confiding in this good, strong, oh-so-kind woman when we, her children, knew nothing about her reasons for hiding and confiding.

Mr and Mrs Starkey had six children: four daughters and two sons. The youngest child, Clare, was the same age as me. Her next sister, Ann, was older than me by two and a half years. Ann and Clare's two brothers were well outside our sphere: the eldest, Gerald, had already left school, while Charlie was still at school but had his own set of friends, so we didn't see much of him.

The big sisters, Pat and Rita, although much older than we were, wasted no time in forging their own link with our family. They were fascinated by our mother and impressed by her style. As Rita later told me, 'I couldn't wait to get over there to see your mum. She was fantastic. My mum used to say, "You can't go again, don't stay long", because I went as often as I could. Your mum was teaching me piano.' Rita described to me our mother's black jersey dress. She thought it was high fashion and promised herself one just like it when she grew older.

While Pat and Rita were gravitating towards our mother, Jackie and I played with Ann and Clare. There was never any doubt as to who was in charge. Ann was the Boss. Undisputed. We only got to make decisions when she was old enough to get boyfriends!

Initially, of course, we played in the gardens. This one or that one – the front, the side or the back. The Starkeys were also in a corner house with three gardens, so we had plenty of space.

The whole estate was lined with lovely, mature elm trees. You could hardly see the other houses. Sadly, when Dutch elm disease was ravaging the English countryside about 25 years ago, they had to be cut down. They were never replaced, contrary to the promise made at the time, so the road has taken on a naked appearance, compared to how it was when it was our living space and our playground. More recently they have built additional housing on the allotments, completely changing the vistas of open sky, which we took for granted.

I don't remember the particular day when I was allowed out of the wooden gate between the high privet hedges at the front, on to the pavement, into the road, on to the Starkeys' pavement and even round the corner, almost out of view, but it happened. I imagine I was about four years old then. As Jackie was only a year-old baby, she wasn't yet a paid-up member of the all-girl gang, but a member-in-waiting. As soon as she got to the grand age of four herself and was deemed old enough for the garden adventure, the crossing the pavement adventure and the almost disappearing round the corner adventure, I grasped her hand and took her along.

Clare and I would be between six and seven and Ann would be nine or ten. Where our mothers lost sight of us, Ann took over. The roads, of course, were clear of traffic. A few neighbours rode their bicycles, even motorised ones, with a little high-pitched buzzing engine on the back wheel, but cars were a rarity. I think my father may have been the first in the road to acquire a car, an Armstrong Siddeley, with a wide running-board. An Al Capone car, for the up and coming man-about-town. Everyone in the road and even the next road, had rides in that car. Up and down the road and round the round the block. I mean the adults! We children much preferred to hitch daily rides on the breadman's gigantic Shire horse, which ambled and shambled around the estate all day delivering bread. One-horse power!

By this time Bobby had become a head-waiter somewhere in town, where the cutlery was silver and had Mecca stamped on it.

He no longer went to work on the tram. He wore a black braided suit, sometimes with tails, a crisp white head-of-waiting shirt, a long camel-hair coat and a trilby hat. Under the hat, his black hair shone, because in the house, just before he left, he had slicked it back with Brylcreem or, failing that, butter. Mummy would sometimes do the glossing and brushing for him, laughing as she stood back to admire her handiwork. He would inspect himself in the magic mirror before leaving the house. It's hard to believe he was going to work.

He wore a pencil-slim moustache and had a bit of a foreign air about him. Nana, his mother, whose name was Gertrude Green, had both black and Jewish blood; she had landed in Liverpool generations back, we don't know when, and become a naturalised Liverpudlian.

I was very excited to think that Jackie and I were perhaps one thirty-second black. But as we grew up later beyond the safety of Springwood, we were accused of having a touch of the tar-brush. Of being dago. I first heard it from Mimi and she was still saying it towards the end of her life. My grandmother's bloodline gave her the most wonderful, olive brown skin, naturally painted dark brown eyelids, with large, deep brown eyes. Eyes that could really see you. Her hair was waist long and grey going white, plaited and wound around her head with long, thin copper-coloured hairpins. She was small and seemed to be everywhere at once and she was fantastically funny.

John was ten years old in October 1950. I don't know whether Mimi allowed him and Mummy to spend this birthday together. I feel certain that Mummy hadn't been able to see him the previous year, when she was pregnant with Jackie, although she may have gone to Mendips. If Mimi had been imposing strict sanctions then, as had clearly been her intention, then Mummy would have been under enormous stress.

Mummy always made a special effort on birthdays. This day belongs to you. No one else can have it. We must do lovely things. Have the birthday tea. Dress up. Laugh and sing and dance and play games. Invite lots of children. The whole road. When we started school, the whole class came too.

I don't know what she was allowed to do to celebrate John's birthday that year. Wear the record out and cry.

When Pat, the oldest of the Starkey girls, was eleven and John was nine, not long after we moved in, my mother asked Mrs Starkey if Pat could go to Mendips with a note. She went on the bus and found the house. John was playing with some friends at the front gate. Pat remembers that Mimi's dog bit her. She cried out and Mimi came out, shouting at her. As far as Mimi was concerned, she was a stranger. What was she doing there! How dare she! Get out of this garden! I can hear her saying it. Pat says she was a horrible woman. To be fair though, when Pat gave Mimi the note from my mother, she immediately took Pat inside and washed the blood from her knee, put a plaster on it and gave her a drink before sending her home.

Pat remembers regularly babysitting for Jackie and me, in the early evenings when we'd just been put to bed, while Mummy went to Mendips on the bus. Mrs Starkey would come over to check on her. My mother would often return very upset because she'd been turned away; Mimi had been shouting at her in the garden; she hadn't seen John – she'd been told to go home. Again.

She would put on her record, 'My Son John . . .' and sit weeping.

She would go over to see Hannah Starkey, looking for comfort. Mummy told her, 'They've taken my son from me. They won't let me have him. We've got to get him back.' I've heard this from Hannah Starkey and her daughters.

My father was on late shifts at the hotel. She would talk to him about it when he came home.

John was the ghost in our house.

I realise now that my mother was grieving as well as living. She went on loving us and smiling and hugging with such warmth while the life was being squeezed right out of her bones.

12: *John Finds a Way*

John was eleven in October 1951. By this time we had been at Springwood for three years and John was asking Mimi if he could go to see his mother. The answer was still no. Mimi, of course, didn't know he had been before, on the secret holiday visits with Stan. And she didn't know that John had begun coming over to see us on his own. He had to sneak over. Our neighbours remember it well, and the children who were in the road, where he was playing, running, hide-and-seeking, tree-climbing and skipping rope, remember it too. They hadn't even seen Mimi, but they knew it was a secret and wild horses wouldn't have got them to tell her.

So Mummy was snatching moments with John, at Mendips, at Nanny's and sometimes, secretly, at home. Making the best of it.

The following September 1952, at the age of nearly twelve, John started at Quarry Bank Boys' Grammar School. This changed things. It changed John's life, and Mummy's life, because he was now able to come to Springwood after school, without Mimi knowing. The three pivotal places in his life were laid out in a triangle. Mendips at one corner, Quarry Bank at another and Springwood at the third. John caught the bus along Menlove Avenue to Quarry Bank. He could then catch the bus along Mather Avenue to Springwood. Sometimes he did this after school, and sometimes he did this instead of school. He had found a way.

My mother was thrilled. John was thrilled. They were making sure they gave and got the love they needed from each other. I can hear the laughter and feel the joy.

I had started attending the primary school at the top of the road in that same autumn term of 1952, when I was five and a half. Jackie was almost three and still at home with Mummy.

I came home for lunch, which we called dinner, for the first year, walking on my own. It either took about five dawdling minutes or two racing, chasing minutes. I quite enjoyed school, but never wanted to stay there for long. Three hours was quite enough at one stretch. That's what Mummy said. She came up to the school gate at playtime, with Jackie, to see if I was all right. I remember not wanting to see her go. Right from the start, if I wanted to go home, I did. I couldn't see why we had to stay if we wanted to go. Or if the sun was shining. Or if my teacher had told me off.

I remember one such time very clearly. My mother took me back to school, opened the classroom door, told me to go and sit down and asked if she could she see the teacher. For a minute, please. I must only have been a school beginner. I can see the sandpit and the playshop. The whole class could hear, as Mummy and the teacher were standing in the doorway.

Julia can read, she was saying. She reads books. Julia can write. She writes with me. Please give her something else to do. Not ABC. Here's a book we've made at home. She left and the teacher came back into the room with a paper book that Mummy and I had made together. She had stitched the spine with chunky red wool and had secured it with a big, loopy bow at the top. I had written a story about a cat, in black Indian ink, with a proper dippy pen. Mummy had drawn some whacky, catty pictures, which I had coloured, in crayon. The teacher asked me to read it to her. I didn't have to do any more A Buh Cuh. Huh!

Was it George Bernard Shaw who said that he had to keep interrupting his education to go to school?

Sometimes, when I went home at dinner-time, John was there, in his school uniform. Sometimes when I got home in the afternoon, he was still there. Or he would arrive after school, and I would greet him and run out to play.

It was at this school that I met Ray, who was to become my lifelong best friend. Her father was in the army and she had been living in Malaya, so she only joined the school in the third year, when we were seven. She lived nearby and we often went to each other's houses to play and have tea. In the years to come she would prove to be a wonderful friend and a provider of desperately needed continuity as my life fell apart around me. Ray and I would go to the same secondary school, seeing our school years out together and remaining the closest of friends throughout our lives.

In the holidays occasionally we went to see Harrie, Liela and David, in The Cottage, around the corner from Mendips. In order to get there, we walked past our school at the top of the road, where we met the bottom end of Allerton Towers, formerly a private estate and now a large public park. We could walk up the country road, outside and to the right of the park's stone walls, or up Blackgates Lane to the left, and arrive at The Cottage at the top of that road. There was a bus that would have taken us right up the road, from one of the park gates, but we usually walked.

In retrospect, we probably didn't go to The Cottage often because it was too close to Mendips. Mimi didn't want us there, in Woolton, and anyway our mother wouldn't have wanted to be so near to John yet without him.

Instead we went to Nanny's house. The big house with the big garden. The long journey there was part of the fun, part of the day out. We caught the tram into town and then we had a choice.

To get to Nanny's, you have to cross the River Mersey. If it was a lovely, sunny day, we would walk down to the Pier Head to catch the ferry across to Birkenhead. We would stagger up the steep stairs to the first deck and climb the white-painted iron rails, standing first on the bottom rail and then stepping up to the next one, daringly. Mummy would be hanging on to us tightly. We watched the great hemp ropes being unwound from the capstans, this way and that, by the seamen on the pier. The men on deck would already be hauling on the ropes at the side of the gangplank to clear the pier. Just before the gangplank was completely upright on the boat, these burly, tattooed men would leap across the moving gap. The engines were roaring and the boat was already drifting away from the pier, sideways on. We were waiting for them to fall in, but they never did. We could see the biggest, fattest tyres, now. The ones chained to the pier to stop the boats crashing and splintering as they docked, a thousand times a day.

As soon as the ferry reached the Woodside terminal, we would race downstairs to stand on the painted, 'don't step over this line' line, or lean over the edge at the side of the gangplank, to watch the fascinating process that brought the boat to the landing stage. The ropes would be unwound from the capstans on board, this time with much heaving and ho-ing, and then flung on to the pier. The seamen would follow them in a flash, leaping ashore as the boat was still edging towards the pier, and start the figure-of-eight swirling and whirling of the ropes around the pier capstans. No sooner had the broad, planked gangway been lowered with great clanking by the sailors, as we thought of them, than we would run across, the three of us, Mummy in the middle, tightly holding hands. Lots of people did this, the weight pushing it down on to the pier with a thud. Some even jumped the gap behind the sailors. We would then catch a bus to Nanny's house.

If it wasn't so warm, we would cross the road from the tram station and go down underground to catch the train – and go *under* the Mersey. That was really exciting, in a scary way. The first thing we had to do was go into the lift that dropped us rapidly into the underground train tunnels. We would walk in through one door and wait for the lift to fill up. First in, first out meant being pushed across to the opposite door, and then the wait. Sometimes they let it go down with only a few people in it. That must have been during off-peak times. At busier times, the lift was bursting on all four sides, which is frightening when you are knee high to a chicken. The criss-cross metal doors would be closed, and then there would be the zoom. The one that left your tummy at the top. The lift always seemed to go a bit further than it meant to go and had to heave itself back up, after it had regathered its strength. We would wait with bated breath. One time, it mightn't shunt up.

The walk in. The wait. The zoom. The tummy. The wait-in-panic. The walk out. We enjoyed this scare.

Then we caught the train. We were already underground but it was the train in the tunnel that made you realise you were far from ground level. The station was dimly lit, dingy. We got on the train and huddled close. The doors closed and we headed towards the black night. Even though the carriages were lit, we thought we were in the dark. As we went through, Mummy used to have us looking for fish through the black reflection of the windows. We counted them out as we went. We saw lots. Goldfish, mainly, swimming past the windows. We checked to see that they were closed. We were under the Mersey, but we believed we were in it a wonderful, magical version. When John was with us, in his teenage years, when Mimi's laws were splintered, he saw sharks and whales. And cod and haddock. He would be laughing with Mummy. As soon as we left the tunnel to come out into daylight, we would all be laughing. We had lived to tell the tale. What a journey that was. A short walk and we were there.

Jackie and I were living in a bubble. A glorious, rainbow-coloured bubble that expanded with our needs. We didn't know it then, but life wasn't going to get much better than this. We knew nothing of nostalgia. We only knew the present and it was good.

Gabriel García Márquez says that before adolescence,

memory is more interested in the future than in the past, and that recollections are as yet unclouded by nostalgia. I was not yet pining for this house and our life in it. I was living and loving it.

13: *Foster Care*

When I was about seven and Jackie was four, we were woken up in the blackest of black night to the thuds of feet on the stairs. I screamed and ran into my parents' bedroom. Mummy was slumped over the edge of the bed, rocking, crying. She was in a pool of blood. Daddy was kneeling in front of her, crying, trying to cover her with a blanket, talking to her. 'They're here. It's all right. It's all right.'

It was a devastating scene. I couldn't take my eyes off the blood on the bed and the floor.

Two ambulance men unfolded Mummy and carried her downstairs, where they put her on a stretcher and took her away. That night, instead of going to work, Daddy had to stay at home, with us.

The next day Jackie and I were taken to another house, where there were people we didn't know. We have had many instant, inexplicable flashbacks to this place, even before we understood it. The long, gloomy, unlit hallway, with the mosaic floor, with no light to reflect its beauty. The dark brown stairway. The back room upstairs with the table, with the food we didn't eat. The attic bedroom where, in desperation, the caring couple locked us in to stop us escaping.

I knew which part of Liverpool we had been taken to. I had seen through the letterbox, before they pulled us back and up, when they let my father out.

I tried to open the door, but I was too small. I was trying to take me and Jackie home. Daddy came in the mornings, before he went to the hospital, and before he went to work. Previously he had been going to see his very sick father every day. I don't know when he was managing to see him now.

If he hadn't carried on working, paying the rent and bills, there would have been no house for anyone to go back to. He explained that to us, on his knees, in the gloomy, unlit hallway. I'll be back tomorrow, Hen. Big kisses from Mummy. She can't wait to see you. Look after Jackie.

Then the big door was opened and he escaped. Bolt, bolt.

We were living out eternity, in a strange place, waiting to go home. Jackie was crying all the time. I had to get us out. I had decided on the day and the way. The next day, as soon as Daddy left us, we were going willingly upstairs. And out. I leaned almost right out of the bedroom window and saw how far down it was to the yard at the back. A long way. There was a drainpipe right there. I was already climbing trees, but Jackie was so much younger. I knew that I would have to go first and drag her down by her ankles, bit by bit. If she could slip down to sit on my shoulders, that would be even better. We would be out. We would deal with the problem of the giant back gate when we got there.

Our dream of escape never became a reality – I was still plotting and planning when Daddy arrived the next morning, singing and clapping and hugging us in the dark hallway and took us home.

I think our stay in foster care lasted about three lifetimes, known as weeks. But although it didn't last long, it had such a profound effect on us that we had plunged it deep into an abyss and wiped it right out of our conscious minds, for many years. I don't know that John ever knew of it. I think not.

I am not certain exactly when the fostering episode happened. I just know it was summer and I was about seven, so it would have been 1954.

In retrospect, the only explanation I can think of is that Mummy had had a miscarriage. When I asked her, Nanny said that she knew nothing about it. She also said to me that we had never been in foster care. But maybe they didn't know. Nanny was good at remembering. If she had known about the fostering, she would have told me, or at least agreed, with a tart comment. What was your mother supposed to do? What were we supposed to do? I think she didn't know. I think that none of my mother's sisters knew. I think that if I were my mother at that time, the last people on earth I would have entrusted my children to would be my sisters. You could be taken into hospital, sick and incapable, and come out in three weeks to find you had no daughters left. I think my parents talked this through in a nano-second. I think that Bobby wouldn't let Judy's sisters near his children. If his mother couldn't look after us, then he had to find another way.

In my recent investigations, I went to find the house. I knew exactly where it was. I recognised the big, forbidding door. I tried to look through the letterbox, but it was blocked off. The whole building had been a bank and was now being renovated for offices. I spoke to a workman outside and asked him about the hallway. He said it had an old mosaic floor.

However we coped with the short fostering episode, as a family, we seemed to pull through together, and happy times followed the sad ones. I have memories of Jackie and me in our parents' bed, at this age, reading stories, playing I-spy, with Mummy's beautiful big brown eye, drawing, playing word games, the can-you-remember-what-is-on-the-invisible-tray game, adding another item each time. Daddy always put ridiculous things in like cars and boats, which made us laugh. They also made the game easier. All of us in their bed. We all slept together. I didn't have to get up to go back to school. I had quite a long time off during that term, and no sooner had I returned to school than it was the beginning of the long summer holidays. Bliss.

14: *My Son John*

1954 proved to be a groundbreaking year. Following the fostering fiasco, when my mother must have been in fear of losing all her children, she rose from her sick bed stamping her feet.

It was evident that John, now 13, was too old to be kept from his mother any longer. Mimi couldn't lock him up. John wanted to be with us and he was coming to see us as much as he dared, encouraged by both my parents. The record was getting less of an airing because 'My Son John' was becoming more a part of our family life.

As his visits increased, he became less circumspect with Mimi concerning where he was spending his time. This caused rows between them, but it also brought a certain clarity to the situation. I don't remember Mimi ever coming to Springwood while my mother was alive, and none of the neighbours remember seeing her, only hearing about her from John, so I imagine that Mummy went again to Mendips, this time not to be rebuffed. John was coming often. He was truanting from school to come. He was staying at the weekends, when he could. Mimi knew where he was. She had to wake up.

However it happened, the sisters obviously came to some agreement, because for the first time we began to visit Mimi ourselves, going to Mendips with Mummy. I can remember being in the sunny garden, playing, while Mummy and Mimi sat on the grass, drinking tea, so I imagine that this was during the summer holidays, only a short time after Mummy's hospital stay.

That summer we saw a lot of John. He stayed on and off throughout the holidays, and we went to Mendips and read and drew with him in his bedroom. We made paper skeletons and hung them from the ceiling, to frighten Mimi. We thought this was hilarious.

John took me to the wasteland at the end of the row of houses and showed me where he played cricket with Pete Shotton and Ivan Vaughan. Jackie, not yet five, wasn't allowed out of the gate, as Mendips was on a busy main road.

This was a truce. The cold war was clearly over, and the wall could be dismantled, brick by brick. Whatever had happened between Mummy and Mimi, some sort of peace had been declared. From that summer on, John came to Springwood much more, with or without Mimi's approval or permission. He sometimes brought friends with him.

For Mummy the joy of having John with her so much more was enormous. Whenever he was there her pleasure was palpable. At last her beloved son was able to be part of our family in a way that had been strictly limited until now. He even came with us that summer to visit Nana's holiday cottage in Wales for a few days. Along with her two sisters, Maggie and Florrie, Nana owned a small holiday cottage on a farm near Dyserth, in North Wales. We called it The Bungalow. We went there from time to time, to be in the countryside and to play in the big field. We rolled giant hay bales around with great difficulty, to construct dens and playhouses, where we could have picnics and think we were hiding. When John came with us that summer, the only time he ever came, he helped us build a mini village, more than we'd ever managed before.

On hot days, we would travel along the seaside coast from the village on an open-top bus, loaded with our swimming costumes, towels, brightly coloured buckets and spades, drinks and butties in a huge shopping bag. We sat upstairs at the front, squinting into the horizon, wanting to be the first to spy the sea, jumping up and down in excitement. On colder days, or wet days, we would stay inside and read, tell stories, trace and draw pictures, colour in books, do jigsaws and make dens on the bunk beds. That summer my father tried to teach my mother to drive on the field, where it was safe. She hit two cars before we left. I think that the lessons ended there.

We would only ever stay for two or three days at a time. I imagine this was as much time as my father could take off from work, and having a car made it feasible to have a short family break.

On John's fourteenth birthday, in the October following the summer of peace, Bobby made him a cake, with orange and lemon peel – his speciality. We had a birthday tea in the kitchen, when Mummy and John played instruments and we danced.

15: *Snapshots*

Ours was a happy home although from time to time my parents quarelled. They had a passionate relationship but they always seemed to resolve things in the end. When we came in from school Mummy was always there, often singing to herself in the kitchen. She would never have let us come back to an empty house.

She was a good cook, but stuck to straightforward things like stews and roasts. It was Daddy who did the fancy stuff like cakes and puddings. Mummy never wasted more time on housework than necessary, she couldn't see the point. She refused to have a washing machine when Daddy offered her one, because washing, starching and ironing the dress shirts and stiff collars he needed to wear for work was not her idea of fun. She sent the lot to the Chinese laundry.

What Mummy always had time for was us. She was an artist and an entertainer. If she had been born into another time, she might have exploited her talents outside our home, but as it was, we were the beneficiaries. Outside the house, she could ride bicycles with her feet in the air, run races, skip, juggle with three balls, do head-stands, hand-stands, the upside-down crab and cartwheels. Inside the house, she could draw, paint, sing, dance and play instruments. These included the banjo, the ukulele, the piano and the piano accordion, with all the keys and buttons and pleats, à la Edith Piaf. We spent hours dancing as she played and sang to us.

Though not vain, Mummy cared about her looks and took trouble over her appearance. She always wore bright red nail polish, on her toes as well as her hands. And she gave herself regular oatmeal face-masks and kept her hands white with lemon juice. She also took brewer's yeast tablets for her complexion. My father adored her. He was what was called a dapper man; he wore a camel-hair coat and a brown trilby set at a rakish angle. He was very tactile, with Mummy and with us. He would lift me and Jackie on to his knees for cuddles – his little girls.

Because he worked during the evenings we often saw little of him for days at a time. He'd be there for breakfast, but would be gone by the time we came in from school, and would come home long after we were asleep. He usually had to work at weekends too, so his days off, when he was at home to play with us and cook us treats, were special. Daddy loved messing around in the kitchen, up to his elbows in flour, baking us apple pies or sticky cinnamon buns.

John always got on well with Daddy. He called him Bobby, but to his friends he called him Twitchy, because Daddy had a nervous little cough, like a tic. I think he had been very ill as a child and this was the legacy. Daddy always gave John pocket money when he came over, and the two of them would joke and play together. I do remember one time, though, that Daddy was, quite rightly, furious with John, who'd been smoking in his room and accidentally set fire to the mattress. 'You could have burnt the house down!' he shouted. John was apologetic in a sort of mumbly teenage way.

Both my parents were strong characters and at times they rowed loudly. Other times they gave each other the silent treatment. Jackie and I would keep out of the way until it was over, then we'd walk in to find Daddy with his arms around Mummy, as they kissed and made up. We always knew they would.

Our family of four extended often to include Nana or John. When Nana came to stay, which she often did, she shared my big bed. She would come to bed after me, of course, when I was meant to be asleep. I would hear the door being gently pushed open and her quiet, low breathing as she felt her way across the bottom of the bedrail to the window side of the room. I would lie there in the half light and watch the divestment. This was a fascinating process, involving concentrated fiddling with the tiniest hooks and eyes which tied together whole-body wrappings of whalebone, edged with pink satin. When she had freed herself, she would pull on a long, white, embroidered cotton nightie and lower herself slowly into the bed, facing the window. I would wait until I heard her breathing become steady, then I would roll myself into her large, soft back and know nothing until morning.

When John stayed, Jackie and I slept together, so that he could have the other room. We whispered and played guessing games and story games until we drifted off to sleep.

John had little peace from us when he stayed. We jumped right into his room and right on to him. We pulled the covers off, shouting for games, bouncing and pouncing on the bed, giggling. We had one game where John raised his knees and we would sit on top of the hill. He would count odd numbers in any wrong order, which made us shriek with laughter, then he would drop his knees flat, grabbing our arms so that we wouldn't crash to the floor. John was wounderful fun.

On weekday mornings John dressed in school uniform, like me. He had to leave before me, to catch the bus at the top of the road. I only had to cross the road by the bus stop and I was there.

If it was a glorious Saturday, we could make plans. This often included the park and the cinema, or the pictures as we called it then. Those were the days when you had the little picture, followed by Pathé News, followed by the big picture, often followed by the little picture again. There were times when John took me and we saw the entire programme twice over. I was sometimes abandoned, with an Orange Maid lolly, while he disappeared into the black, to meet his friends outside. I think they were smoking. There were a lot of cowboy films and then, later, there were the many times that we went to see the first Elvis films, *Loving You* and *Love Me Tender*, accompanied by our mother.

69

One particular memory of John's schooldays from about this time is when he was booked in to get the cane, as a punishment for some misdemeanour or other. It was probably one of many occasions, but I remember this one because he had a defence strategy. Two pairs of trousers! Padding against the whacking. We were treated to a very funny demonstration of how he would enter the room, saying what a nice day it was and asking how the teacher was and what did he want. When the imaginary head teacher exploded with anger and reached for the weapon, John bent over the kitchen chair and held his breath, waiting for the inevitable impact. We laughed ourselves silly at the scene, which was to take place for real on the following Monday. I am sure that John was being a lot more blasé that he actually felt, and that making light of the matter with us was an attempt to lighten his own load. He even said 'Thank you very much, sir' as he stood up. In the kitchen, I mean.

Sometimes, when we had started to go to Mendips to see Mimi and John, he would take me out through the front gate. There were two places to go. One was the waste ground or tip, just at the end of Mimi's row of houses, where we could run about, hide or play cricket. The other was to play 'get the golf-ball', a common pastime for many of the local youngsters as a pocket-money aid.

The golf-links were immediately opposite Mendips, on Menlove Avenue which rolled its way down to Allerton and came out directly opposite the high school I was to attend in a few years. We would cross to the golf-links and walk along the edges of the fairways and greens, waiting for a ball to fly or roll in our direction. Sometimes we could just see white golf-balls in the long, rough grass at the sides. John slipped these quickly into his pockets. He and his mates would take them home, clean and bleach them and then sell them back to the golfers in the club-house, or even as they were playing, for a shilling – which was a whole week's pocket money for me. If a ball appeared by chance, zooming through the air and then landing close by, out of sight of the golfer, John would push me forward to collect it. Sometimes, you could actually see the owners of the 'lost' balls coming along the fairway. If I thought I was going to be caught, I wouldn't go, and John would have to race on to the grass himself.

Running all the way down the left-hand side of the golf-links, the left-hand side from the Mendips end, that is, was a real country lane. Blackgates Lane. The same lane that we walked along with Mummy when we started to visit Mendips, and the same one that took us, if only rarely, to see Harrie and David in The Cottage. The lane was, and still is, full of fruit bushes – blackberries and blackcurrants – which we gorged on when the season was right. Or even before the season was right. It is about three-quarters of a mile long, but then seemed endless. However, there were distractions on the lane itself, and not just fruit-picking.

One was a Nunnery. We often saw the nuns in their long black garb, seemingly floating up to Woolton or down to Allerton. You had to look hard to catch a glimpse of their black lace-up shoes. They always appeared to be gliding. I used to try to imitate the float, but you really needed the long outfit to make it work. They took on the same illusory appearance as someone who rides past on a bicycle, behind a hedge or a wall, and appears to be gliding along unaided. If we'd had a close shave, trying to get a golf-ball, we could run like hares through the hedges into the lane and disappear into the Nunnery grounds, where we would hide from the nuns. Guilty consciences!

John showed me the other hiding place, which was a stable. You had to stroll in there, as if you had a horse of your own, as many families did. It was a brave thing to do. Once in there, you could get right up to the horses and stroke their noses and all down their long necks and feed them grass. I just loved those horses and so did John. He must have found all this with Stan, a few years before, when making their way along the lane to

Mummy, in the days when Woolton was still out of bounds to us. When we started to go there, after the sanctions were lifted, we lost no time in showing each other our discoveries in the lane. I already knew about the nuns, as we had passed them before, but the horses were the real find. I didn't know then that I was building a fortress against loss, but I was. In later years, after Mummy died and we moved to Woolton to live with Harrie, Blackgates Lane became such an important place for me. Every day I walked down it to school it took me in the direction of Springwood and memories of Mummy. It became my private comfort zone.

16: *Part-time John*

John had problems in not living with us full time. One of them was explaining the situation to other people. Children are sheep and have a flock mentality. So his friends and our friends all wanted to know this: why did he live with his aunt when his mother was just down the road?

But he had no answer. Neither did we.

The very fact that you have to explain it to people just wears you out. You have to make it up because you don't know why yourself. They are making you face the problem you can't define or fix. And in the end, you want to hit them just for asking. And for pointing out that you're not normal. It happened to me and to Jackie. So I'm sure it must have happened to John, all the time.

I remember wondering why John had to leave our house and our Mummy and go somewhere else. I started to think about it for myself when I overheard John and Daddy talking in the kitchen one day. I froze at the table, making myself small, as children do, the better not to be sent off or to miss a word.

My father was telling John to stay if he wanted to. He was holding his shoulders, looking right into him, the way Nana could do. He was saying, 'You don't have to go, John.' He would go to see Mimi, himself, right now, he said. This can't go on. Let's sort it out, once and for all.

This was the summer term of 1955, when John was fourteen. Although he was visiting us openly and more often than before, he still had to go back to Mimi's at the end of each visit. And he was becoming more distressed at leaving our mother. At leaving us.

This time he had shouted and cried. That's why Daddy had taken him into the kitchen, away from us, to talk. John was sobbing, Daddy was holding him. 'I can't, I can't,' John said. 'I'll be in so much trouble, I've got to go. But I'm going to stay all summer.'

But John didn't get to stay with us all summer. He was sent to Scotland with Nanny and her son Michael, to keep him away from his mother and the house of sin. He had been to Scotland before, of course. In fact, he had been that Easter, but he had never been sent with Nanny before.

I have mentioned that Nanny poured her entire being into her only child. Michael was never going to be the middle child like she was. The Misfit.

I think that although Nanny never forgave Julia for having the affair that led to Victoria/Ingrid, and absolutely never forgave her for living with Bobby while married to Alf, before she had a child of her own Nanny had actually tried to smooth things over with Mimi. She tried talking to her, on Julia's behalf. She could compare John's treatment by the adults with her own when she was growing up. She was the one who collected John and took him to his mother, which was a journey. And her home was always a meeting-place. But once she had Michael, she became a single-minded, intensely focused tigress. No one else mattered. Michael could do no wrong, we were all aware of that, even as children.

On that trip to Scotland Nanny devoted all her time and energy to Michael throughout that entire summer. She coddled and cuddled Michael and ignored John. She bought Michael ice-cream and sweets but not John. She sat with Michael and John in the back of the car on the long journey and ignored John. Bert and Mater were seething when they returned to Edinburgh. They told everybody. During the holiday they had remonstrated with her, trying to make her see what she was doing. In the end they came home early.

That was to be John's last summer trip to Scotland. He spent the next summers with us. He went to Scotland once more, when Mimi took him to spend Christmas with Mater and Bert the following year, and that was his last time that he was sent there to keep him away from his mother. He did return to Scotland, however, on tour with Cynthia, and in later years with Yoko. John had to face another ordeal after returning from that holiday. His Uncle George, Mimi's husband, had died while he was away, collapsing as he came downstairs one Sunday afternoon to go to work on the nightshift. Mimi and one of the lodgers, Michael Fishwick, called an ambulance and George died a few hours later. He had suffered a massive liver haemorrhage.

I only remember Uncle George as a mild-mannered, white-haired man, who, despite his imposing size, was a mouse about the house. Because of the hours he worked he was either in bed or going to bed whenever we were at Mendips. It was the older children who had a relationship with him. Stanley, Liela and, of course, John. Liela remembers that no one had known that he was seriously ill and that it was a terrible shock to them all. She describes him as the most kind, pleasant and non-aggressive man, who never said a cross word, and remembers that he and John always had 'little secrets' going on between them. He was affectionate and always gave John 'squeakers', his name for kisses, at bedtime.

George had been John's friend and ally at Mendips, and it would have become a colder house without him. John had looked on George as a father figure and must have been distraught at his sudden death. John himself recorded how he felt, when he said, 'I've never learned to be sad publicly, what you were supposed to say and all that. So, I just went upstairs with Liela and we both had hysterics. We just laughed and laughed. I felt very guilty afterwards, because I did care very much about George, but I just couldn't show it. George had always been exceptionally kind to me.'

I'm sure Mummy would have comforted John over George's death, and all Mimi's sisters would have rallied round her at the loss of her husband, still only in his early fifties. At 49 Mimi was now a widow and it must have been hard.

I knew nothing of what was happening over at Mendips. I was still immersed in the world of Springwood, where one day Daddy came home with an LP. We'd had a record-player for a long time, with a heavy contraption holding the needle. A monstrous piece of walnut furniture. He wanted to know if he had brought the right one and within a minute we were listening to 'Hound Dog' at full volume. This was soon followed by 'Heartbreak Hotel', and the front room was rocking to the sounds of Elvis Presley, the new singing sensation from America. My mother was mad about Elvis. She danced with my father, with John and with Liela when she stayed with us. When Stanley was there, he would join in too. Jackie and I would watch and try to join in. This was our introduction to the King of Rock and Roll and the beginning of hero worship for John, and for all of us.

My parents were good dancing partners. They went and did Latin American dancing somewhere in town, and they loved the tango and the rumba. Mummy had a fairytale dress for these occasions, a pink satin creation, covered with silver stars, with pink, layered netting over the full skirt. She looked like Cinderella about to go to the ball. She was a Princess. That dress hung in her wardrobe, behind an everyday, navy blue shirtwaister dress with white polka dots and a neat black jersey day dress with long sleeves.

Recently Jackie and I were browsing in London when I spotted a pink, starry, floaty affair on a hanger. I pointed it out to Jackie and asked her whether it brought back any memories? Her reply was instant: Mummy.

Despite her admiration for Elvis, the favourite record, the most played song in my mother's collection was still 'My Son John, To Me You Are So Wonderful'. Even after John came to see us more often, and for longer, she would sit and listen to it after he had returned to Mendips, that fifteen-minute walk across the horizon.

Mimi as a young woman,
in the 1920s.

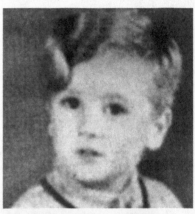

This is a lovely early
photo of John. He's
about two and a half.

My mother in Nanny's garden in the summer of 1950.
She's holding my sister, Jackie.

All of us cousins were close. This was taken in Nanny's garden in the summer of 1949. John is in the back row on the left, next to him is Liela. Then in the front, left to right are Michael, David and me.

Me, David and Jackie outside The Cottage in the summer of 1958. Stan had just brought us back from Scotland, hence the tartan.

I love this photo of John: he has such a cheeky grin.

Me and Jackie, 1958, in the gardens at Wooton Woods, where we went to live after our mother died.

We were often dressed almost identically. People used to think we were twins. This is me and Jackie again in 1958.

These four photos are of John on a Dovedale Primary School trip to the Isle of Man, in the summer of 1951. He's right at the bottom left corner, with the white shirt.

I love this seaside shot. John is just off to the left of centre, in the foreground, with his swimming trunks pulled almost up to his armpits!

Most primary schoolchildren at the time got the opportunity to go on the holiday. I went myself, another year. John is all the way over to the right, in the middle.

It looks like John had non-stop fun. In this one, he's squished into the very top of the left hand window . . .

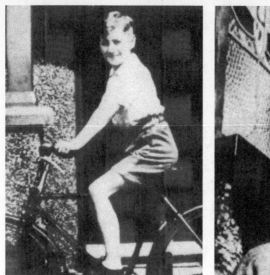

These two shots of John were taken outside Mendips when he was about 11.
In one, he's riding the bike Uncle George gave him.

This was taken in 1951 in John's final year at Dovedale Primary. He's in the top
row, fifth in from the left.

John with Mimi in the garden at Mendips.

Stanley in the front porch of Mendips, aged 16, despite looking very grown up in that coat!

Mimi, John and Michael Fishwick outside Mendips. I find this photo
extraordinary, knowing what I know now.

We had watched her listening, in sadness and despair, to that song, starting back in the days of no visits by John and her own hopeless visits to the unbending Mimi. Was she thinking about the daughter she couldn't talk about, as well as the son who kept leaving her? Was she contemplating her own helplessness? I only know that she would sit in the evening shadows, listening, and we would have to leave her be.

Since my father was a good cook and an enthusiastic baker he would sometimes have us help mix and beat in the kitchen. Looking back, I am sure that it was to occupy us and to leave Mummy with her sadness.

17: *The Unconscious State of Bliss*

As John was trying to deal with the problem of his abnormal life, Jackie and I were living unconsciously in a state of bliss. We didn't know then that soon we were going to be not-normal too. That a tidal wave was on the way – with no warning, no chance to get to the high ground.

That your Mummy could leave you and never come home.

We lived in a house with our mummy and our daddy and our brother, who came and went, but who now stayed more and more, for longer and longer. How is it that when I look back on that time, I see sunshine and not tears? That I feel loved and happy? It has to be because Mummy is there, protecting us from the pain she feels at her part-time son and torn-away daughter, hugging it to herself, so that we can have a chance at being normal.

We were living in the glory days of the Fifties. We were the Baby Boomers and we were blooming, as the post-war system was being built around us; education and the National Health Service. Never again would the call-up for war reveal a sickly, uneducated young population. They had said it after the First World War and hadn't fulfilled their good intentions. The Depression put an end to that. Now they said it again and meant it.

My generation are the beneficiaries and have had the most charmed existence of the twentieth century. We have carried on forging new pathways for the next generations. We are still doing it.

My primary school was known as The Scholarship Factory.

We were in classes averaging 54 children, with one teacher and a squeaky blackboard, with crumbly white chalk. We learned and fast. In the last year, we did a scholarship paper every Friday morning, before playtime. We did spelling tests from words taken out of the *Encyclopaedia Britannica* by the teacher, who was sitting on the desk in front of us, flicking through the tomes, seeking out the most difficult words. We would take the carefully written lists home and sit muttering and memorising and being tested by parents, until we were sure of getting a ten-out-of-ten. John tested me many times. He could spell too.

The other vital memory game was the times tables. The twelve times tables. We were, of course, still using imperial measures. We learned our tables everywhere we went. At home. In school. Always testing, testing, until we knew them inside out and back to front, sideways on and upside down. We could have chanted them standing on our heads.

We had one veritable monster of a teacher who delighted in testing us up to the sixteen times table. But I can say with all honesty that knowing these tables has been one of the most consistently useful things in my life.

Mummy would be peeling potatoes and chanting, once two is two, two twos are four. You had to listen hard because when she stopped, at any point, you had to take over, without breaking the rhythm. Then you could do the same to her and she would take over. I knew up to the twelves by the time I was six.

I practised everywhere. The breadman, the milkman, the insurance man and the rag-and-bone man – they all had to listen to my tables. John would pull any table question out of the air at any time and I had to be on red alert to bounce back with the right answer. Eight sixes. Nine sevens. Twelve twelves. Easy peasy. I did the same with my own children and when I was a classroom teacher. Good habits die hard.

We did art at school too. A messy business, saved for Friday afternoons, when we could relax. It was a reward for having done an eleven plus paper in the morning. We had paint in all the colours, mountains of paper and dads' old shirts to wear, and we were given free rein to be artists. The results were tacked to the walls and changed every week, so everyone had the satisfaction of seeing their work on display. We received gold and silver stars in abundance, lines of them stretching out beside our names on the wall by the door.

One day we heard there was to be a painting competition at school. We could paint anything we liked, at home, and the headmaster was going to look at them in assembly and award the prizes. I rushed home to tell Mummy. She loved to paint. She painted me a wonderful seascape. A yacht on the water, with the sun going down over the horizon. And a reflection of the yacht in the rippling waves. I was thrilled. I did dabble at it, but it was Mummy's masterpiece. Rather naughtily, I won first prize and it was framed and hung in the headmaster's room. The most difficult bit was when he asked me how I had done the reflection. He had to wait until the next day for the answer.

We did geography and history, learning about Eric from Norway and the Phoenicians and Egyptians. We were imbued with curiosity. We loved to find out, to know more. We read books as a class, all taking turns to read out loud, professing to hate it. When a reader had been reading for several minutes, you had a hammering heart. You could be next.

A quick flick of the eye down the page, maybe even turning over to the next page. Looking rapidly for any words you might stumble over. The teacher didn't like that. His eye was roving. It stopped. Michael, please. Jane, please. A reprieve. But when you were chosen, you rose to the occasion and read as if the Queen was listening. We loved it when we read well and had praise. Well read. Thank you.

We wrote so many stories. About our brothers and sisters, our cats and dogs, or our weekends. Every start of term had us writing at length about Christmas, Easter and the long summer days. We wrote with what now call calligraphy pens and in blue-black ink from the inkwell sunk into the top right-hand corner of the desk. We made many blotches, despite the pink blotting paper. Sometimes, I would write a whole page without a single blob, then turn the page over too quickly and ruin it all. My handwriting was always large-to-giant, sometimes only three words to a line. I sat hunched over the exercise books and wrote with my tongue sticking out. I loved to write. I wrote stories at home in bed, by the landing light if need be. In story books there were always blank pages, begging to be written on.

Mummy's writing paper would disappear and then reappear later with a story for her, about what we had been doing at school, in the park, down the road. She would read them while she was cooking and show them to John and Bobby. Then I would get a letter back, from Mummy, at the front of a story book, as a surprise, or on her writing paper.

John would sometimes read my stories out if I was there, holding the paper too high for me to reach, teasing, or even singing the words, to have me leaping up and down.

He was writing himself, all the time. John didn't enjoy school-work, and stayed in the bottom stream, despite his brilliance, simply because he couldn't be bothered. But he channelled his enormous abilities into things he liked and enjoyed, such as 'The Daily Howl', a satirical look at life which he created. And he wrote stories and drew and painted with Mummy. She introduced us all to long, nibbed pens and sharp, black Indian ink. Even at art school, John hated using colour. In a way, he was still doing artwork with Mummy.

My tenth Christmas present, in 1957, was a typewriter, with a blue and red ribbon. I still get excited by the sight of a clean, crisp sheet of paper and a black pen. Maybe one day I'll feel the same about a New Blank Document on my computer. But I doubt it.

At school we had PE, in the hall if it was cold and wet, or outside if it was warm enough. We ran races, played rounders and cricket and did athletics. We ran a lot, in all sorts of races: the hundred yards, the relay, the hurdles. Round the outside of the field. For the class team. The school team.

Every year we had Sports Day, when the parents were invited to join in the egg and spoon race. My parents never won the race, they were laughing too much. Mayday was another annual event. This was really exciting, and we danced around the bright, stripey maypole, twisting the long ribbons in a certain order, then turning round and untwisting them. It may have looked easy on the day, but we had half strangled ourselves over and over in practice.

Our house was near the Police Training School, at the back of Paul McCartney's house in Forthlin Road. They trained police officers to ride horses and work with dogs, usually German Shepherds. We loved this. They were the star attraction at school every Mayday. The horses would arrive amid a fanfare from the whole school. They would be put through their paces, jumping fences. The dogs would jump through hoops of fire and leap on pretend robbers, who were wearing protective, leather armbands which were chewed aggressively, until the order was given to stop. We loved this display. It was school at its best. And, to top it off, you could go home with your parents at the end of the afternoon, without going back into the building.

We would go to the Police Training School after school and at the weekends, sitting on people's garden walls to watch the dogs and horses. We took butties or sweets. It was like a day out. We felt as if the animals belonged to us. The policemen never chased us away. They would wave to us and we waved back. They probably loved the audience, as they were prancing about and shouting orders, and we loved the free show.

We played all the playground games that there were. People

now conduct research into our games. We just played them. Skipping. Not just any old skipping, but skipping with a purpose. Accompanied by complicated rhyming that you had to get right or you forfeited the rope straight away. And there were plenty of children waiting for their turn. We took no prisoners. You got it right or you were out. O-u-t, out. We were learning the art of arguing, winning and losing, with and without grace, all through school. Children are the best teachers for these skills.

We skipped in the road at home after school. Practising. Sometimes, if we had a long enough piece of washing line, taken down from the garden, we would tie one end to one of the elm trees and the other to a tree on the other side of the road. This meant that, on the rare, rare occasion when a car came, it would slow to a crawl, then stop and wait for us to untie one end of the rope, and the driver would bump the car over it and we would tie the rope again. We knew all the drivers. Sometimes, they even found a packet of sweets for us.

We all had our own skipping-ropes, with small ball-bearings in the handles, that rattled a rhythem as we skipped. We were like boxers in training. Sometimes we took it in turns, with the skipper in the middle of a chanting circle. We were counting the number of skips. Faster. Faster. Double skip. Skip backwards. Faster. Let another person inside your rope, keep going. We were hard on ourselves and very competitive.

We also played a game with the rope called Higher and Higher, which is a bit like a game of dare. Two people would hold the rope, not turning it for skipping, but holding it still, so that we could queue up to jump over it. It always started out on the ground, giving you confidence, then gradually it was raised higher and higher, until you were eliminated from the game, either by tripping on the rope, even slightly touching the rope or – the worst indignity of all – falling flat on your face on to the concrete. Maybe even needing a plaster, after having the grit washed out and swabbed with pink healing ointment.

Mummy used to say that we'd be sorry about these knees, these knobbly shins. We were permanently covered in bruises, from black to shades of blue and grey. We knew the course of the colours well. We could diagnose for ourselves when they would fade away. Only to be replaced by the bruise-in-waiting.

John joined in these street games with us. He was a dab hand at rope turning. And he was good at solving disputes. Particularly when you just knew that you hadn't even tipped the rope and they wouldn't let you have another go.

Another rope game was to make our own maypole around the iron lamp-post at the corner of the road. One of us would climb the lamp-post and tie the rope around the T-bar at the top, just below the large bulb in the glass globe. Then the rope would be wrapped around the length of the post, spiralling down. The victim – and that is undoubtedly the correct terminology – would take the bottom end of the rope and run round and round the pole until the force of the speed and the unravelling of the rope made you into a projectile. You were off – and often off the rope, too, into the road. More plasters, please. Smaller people, like Jackie, were taken even higher by grasping the hand of victim number one. They really flew.

You could also swing like a monkey on the T-bars. It was a long way to fall. We fell all the time, often on top of one another after four of us would hang on two bars and get our legs in a tangle.

The park, of course, presented even greater opportunities for hospitalisation, which did happen from time to time. Clare Starkey was taken in an ambulance directly to the local hospital. She had broken her arm when she lost her grip on the swing, having been pushed so high that the back pusher was herself swinging up and away, hanging on to it – the pusher's reward. But when the seat of the swing was right out of reach of the pusher, Clare jerked herself so high, that the long chain buckled and threw her right off and she crashed hard down on to the concrete. The parkie knew his job. He called the ambulance and her sister Ann went along with her to the hospital while we flew home to break the news to her mother.

I remember coming off the jerker, when we jerked ourselves hard enough to hit the beam. You were being taken to the beam, bang, bang, with your head just missing the frame. I tipped right off, but luckily was cushioned by one of the bigger girls.

The Maypole in the park was a disaster area, but we couldn't keep away. The long chains hung down the length of the pole, limply, until six of us took a wooden handle each and walked round and round the pole right behind each other, the handles getting higher and higher as the twist became tighter and tighter. The tallest person had to be holding the last chain, the one that went the highest up the pole. Then the run started and built up faster and faster, until the last person was swung to heaven and possibly dropped to hell. When you fell off that, you went horizontal like a rocket, before dropping like a stone, crashing down on to cracked concrete. The aim, of course, was to hang on like grim death until your chain slowed down enough for you to jump off, triumphant. Rare but excellent credit rating. John was very good at this.

The monkey bars were a set of horizontal iron ladders, set about twelve inches apart, about six feet off the ground, so that you swung in mid-air. You climbed up to the second thin, round iron step at the side and if you hadn't already slipped right off and crashed to the ground, you had to hurl yourself into space and grab a horizontal rung, then monkey swing the whole length.

The real test, though, was to jump to a rung shouted out by someone else. So you were slipping about on the side rung, waiting for Ann to shout three or even four, and then you had to grasp only that rung, with the audience gathered round for each act.

Then there were balls. We played two balls and three balls, into the air, against a wall and to each other. My mother was brilliant at this. She could even juggle – and did, for all the children. She taught us all to play two and three balls against the coal-shed door in the back garden. We could even throw the balls against the door and turn around super fast and be in place to catch the next ball, without falling over.

John was no good at this, but he was good at cricket, another game played right in the middle of the road. He was a fast bowler and a terrifying batsman. The trees served as everything in our games, they were an integral part of our outdoor lives. In cricket, they were stumps, or markers for fielders. First fielder, second fielder, positioned at the first tree and the second tree. We played with a proper willow cricket bat and a proper leather ball, so there were plenty of injuries. But a tennis ball would never have cut the mustard.

We also played French cricket, where the batsman stands in the middle and bats out wildly anywhere, often hitting the fielders full-on. This was John's speciality. He could make the ball disappear right into a garden.

We had a meeting tree, a large oak, just at the corner of the next road. All the children of the neighbourhood gravitated to that tree, it was the place that we were aiming for when we left the watchful eyes of our mothers and became Ann's charges. Our mothers always knew where to find us.

We held pow-wow there. We collected the acorns every year and counted them into the thousands, often burying them back underneath the tree. We took books to read and paper to draw on. We even took bread and butter and jam butties and had picnics.

In the long summer evenings, when our mothers came looking for us, to feed us and bath us and put us to bed, we begged: five more minutes. Pleeease. Everyone else in the world is staying out.

Just five more minutes. I don't ever remember being refused this extra time, which would extend as far as we could make it.

Elastic, summer time.

Heaven.

18: *Making Music*

I don't remember the day the Beatles were born, but the seed was planted in Springwood. Our mother was the sower and John the reaper.

As John entered into his teens and spent more time with us, she started to teach him music and he loved it. Their inborn, shared artistic talent became their renewed umbilical cord and it was soul-strong.

I can see John so clearly, concentrating intently on the mother-of-pearl backed banjo that had belonged to his grandfather, who had brought it back from a sea trip and then left it to our mother. She would stand behind him, leaning over his shoulder, and raise the neck of the banjo high. She would place her hands over his, their left hands on the neck of the banjo and right hands in the strumming position over the hole, and notes would happen. Sometimes, to get it right, she would tell him just to concentrate on the left hand and she would strum, or finger pluck. Sometimes she would press the strings herself to change the notes and John would strum and pick and pluck as loud as he could, making music. They would roar with laughter and he would be delighted with himself. Other times, our mother the musician would place his hands on the strings in the right position, come round to face him and then carry on instructing from there. Sometimes a record would be playing, slowed down to the slowest speed, sounding weird, while John strummed slowly but loudly along to the ghostly refrain. Then Mummy would take the banjo herself, return the needle dial to normal speed and play along, with John staring at her fingers on the strings, playing air guitar, before he had another go.

The skiffle craze was sweeping England as it had already swept America, along with rock and roll. Thanks to Lonnie Donegan a new dawn was being ushered in through the medium of music from the States. The whole bright day still lay ahead, waiting to change the existing world order. And in Liverpool, in our house, our mother played Elvis on the huge gramophone and Buddy Holly sang 'That'll Be the Day'.

Years later, in an interview, John said: 'The very first tune I ever learned to play was 'That'll Be the Day'. My mother taught it to me on the banjo, sitting there with endless patience until I managed to work out all the chords. She was a perfectionist. She made me go through it over and over again until I had it right. I remember her slowing down the record so that I could scribble out the words. First hearing Buddy absolutely knocked me for a loop. And to think it was my own mother who was turning me on to it all.'

The ukulele was used too, although I don't remember John wanting to learn it, as he did the banjo. Mummy played it really well. She had a wonderful repertoire as a one-man band, including a fantastic impersonation of George Formby. We would be encouraged to sing along, as she strummed and finger-plucked the strings of the ukelele and danced around the room. Jackie and I would be running round in circles, turning this way and that, thinking we were dancing.

Then Mummy would sit down and twist and turn her way into the piece of furniture that was the piano accordion, pushing the wide straps over her shoulders and lifting the whole instrument up and away from her body, shifting until she was happy with it. Then she would slowly raise herself to her feet and peer over the top, to check where she was placing her fingers at each end, and start to play. The piano accordion played like the piano, only upside down and sideways on, but there the resemblance stopped. The other arm was pushing the long pleats in and out, sweeping in an upwards and downwards arc, making different sounds as her long fingers jumped over the brown buttons. Sometimes it was exciting, like dervish music. Sometimes it was a haunting sound, slow and deliberate. Mummy didn't dance with us, she just swayed and hummed. I couldn't even lift it.

Years later, I studied French and went to Paris. It sounds like a cliché, I know, but my first trip on the Métro confirmed that I was truly in France – the France I knew from the schoolroom and the cinema. We had been devouring French films for the past two years. *Et bien, nous voilà*! The whole of the underground maze and everyone down there seemed to reek of the garlic they lived on and the Gauloises they were smoking. There was no escape. And then there were the accordion players. My mother had died seven years previously but when I heard the instantly familiar music coming from a distant tunnel, my chest was pounding and out of control. I had not heard this sound since we left Springwood. I followed it to where I could see the musician and listen without looking, and I sat down with my back to the wall and cried. I was unable to tear myself away for the rest of the afternoon, in a strange state of happiness and desolation.

The other instrument in our main living-room was the piano. John didn't learn to play it at that time, although we all hit the keys discordantly from time to time. His playing it to accompany 'Imagine', however, is one of the most enduring memories we all have of him.

I can't remember our mother ever reading music. I remember her sitting on the stool, practising, singing the notes she wanted to reproduce, but she was playing by ear, which would be more than difficult to teach, if not impossible.

The piano would be used as a background to some of our downstairs fairy stories. 'Goldilocks and the Three Bears' lent itself admirably to the Mummy and Piano treatment. Each bear had its own set of noises, from the deep growling of Daddy Bear, down on the low keys, through the middle C thumpings of Mummy Bear to the high-pitched tinkering of Baby Bear. Mummy did Goldilocks herself, turning round to make the faces.

And, of course, there was 'The Teddy Bears' Picnic. That opening sequence of four low descending notes could bring a girl running into the room, to creep around invisible trees, in pretend disguise, hiding and then joining in the singalong, only waiting for the final 'piiiiiiiiiic-nic!'

It was probably our mother's dinner-gong.

Another instrument associated with John, right through his musical career, is the mouth organ. The Liverpool slang for this is the 'gob iron'. Mimi's husband, Uncle George, gave John his first mouth organ, when he was about fourteen years old. He loved it. He would carry it in his pocket, or in his mouth and make a noise. He brought it over to show Mummy, who couldn't play it herself, but knew a neighbour who played it well, Arthur Pemberton. He lived next door but one and our mother sent John there, to learn the basics of puffing and blowing. He lived with it as an attachment for some time, even while he was practising the banjo, as he could still grip it with his teeth and suck and blow air, creating a din, until something resembling a tune began to emerge.

When the Easter holidays arrived, John was sent to Edinburgh on the bus, to see Stan and Mater. He entertained the passengers all the way up there, sitting just behind the driver. I can only think that he must have gained some proficiency by then, as no one took it away from him or, even worse, threatened to put him off the bus. In fact, the bus driver was impressed enough to make John an offer. Someone had left a good mouth organ on a bus sometime before and it was lying unclaimed in lost property. If John could come back to the bus station the next morning, he could have it. Stan took him back there the following day and John became the proud owner of a decent harmonica. I think he used that same one for many years. It certainly would have carried wonderful memories for him. And boy, he did improve!

19: *From Bands to Groups*

Before 1954 there were bands. A band was an orchestra, a brass band, a blues band, a jazz band or even a backing band. Then the new music disclaimed the band and adopted the group. Suddenly, bands were out. Infra-dig. Groups were in. Dig this.

It all began with skiffle, which had its roots in American music of the early twentieth century but really took off with Bill Haley's 'Rock Around the Clock', released in the spring of 1954 in the States. It was 1955 before its influence swept across the Atlantic, though. It emerged in Britain as the theme tune for the film *Blackboard Jungle* and excited unprecedented interest in the newly self-defining teenage population.

In January 1956 Lonnie Donegan and his skiffle group released the single 'Rock Island Line' and embarked on a nationwide tour, including an appearance at the Liverpool Empire. Paul McCartney attended that concert at the age of fourteen, and John bought 'Rock Island Line'. We had it at home and it was played almost to extinction before John sold it to a school friend.

The dancing was also new. Meaning it wasn't a waltz or a fox-trot, or even a cha-cha-cha. The new dancing was inextricably tied up in the whole skiffle/rock phenomenon. It grew its own name. The Jive.

While Jackie and I were bouncing around up and down and from side to side, having a great time, Bobby, Julia and the older children had a job to do. They had to learn the new steps! And practise them until it looked natural, as if they had been born jiving. My parents, who already loved Latin American dancing, set about mastering the latest craze, twirling and whirling on the sheepskin rug in the larger living-room, where the piano lived. They held hands and swung back, away from each other, then seemed to rush forwards at each other, twisting their bare feet. Then my mother would hold my father's hand and twirl around on the spot.

John and Liela watched my parents and followed suit. John and Mummy. Liela and Mummy. Liela and Bobby. John and Bobby. And Stan, when he was there. I can see him jiving with Liela, Judy and John. All of them dancing with us smaller girls too, indulging us, when we thought we were dancing, when they really wanted to master the art of jive for real and look good at it.

This outbreak of skiffle in January 1956 was followed immediately by Elvis and his 'Heartbreak Hotel', which sold more than a million records worldwide and earned Elvis his first Gold Disc. His first album appeared in March, and June saw the world rock wide awake with the release of 'Hound Dog' and the sight of Elvis's unforgettable hip swivel. It has never recovered. The King was born and there was no going back.

It wasn't long before mimic groups were sprouting all over the country, and Liverpool was no exception. All over the city the mad music craze was taking over, subverting the more than willing young. It was a roller-coaster about to start and they were all on it, waiting for the revving engines to let go and begin the run that was to blast through the global status quo.

You could ask anyone who had a brother what instrument he played. He played something. Even the front singers played. And they were practising in any space where they were tolerated, normally at home, in the garden shed or even the bathroom. Although we didn't realise it at first, this phenomenon was taking the whole country by storm. I have a fantasy image of a skyline of raised roofs rocking and rolling as a cacophony of sound hits them time and time again. What an innovative and exciting era: the birth of the Sixties in the Fifties.

John's first ever group consisted of Julia and John. Teacher and student. Artist and son. And as John's passion for the new music grew, so did the time he devoted to practising. All his friends were of a like mind. For some time they had been turning up to see him or to go out together, just to do the teenage hanging about. Now, they began to arrive with guitars. There was also a washboard, just like the one in Lonnie Donegan's group. I have memories of my mother playing it to accompany John and his friends, with her silver sewing thimbles on the fingers of her right hand, while holding it up with her left.

This budding group also boasted a real home-made instrument, a tea-chest-cum-bass, with a long string stretched as taut as it would go. I even remember someone staggering up the garden path under an old set of drums.

So the group that was eventually to lead to the Beatles had its beginning here, in our house, with John's diligent practising on the banjo and the harmonica. It was a multiple birth, however, as it was also in its infancy in Paul McCartney's house, where his patient father, Jim, allowed him to play in the house, garden and loo. And in George Harrison's house, where he was rapidly becoming an impressive guitar player. And in the house where young Richard Starkey had just come out of hospital after being treated for lung infections for two years, and taken up the drums. They just hadn't met up yet.

John made a transition at this point which, in retrospect, was a vital career move. He started to play the guitar. However, he often found himself reverting to banjo chords on his newly adopted instrument.

Meanwhile John formed the Quarry Men, named after his High School, Quarry Bank, in the Penny Lane district. Right at the beginning, in January 1956 when John was fifteen, they were called the Blackjacks and, to celebrate this name, they wore black jeans and white shirts, but that name only lasted a few weeks.

The first official Quarry Men group in the late autumn/winter of 1956 comprised John (banjo/guitar), together with his good childhood friend Pete Shotton (washboard), Eric Griffiths (guitar) and Bill Smith (tea-chest bass). It was Eric who introduced Rod Davis (banjo) and Colin Hanton (drums) into the group and at the same time Bill was replaced by Len Garry, also playing the tea-chest bass. He was sometimes joined in this performance by another great friend of John's, Ivan Vaughan. Practising took place at Springwood, Mendips, Eric's house, Rod's house and in Pete Shotton's air raid shelter.

Rod Davis remembers that John and Eric were playing really cheap guitars, trademark Egmonds. George Harrison's guitar, they later discovered, was identical. John's was a reddish sunburst and I can remember it myself. Eric's was, in Rod's own words, 'two vile shades of brown'. He thinks that John's may have been borrowed from a friend.

Our mother bought John's next guitar, so although it was his second one, it was the first that he had owned. This was a Gallstone Champion guitar, 'guaranteed not to split'. It was bought through an advertisement in a popular magazine, *Reveille*, for the grand sum of £10.19.6d.

Mimi put up the deposit for his third guitar, bought from the Liverpool music shop, Frank Hessey's, under a hire purchase agreement. It was John's first electric guitar, a Hofner Club 40. This progression from acoustic to electric guitar was absolutely necessary for the rampant volume demanded of a rock and roll group. Rod Davis remembers that when he started to come to Springwood with his banjo, to practise their repertoire, Julia would borrow it from him to join in. She wouldn't play the guitar. Stanley thinks that her own banjo was, by then, in a state of disrepair with broken strings, following John's primitive attacks on it, and that Mummy would have stored it away for future fixing. I can remember it being up-ended at the back of the clothes cupboard in my bedroom, so that was probably where it went to live in the meantime.

When John's guitar strings snapped – as in those pre-amp days they thrashed the living daylights out of their instruments to get volume – Rod would quickly pass him his banjo to play, while he changed the string. Of course it produced a completely different sound, but no one seemed to care.

They played mostly skiffle and rock songs, but Rod also remembers John singing the haunting 'Nobody's Child' often and with great emotion, as if it was his own song. It's easy to see why the song's poignant lyrics had special meaning for him.

No Mammy's arms to hold me or soothe me when I cry
Sometimes it gets so lonesome, yes I wish that I could die
I'll walk the streets of heaven, where all the blind can see
Where just like all the other kids, there'll be a home for me.
People come for children and take them for their own
I know they'd like to take me but I'm left here all alone
They say they like my curls of gold, they like my eyes of blue
But they always take some other child, and I'm left here with you.
I'm nobody's child, nobody's child
Just like a flower growing in the wild
Got no Mammy's kisses and no Daddy's smile
Nobody wants me, I'm nobody's child.

Perhaps that's what he felt he was – or at least had been.

The bathroom was particularly popular when John and his friends played their loud skiffle and rock, because it was small, tiled and gave out a booming echo. John and one other could fit in. They would stand with one foot on the rim of the bath and the other wedged against the wall, picking, plucking and hammering. There were times when Jackie and I were taken out of the bath to let them in. The other favoured room was the kitchen, which was spacious when the table was pushed against the wall, and there were the chairs to balance their feet on. I can hear the chair legs scraping on the lino, as they balanced themselves upright with whatever they were about to play.

While they rehearsed in every spare minute, Elvis got truly serious. He released his first film *Love Me Tender* in November 1956. As soon as it came out, our mother took John, Jackie and me to Garston cinema, in a state of high excitement, and we began life anew. We watched it four or five times over two days, at a time when you could hide in the dark of the cinema all day if you wanted to. By the time we left we knew all the words to all the songs and the film script too. We were smitten.

Elvis always transcended his black-blues sound and his heavenly, Indian-Adonis looks. Right from the start, there was no age barrier. Six or sixty, you came alive. And swooned with simultaneous ecstasy and jealousy when he kissed Jana Lund in *Loving You*, first released in early 1957. We went to see that and, later, *Jailhouse Rock*, time and time again. Sometimes, John took us by himself and he would always nip out to smoke, when the cartoons or Pathé News came on.

A stray cat adopted us. Mummy called it Elvis. She had six kittens.

That's how mad things were. Mad happy.

The musical storm sweeping the country was also reflected in the new, rebellious fashion. Teddy boys ruled, OK. I can see John now, with his black leather gear, black winkle-picker shoes, big, greased quiff and DA (duck's arse) hairdo. I can see him striding down the road, coming or going, guitar swinging in his hand, shoes pointing the way, clack clacking.

This new apparel, however, was no defence against welcoming hugs and twirls for us girls, in or out of the house. We loved him to bits, and ran at him, wherever he was.

One extra thing that both Rod Davies and John shared was myopia. Neither of them could see much beyond their noses. John hated his glasses, and even when he wore the black frames made famous by Buddy Holly, his hero, it was only as an emergency measure. Glasses did no favours for the Teddy boy get-up and I remember John black-leathered and bare-faced. He would only put them on when he got into the house. We all knew he couldn't see without them.

We put them on to try them out, to see the world through another window and to bump into things. That's what Mummy said would happen. Except that I didn't bump into things wearing them, and in fact the trees beyond the magic mirror took on a clarity I was forgetting. I was diagnosed as short-sighted via the school medical at the age of ten. My mother was there and she cried. What I didn't know at that time was that we had inherited this condition from her. We didn't know because she never wore glasses. Goodness knows how she managed without them – she can't have been as short-sighted as John and I were. She did have a pair with no lenses in, that she wore to make us laugh, though.

20: *Teenage Muscles*

As John was growing muscles, as he liked to call them, he enjoyed demonstrating his teenman prowess. And what better way to show off than to fling two small, squealing girls about?

My father used to play quite rough games with us. But he could throw us around in front of John and of course, John wanted to do the same, although he was forbidden. The wrong words were, 'You're not strong enough to take their weight, to swing the girls round, to swipe them through your legs without hitting their heads on the ground. You're not tall enough for that yet.' What an incitement to arms.

We had several throwing games we loved. Daddy would stand like the lamp-post at the corner of the road, with his arms stretched wide, and Jackie and I would cling on and swing. If he thought we were doing too well, or he wanted us off, he would slowly turn around until we fell off!

Then there was the aeroplane. The swing park brought to the garden. One arm, one leg, swung from the ground and then suddenly, you were flying loop-the-loop through the air, with the flowers and bushes spinning past until you had to close your eyes against the sick-tummy feeling. You would be lowered to the floor and you would roll on the grass until you felt human. It was fantastic.

The most dangerous game, and therefore the most wonderful, was nameless, but I think of it as the Swipe. You stood back-to-back with the adult in the equation, Daddy. Then we both stooped down to floor level, with our legs wide apart and grasped each others' wrists as hard as we could. Ready? Curl your head under as far as you can. One, two, three and 'swipe'. A second later you're standing up facing each other, still holding hands, in a laughing sweat. You didn't even know how you got there. It happened in a flash. It was a show-stopper.

So John had to try to do them. Of course. The arms outstretched part was a no-go from the start. He tried it a couple of times and dropped his arms straight away, even with only one sister on board. He had no balance at all then.

He was pretty good at the flying aeroplane, although not when he tried to do the dive-bombing that Daddy seemed to find so easy. But he got us airborne and that was the name of the game. You didn't feel so sick either, as it only lasted two turns. And he only let go once that I can remember, but I just dropped on to the grass.

But the Swipe was a disaster. When he did it with me, or rather to me, the first time, instead of ending up standing facing him, we lost the tight hold of our wrists, after I had been swiped through his legs to face him. It hadn't been a fast enough jerk to pull me up and I ended up landing heavily on my derrière. Sore! Sweat overcame nervous laughter! John demanded another try immediately and I took up the position. Back to back, lean right down, grab wrists tightly. This time there was no 'Curl your head as far as you can' or 'Ready? One, two three'. John thought he knew where he had gone wrong and was eager to do it without the boring preliminaries. I was swiped without warning and my head smacked the kitchen floor with a thud I can hear to this day. Scream, scream. I had to spend the rest of the day in bed, and John came to read to me – sent by Mummy, I might add. I made him read loads of Brothers Grimm. Looking back, it was appropriate. I had a tennis ball bump on the side of my head and ultra-maximum, hands-on, scrumptious loving.

Another game, one we didn't play that day, was using my big bed as a trampoline. We would bounce on it in turn, my sister and I, and sometimes John. He would be aiming to hit his head on the ceiling, while we were just trying not to fall off and hit the floor. He taught us the art of trusting collapse, as when you trust a friend to stand behind you and fall as a dead weight into their waiting arms. We all played that game, even in the road. On the bed, you moved the bolster and the pillows, leaving the soft eiderdown, to give all the available mattress length. You had to remember the rails at each end of the bed and choose your stance. Either facing the foot of the bed so that you fell face down – really frightening – or facing the head of the bed, feet tucked up as far as possible and collapsing freefall-style, landing backwards – also really frightening. This was no game for scaredy-cats. In either case, a brutal injury was a distinct possibility, but that didn't stop us. As I said, we grew up covered in cuts and bruises. We loved having the poultice – once the initial burn had eased – the lie down and the fuss.

I used to trample hard in any available puddle, scooping the water right in over the tops of even my knee-length wellies. When my feet were thoroughly soaked, I would squelch home and flop and slop into the kitchen. The result was fantastic. Hot soapy water in a washing-up bowl in front of the fire. Hot, sweet drinks. Lots of temperature testing, soothing of brow, back stroking, hummimg and ha-ing, cuddling, stories, getting the pens and paper brought to you. Particularly if I had been shopping for Mummy, helping her out, carrying big bags, bringing the right change. It never occurred to me that she might suspect it had been deliberate, even when the bowl was already waiting in front of the fire, and the very books I wanted were right there. Mummy was so good at tending the down and out, until you were up and out.

Meanwhile music and flexing his new-grown muscles weren't the only things on John's mind – he had also acquired his first girlfriend. For years he had attended Sunday school in St Peter's Church in Woolton village. An exercise in disruption for John, and a trial for the teacher. The one attractive teenage girl in the group was Barbara Baker. All the boys had an eye on her, but it was John who made the grade and dated her when he was fifteen. They went out together for more than a year and she was certainly his first serious relationship. One day John brought Barbara down to Springwood, to meet our mother. We peered at this new thing in John's life . . . a *girlfriend*. She was very pretty, with blondish hair, and sat talking to Mummy about school.

On one particular occasion, they came in the house, had a cup of tea and a sociable chat and then left the house. I watched my brother and Barbara walk up the road, hand in hand. Ann and Clare were watching with me. On a whim, we suddenly ran after them, skulking along the hedgerows, careful not to be seen and sent packing. They crossed the road to school and turned right, walking towards Allerton Towers, with its woods and parkland. We trailed them to the beginnings of a clump of trees, almost the first lot in the park, where they suddenly flung themselves down on the grass and started the strange business of necking. This was fun and we moved in closer, to get a better view. John saw us and shouted for us to 'come here'. He then gave me half-a-crown, to go away and not tell anyone.

We couldn't believe our luck. This was a fortune and we went straight to the sweet shop with our ill-gotten gains. We never caught John and Barbara out again.

A few short years later, however, I came across John, in a carbon-copy action, in Woolton Woods. This time the glamorous, blonde Brigitte Bardot look-alike was Cynthia.

21: *Mimi's Secret*

None of us knew at the time, but from the autumn of 1956 Mimi was living a secret life at Mendips. If my mother and father or John, or even Mimi's sisters, had known, how different things might have been for Mummy and John. As it was, none of them ever found out.

I heard the very first suggestion of Mimi's secret only a few years ago, long after Mummy, Daddy, John and even Mimi herself had died. It was on one of the visits I made to Nanny in 1997 that the first hint was given. Now 84 and nearing the end of her life, Nanny told me, right out of the blue, that 'Something was going on with Mary. Mary and George.' I assumed of course that she meant Uncle George and I said so. I reminded Nanny that Mary had been married to George. George Smith.

'Not *that* George!' was the reply. 'New Zealand George! I think that Mary was going to marry New Zealand George!'

I was more confused than Nanny. We all knew that Mimi kept up a correspondence with relatives in New Zealand and that one of them had been her uncle, George Millward, who had gone out to see his outcast sister and decided to stay. But he would have been an old man, apart from being their mother's brother.

But Nanny was not to be deterred. 'Something was going on. Mary was going to live in New Zealand. After George Smith died. I'm telling you, there was something going on.'

Well, Mimi's husband George had died in July 1955, so it had to be some time after that. I travelled home thinking about this. Nanny had obviously been on the scent of some mystery. But what could have been going on? And when? And why was she telling me now?

We must both have been trying to unravel this conundrum. I had been wondering how to bring it up again, but when I next visited her I didn't have to ask. She launched in straight away.

'I think Mary was going to marry George.' It was almost as if she wanted me to challenge it. I asked her when that would have been.

'After George Smith died. Before your mother died.'

'What, Nanny? What about John? He was only fifteen when Uncle George died. What would have happened to John?'

'John was spending most of his time with your mother. Mary was having the devil's own job with him.'

A couple of months after this conversation Nanny died. She never alluded to it again and neither did I, for fear of upsetting her. But it had planted a seed in my mind.

I started thinking more and more about her revelation that 'Mary was going to New Zealand, to marry George.' There was something in there but, like Nanny, I didn't know what. I was determined to get to the bottom of the mystery. She had planted the idea and left me to sort it out. I wish Nanny could have known what I did unearth, seven years after her death.

I sat and thought, and walked and thought, and dreamt and thought, and the clouds began to lift. I began to see.

Mimi had had a lover. That's what Nanny had sensed, without actually knowing. Nanny had an inkling, a feeling that there was something afoot, and now I was sure that she was right. But it wasn't an old uncle in a far-off land. Much nearer home. If Mimi had had a boyfriend, he had to live very nearby. She never went anywhere.

Mendips is in a long row of semi-detached houses. Immediately next door had lived some relatives of her husband, so it wasn't there. Mendips had originally been on one end of the row, with waste land next door. This had been built on, however, some years before and the Mayor of Liverpool, Louis Caplan, lived there with his wife. What about him? I was on the wrong track as it turned out, but my instincts were correct, as I was about to discover.

All of us in the family remember the students in Mendips. I had peeled buckets full of potatoes and apples for them in my teens. There were many of them over the years, but there was one student who had lived with Mimi for nine years, although towards the end of his tenancy it was more sporadic. Michael Fishwick was there from September 1951 right through until 1960. I decided to track him down. I wanted some insight into what was going on within the walls of Mendips during those years and, as a long-term tenant, he might be able to throw some light on it.

To my delight, I received an immediate response to my letter. Michael had been very fond of John, regarding him a little like a younger brother. When Michael arrived at Mendips, in September 1951, John was in his first year at Quarry Bank High School. Michael was nineteen and had just left home for the first time, to study bio-chemistry at Liverpool University. Mendips was his student lodging and his father had come to inspect it before he moved in and had decided it was suitable.

He remembered Jackie and me playing in the garden and told me how much John loved us and talked about us. I asked him outright if he knew who Mimi's boyfriend was.

'Boyfriend? What makes you think that Mimi had a boyfriend?'

I told him what Nanny had said and that I was sure she was on the right track. Could it have been Louis Caplan from the bungalow next door? He laughed and said that we ought to meet up.

We met the very next week in Liverpool. Michael was researching some of his own family history and wanted to go to Wigan to do some investigations. He altered his travel plans to meet me on the way.

I recognised his face immediately, even though he was now 72 years old. We went straight for a breakfast coffee on Liverpool's Albert Dock. As we sat in a café, I came right to the point. I asked him again about Mimi's love life. He was fiddling with his cuff, under his coat sleeve. I thought that he needed help to button his shirt cuff and was just about to offer assistance when he put a gold cuff-link down in the middle of the table.

'Have you seen this before?'

'No. Should I have done?'

At that moment I had a blinding flash of realisation.

'No! She was in her fifties and you were . . . in your twenties! No!'

But I knew it was the truth. I had been looking for someone outside Mendips but as near as possible, perhaps next door, as she so seldom went anywhere. But her lover was even closer than that. He was inside Mendips and they were sleeping in the room right next to John's.

There are no words for my feelings that day in the café. I felt as if it had lost its floor and walls; we walked along a river without water and sat down again. There was no noise other than Michael's voice, talking, talking. White noise.

Michael and I spent the whole day together.

The gold cuff-links had been an engagement gift from Mimi to her young doctor fiancé, in 1932. Mimi had given them to her student lover before he left for good in 1960. When he had moved in as a young undergraduate in September 1951, Uncle George was still alive. After George's death in the summer of 1955, he returned in the autumn term to a Mendips with just Mimi and John. They developed a close friendship, which grew a year later into a full-blown love affair. Mimi told Michael she was 46, although she was 50, and he was by then 24.

What had he seen in a woman so much older? Certainly not experience, because it turned out that Mimi was a virgin. For whatever reason – we shall never know – Mimi and George had never consummated their marriage. But Michael told me that he and Mimi had 'clicked' as intellectual friends from the start, and that she had been a very attractive woman.

In the first throes of her love affair, the Christmas holidays arrived and Mimi took sixteen-year-old John to Edinburgh to celebrate the New Year with Mater and to keep him away from Springwood, where he was now spending so much of his time. After Christmas, Michael returned to Mendips early to continue with laboratory work, and contracted Asian flu. He telephoned Mimi in Edinburgh to tell her he was back early and ill. A secretive phone call, as Mater was right there and Mimi had to be guarded. The very next day, Mimi left John in Edinburgh and returned to Mendips, so that they could have the house to themselves.

I am thinking of my mother in Springwood, in the despised House of Sin. And Mimi in Mendips, the house she called the House of Correction, where children were taken to live, away from the disgusting immorality of a common-law relationship.

I am thinking of Mimi leaving John in Scotland so that she could be with her young lover, eight years older than John.

I am thinking of the greatest possible hypocrisy.

I now feel so sorry for Mimi. What a figure of pathos she turned out to be.

And as Michael explained in a letter he subsequently wrote to me, New Zealand had indeed been an option. Nanny had got that right. She had picked up on the lover aspect, without knowing the detail.

In his letter Michael explained that Mimi had faced a moral dilemma. This was not because she was having a love affair, since both parties were single and free to marry – although the age difference was shocking – but because she was living under the same roof as her lover, and John was living there too. This was the exact same situation Julia had been in, when Mimi used it to gain custody of John. The only difference had been that Julia was still married. And, of course, that she was John's mother.

Michael explained that although the parallel wasn't lost on Mimi, she was not prepared to end the affair – or to give up control of John.

Then, in 1957, Michael Fishwick was offered a three-year research post in New Zealand. He told Mimi, who jumped at the chance to go with him. She told Michael that she owned a property (The Cottage) and that if they went to New Zealand to embark on a new life together, it was all his.

Mimi knew that John would soon want to move in with his mother, stepfather and sisters permanently. She was ready to let him go and pursue her relationship with Michael. The plan fell through when funding for Michael's research post was refused. This meant he would no longer be exempt from National Service, and a few months later he left Mendips to join up.

He told me that had they gone to New Zealand, marriage was a distinct possibility, though later he realised that he might have lived to regret it, as it would have ruled out having children.

Although he continued to return at regular intervals, Michael said that his failure to secure postgraduate funding to go to New Zealand, followed six months later by the tragic death of my mother, spelled the beginning of the end of the romance. Michael and Mimi gradually reverted to a friendship, and in 1960 he met the woman he would marry.

Have I said before that I was flabbergasted? I was stupefied with horror. Now a whole new light is thrown not only on Mimi's condemnation of my mother and father, but on her role as John's moral protector.

No wonder she was to refer to herself on her deathbed as 'a wicked woman'.

22: *Launch of the Quarry Men*

Meanwhile, oblivious to the secret Mimi hid from the world, Mummy continued to delight in John's company, at Springwood and also at Mendips. Michael Fishwick remembers that while Mummy was banned from Mendips John 'adored his sisters'. This was a delight to hear, so many years later, from someone who knew us all back then. And once Mummy was allowed to visit he recalls relaxing and laughing in the garden at Mendips with Mimi and my mother. He and Mimi would have been together as lovers, after my mother had gone home.

At Springwood, with Mummy's wholehearted support, John continued to practise with his group. And the practising began to pay off. The Quarry Men started to get some bookings.

Probably the very first public performance ever, by common agreement if not by distinct memory, took place at Lee Park Golf Club, in Childwall, on the outskirts of Liverpool. A friend of John's, Nigel Walley, who was working there as an apprentice golf professional, was credited with getting this booking for the group. He took upon himself the role of manager, and even had cards printed.

Colin Hanton, the drummer, remembers early 'bookings' at St Peter's Church Youth Club in Woolton village. We all attended that over the years. John, Pete, Rod and Eric had all attended Sunday school in the Church Hall, so in fact they were members, playing for nothing because they just had to get up there, anywhere, and let rip. They got themselves thrown out for complaining that there was no microphone. It was only the size of a school hall, and with their energy I can't believe that a

110

microphone was essential. I imagine it was more a matter of them wanting to be considered professional enough to have one.

Another booking remembered by Colin Hanton took place at the Vespa Scooter Club, where my mother went along and sat at the front of the stage. There was hardly anyone else there. She clapped loudly at the end of every song.

Julia was their greatest supporter, as John knew.

They got to all their bookings, like all the other groups in Liverpool, by bus. Liverpool Corporation buses played a vital role in the launch of British rock and roll. Groups couldn't take a booking unless it was on a bus route. Crude drum kits, tea-chest basses, guitars and banjos were being transported from one dance hall or club to another across the city. These were the days of the double-decker bus. The instruments would be stashed in the cubby-hole meant for prams and parcels, while the budding musicians headed upstairs to smoke and plan. Sometimes the instruments would be loaded on to the bus at one bus stop and taken off by people waiting at the bus stop nearest to the venue, while the group would arrive later, on another bus.

A new club opened in the centre of Liverpool in January 1957. This was the Cavern Club, founded by Alan Sytner and named after a jazz club in Paris called 'Le Caveau'. It was to be the club that did more than any other to promote the revolution that was to engulf Liverpool over the next two decades.

The Quarry Men first performed there in the early part of 1957. At the same time they were entering competitions. Rod Davies remembers appearing on stage at the Liverpool Empire in June 1957 in a skiffle competition, promoted by the Carroll Levis TV show. They had to attend a preliminary round on a Sunday in order to get through to the next round with a real audience the following Wednesday. The Quarry Men were allotted five minutes to display their talents but lost the competition to another skiffle group.

As they got more gigs they began to talk about stage outfits.

Their first came courtesy of my mother, thanks to her eye for a bargain.

There was a market every Tuesday and Friday in Garston, near the South Liverpool football ground. There were stalls to entice the wandering shopper, with everything from treats and sweets to socks and light bulbs, woolly hats and old comics, before they went through the big gates into the football ground.

The entrepreneurial stall-holder would be up on a crate-stage, often under a makeshift awning, trying to attract the punters. He perched tall on the wooden crates, the better to scan the crowd, keeping the all-important eye contact with his prey, who were mainly women. He was often accompanied by a sidekick who moved among the crowd watching like a hawk for a face that might twitch, indicating a possible sale, always ready to change direction when the man on the crate said 'Over there' or 'The lucky lady in the red coat'. He wrapped the goods and took the money before anyone's mind could be changed. They could have sold you anything, whether you wanted it or not. In fact it always seemed that part of the challenge was to make the customer part with cash for exactly that – what they didn't want! They sold fish on Fridays to all religions, sides of meat, fat rings of sausages from Cumberland, whole dinner services, sets of towels, pots and pans and boxed sets of cutlery. Women went in bravely on their own or in gangs to banter, heckle and sometimes leave with things they never intended to buy. Most of them laughed until their sides ached. It was a show and we were all part of the performance.

The funniest one I ever heard, when I was at the market with my mother, was from an underwear salesman extraordinaire. He was selling knickers and underpants for all, brandishing the wares over his head, while his runner was racing among the women with ready made-up parcels. The laughter was already raucous as he shouted the colours, sizes and the never-to-be-repeated give-away prices, and then he announced, 'If you can't be fitted here, madam, I'll get you an appointment for a fitting with Cammell Laird' (the Liverpool shipbuilders)! It was worthy of an Oscar and the audience gave him a standing ovation.

We were at Garston market one day when my mother was drawn to one such rowdy auction. They were selling 'the best genuine cowboy shirts outside America'. We stopped and edged our way into the crowd. Mistake. Unless my mother meant it. The runner was there in a trice with several folded coloured check shirts. Straight from America. The game was on. I stood and gaped as Mummy bought not one, not two, but three of these shirts.

You can see the boys wearing them in both the Roseberry Street and the Woolton fête photographs. Quarry Men cowboys. John loved those shirts. The Roseberry Street party was an outdoor affair. It was a part of the street party celebrations for the anniversary of the granting of Liverpool's Royal Charter, by King John, back in 1207. We wrote the stories and drew the pictures in our exercise books in school. Booklets were given to all the children, in pale blue, with a black Liver Bird on the front cover called *The Story of Liverpool*. We were learning to be proud of our city.

Our Sunday school, All Hallows, near Springwood, had organised its own celebration. A bus ride from the church hall to the bottom of Helsby Hill, followed by a long hike and climb to the top, where the prize was a ride and slide on the helter skelter. There is a fantastic view over the Mersey estuary from the top. It's well worth the climb and is still a popular day out.

Mummy had walked Jackie and me to the church in the morning and waved us off on the bus. She was standing there, still waving and smiling, when we arrived back many hours later. We assumed that we would be going home, to eat, bath and bed – but no! Excitement! We were going to watch the results of all the previous weeks' home rehearsals. We had known that the Quarry Men were playing at one of the celebration parties on Saturday night, but this was the first time that we'd been allowed to see the musicians perform to anything other than the tiles in the bathroom or the kitchen walls.

Mummy had the address: Roseberry Street, off Princes Avenue. She wasn't sure which part of the long avenue we were looking for, so we got off the bus right at the beginning, by the park, and started walking towards town, looking at all the street names on the right-hand side of the avenue. I ran on ahead and found it. Well, first I heard it. The show had already started, but Mummy had had to wait for us to get back from the outing.

I waved Mummy, who was now carrying Jackie, to the right place and went towards the 'stage', which was actually a lorry. It was a cleaned-up coal lorry, I am sure – and not so cleaned-up at that. I could hear John singing at the top of his voice and could hardly believe it. The same songs we always heard! The same thumpings, drummimgs and hammerings. I don't know why I expected it to be different. John grinned at me while singing. I shouted over the noise that Mummy and Jackie were just coming and clambered up on the back of the lorry. The noise was deafening. I looked round and saw people and flags, then Jackie was lifted up too. Mummy went to stand in a doorway with another mother and was soon drinking tea and laughing. We didn't last long up there with the stars before we were lifted down and stood with the crowd.

John came home with us on the bus. I learned much later that the show was cut short, as some more Teddy boys had arrived and were threatening to 'get Lennon' – a familiar refrain to John, who couldn't resist provoking them with taunts. A policeman had been summoned to keep the peace and he accompanied us to the bus stop, presumably to see The Troublemaker off the premises.

The most renowned and popular local newspaper, both then and now, the *Liverpool Echo*, awarded Roseberry Street an accolade for the best decorated street, the result of which was another street party. This time the Quarry Men were not invited!

The next public event was the Woolton fête, an annual festival, held in the gardens of St Peter's Church, over the road from the church hall where the Youth Club was held. The date was Saturday, 6 July 1957, and the day was gloriously sunny.

We set out early and walked to Woolton. The village was already a hive of activity when we arrived just before the start. There were busy people still putting last-minute touches to the costumes and vehicle decorations.

The entertainment began at two p.m. with the opening procession, which entailed one or two wonderfully festooned lorries crawling at a snail's pace through the village on their ceremonious way to the Church field. The first lorry carried the Rose Queen, seated on her throne, surrounded by her retinue, all dressed in pink and white satin, sporting long ribbons and hand-made roses in their hair. These girls had been chosen from the Sunday school groups, on the basis of age and good behaviour.

The following lorry carried various entertainers, including the Quarry Men. The boys were up there on the back of the moving lorry nonchalantly trying to stay upright and play their instruments at the same time. John gave up battling with balance and sat with his legs hanging over the edge, playing his guitar and singing. He continued all through the slow, slow journey as the lorry puttered its way along. Jackie and I leaped alongside the lorry, with our mother laughing and waving at John, making him laugh. He seemed to be the only one who was really trying to play and we were really trying to put him off!

In the church field there were the police horses, who were going to demonstrate their jumping skills, and the police dogs, who were going to leap through hoops of fire and tackle policemen posing as robbers. There were hoopla stalls, fish-for-ducks stalls, candyfloss kiosks and ice-cream vans. There was also a fancy-dress parade and, this year, live music that was not the police band or a local brass band. The Quarry Men had arrived, on a lorry, and would leave that evening as half of the Beatles.

This was the second time we had come to see them play what we heard at home all the time. The sound was more subdued, of course, outside, especially with their creaking sound system. I thought they sounded better in the bathroom. They were playing three times that day. Once in the procession, once again in the afternoon, where we would be in the audience in front of the makeshift stage, and once again in the evening, over the road at the church hall, by which time we would be at home and in bed.

That day Ivan Vaughan had invited his school friend Paul McCartney along to the fête. This was the famous meeting between John, then sixteen, and Paul, who'd turned fifteen a few days earlier. After the gig they got together to play some music, and young Paul impressed John with his guitar playing and his knowledge of song lyrics – John didn't know the lyrics to half the songs they performed and usually made his own up.

Paul looked up to John, especially when he heard that John, who was a voracious reader, had read the entire works of Winston Churchill. And John not only had his own group but was allowed to dress like a Ted, which Paul could still only aspire to. For Paul, John was all that was hip.

John, initially, had different ideas about Paul. He could see that Paul was more outwardly sociable than he was, even though he was younger. Maybe he felt threatened by Paul's gregarious personality, worried that it might interfere with his unquestioned leadership of the Quarry Men. Paul was talented, John could see that, but it took him thinking time to come to terms with this particular newcomer. In the end the good of the group won the day and soon afterwards John sent Paul a message via a friend – he was in.

The official line-up for the Quarry Men now was John, singer and guitar, Paul, singer and guitar, Colin on drums, Len and Ivan on tea-chest bass and Nigel, the group manager, who, as Paul said, managed to get on the stage and play with them! Pete Shotton, John's best friend, was also around on washboard, but as he remembers it was at this time that he and John started to think he should leave the band. Apparently, one night the Quarry Men played at Colin's aunt's party. There was free beer and the boys got rather drunk. John and Pete chatted long into the night, and the inebriated silliness culminated in John breaking Pete's washboard over his head! It was all in great humour: Pete described it as his release from the band.

The first booking that the Quarry Men had with Paul as an official member was to be at the Cavern, on 7 August 1957. And Paul missed it! He presented an absence slip before he even started; he had a prior engagement of his own that he had to attend, at scout camp in North Wales.

23: *College Boy*

John was now sixteen and had a need for money, beyond pocket money. He had been smoking for some time now, so the money that he did have was truly money to burn. Drinks cost money too, as did the vital stage and street gear. So my father decided to try John out at basic paid restaurant work, washing up and waiting on tables.

Bobby was then the restaurant manager at the Airport Hotel, in Speke. The airport is now Liverpool John Lennon Airport and has been moved a mile or so up the road and expanded. Back then, on its original site, the hotel was in a wonderful Art Deco building, which has since been restored as a period restaurant, minus the window-wide views of aircraft taking off and landing, which we loved. We all went to eat there several times, as we did anywhere my father was working. We also had a tour of the control tower in action, which was very exciting. Daddy got John his first Saturday job in his restaurant before the end of his final term at Quarry Bank, after which he was able to work more.

John's academic level had suffered from his increasing absences from school, and he'd spent most of his time at Quarry Bank in the bottom stream because he was either fooling around or absent. John's unofficial absences had started with his playing truant to spend secret time with Mummy. They had increased with his growing interest in music and his obsession with starting up and playing in a group. Our mother encouraged him every step of the way, and all his spare time was focused on practising and acquiring better instruments, more chords, more words and a wider repertoire.

At school he'd soon learned that there wasn't much the teachers could do to control him other than give him detentions and canings, neither of which had much effect on him. When he did turn up to lessons he spent most of the time passing round notes and cartoons and making the rest of the class laugh. So it was no surprise to anyone that, bright as he was, he left in the summer of 1957 with no O levels. Despite his lack of exam success and the fact that he wasn't seventeen until October, he had been accepted into Liverpool College of Art. This was thanks to the perseverance of both Mimi and his headmaster, plus a superb portfolio of the workings of John's mind, translated on to crisp white paper with Indian ink. À la Mummy.

John was warned by Mimi that he was going to have to attend college a lot more frequently than he had attended school, if he wanted to succeed. He promised he would.

The first engagement the Quarry Men had when John was an official art student, rather than a wayward schoolboy, was on 18 October at the new Clubmoor Hall, the Conservative club in the Norris Green district of Liverpool. Both John and Paul wore white jackets. The rivalry was already coming out of the shadows.

Paul messed up on one of his first songs, 'Guitar Boogie', being nervous. John announced that he was the new boy and that he would improve with time! But despite his stage fright, it was obvious to everyone that Paul McCartney had something. For a start, despite being younger, he could play the guitar much better than either Eric or John. John had already recognised that he could be knocked off his pedestal by Paul's musical skills. He even thought that Paul had a look of Elvis about him. High praise indeed. They could see that they were going to have to pull their socks up to compete with him. And the first thing they had to do was to learn more proper guitar chords and relinquish the banjo chords.

Paul's arrival was a giant step forward for the Quarry Men.

He was already starting to instill the professionalism that was to build up until it catapulted the group into stardom.

As 1957 rolled on, the group played many small venues. Some invited them back; others didn't. Paul was soon adding to their range of material. John had already launched into raucous versions of Elvis's 'Hound Dog', 'Blue Suede Shoes' and 'All Shook Up', when he thought the skiffle fan audience wouldn't throw them out. Paul was able to raise the rock stakes even higher with impromptu renditions of his party piece, 'Long Tall Sally', although he kept on repeating the same words.

They entered free talent contests, tempted by prize money of one pound each, hoping that a talent scout would be in the audience. Money, or the lack of it, was a stumbling block. They shared whatever they were paid, and drank more than that. Strangely, although they did their desperate best to present themselves as tough Teddy boys, in both appearance and attitude, they ran a mile whenever any would-be tough guys confronted them. Pseudo Teds.

Mummy had taught John to play several songs, including 'Wedding Bells Breaking Up that Old Gang of Mine', a lovely song called 'Ramona', and 'Girl of My Dreams', 'I Love You, Honest I Do' and 'Little White Lies'. Paul brought in other songs that he knew, and together they began to write their own songs. Almost as soon as they met, John and Paul discovered that as well as being desperate to get up on stage, any old stage, they both wrote songs. It wasn't long before they found mutual inspiration and each began to jot notes down, when they were apart, to run by the other, for continual suggestion and improvement.

Paul joined the musicians coming to Springwood, and rehearsals took precedence over everything else. Our kitchen was increasingly a practise arena for the small clubs and the talent contests that they were entering. When Mummy learned that Paul's mother had died of breast cancer the previous year, she exhorted John to bring Paul home to eat. 'That poor boy. He's lost his mother.'

One day Paul arrived with a new prospective group member. George Harrison went to the Liverpool Institute with Paul and was a few months younger. Normally John wouldn't have considered a fourteen-year-old for the group, but George's guitar playing was exceptional.

George, by all accounts, had already seen the Quarry Men perform at least once, at Wilson Hall, in Garston, a short bus ride from Speke. He was a fan before he was in. He was only a little guy and he came in admiring John greatly.

Meanwhile John's best mate, Pete Shotton, had decided he was definitely going to leave. Pete and John were inseparable in Woolton village and they got into mischief and music together. John had wanted to play music and be in a group, so Pete found an easy instrument, the washboard. But Pete wasn't a musician and he had soon had enough. The evening at Colin's aunt's when he and John got drunk had confirmed that it was fun but it wasn't really for him.

Pete hadn't seen Paul as a rival to his bond with John, and he could see that Paul was good for the group. And another reason for him not to worry over John and Paul's closeness was Mimi's social snobbery. She liked Pete, but Paul was common, because he lived in a council house. So did we, of course. Despite this, in time Mimi came to like Paul and approve of his friendship with John. And of course she was planning a new life with her student lover which perhaps made her less critical of John's way of life.

When Pete told John that he wanted out, rather than being upset, John welcomed his decision. It had saved him the uncomfortable task of telling his long-time best friend that he wasn't musically good enough for the new dynamism that was taking over. Pete didn't mind. He and John remained good friends for many years.

By February 1958, the Quarry Men consisted of John and

Paul, singers and guitarists, Eric on guitar, Colin on drums and Len Garry on T-chest bass. However, change was in the air.

Later on that year, Len Garry left the group after he contracted meningitis, as he was in hospital for several months. Nigel Walley also became ill, with tuberculosis, and was sent to Fazakerley Sanatorium, where he spent the next six months. The group used to visit him every Sunday afternoon with their instruments and have a singsong in the ward. He stayed on as manager and was even able to procure them a couple of bookings from his hospital bed.

In August Eric left the group, unable to invest in the new electric guitar that the rest of the group wanted. He was replaced by George. John Lowe (known as 'Duff') joined them occasionally, playing the piano, and in the late summer of 1958, John, Paul, George, Colin and Duff made a proper recording at Percy Phillip's studio in Kensington, Liverpool. They recorded the original version of a song written by Paul and George called 'In Spite of all the Danger' and a cover version of Buddy Holly's 'That'll be the Day'.

There were now three guitarists in the line-up and a drummer. There was definitely no room for the accordion, nor for the banjo, the instrument that had started it all off. The sound that the Quarry Men were producing had undergone a subtle but irrevocable change. They had started out as a skiffle group. They were still stuck in the bathrooms, the kitchens, the porches and small venues. But they were being reborn as a rock and roll phenomenon.

24: *The Nightmare You Live*

I was eleven years old on 5 March 1958. Although it was midweek, and therefore a school day, Mummy wanted to have the party after school. It had to be on the day. Nana was there and John had arrived some time in the afternoon. He was in his first year at art college then and looked every inch a Teddy boy. My whole class was invited and all the children in the road. One of our teachers had two children at the school, one of whom was in my class, so he walked all the children in a crocodile over the main road from school to our home. I think it was my first 'buffet' party.

There had never been so many people in the house at once before. Bobby had made two cakes, and the kitchen table was groaning with sandwiches, snacks and chocolate figures. There were different coloured jellies on the window sill, setting in the chill March air. Mummy gave everyone a drink as they arrived, and I had to take all their coats upstairs and put them on my bed, making a mountain. Once we'd had a drink, we drifted in through the house and out into the garden. The adults stayed in the kitchen drinking tea and chatting. The teacher had said that he would be back later to collect his daughters, but ended up in conversation and stayed the whole time. I thought it was strange that a teacher was in my house and at my party. When it became too cold to stay outside he organised some games, including Pass the Parcel and Musical Chairs. It was late and dark when everyone had finally gone home, as some of the parents who came to take their children home had a cup tea.

My present from the family was a stack of books, always my

best ever present, and I went to bed late with Jackie to choose an adventure and read ourselves to sleep.

That birthday, which was to be my last with Mummy, was to become a precious memory I would re-run in my mind, cherishing it for its sweetness and its haunting, aching sense of loss. It was such a wonderful day. Mummy laughing and full of the joy of life, Daddy handing out his home-baked cake to everyone, John giving me birthday hugs and swings, and later me and Jackie exploring my new books in bed. Perfect. Too perfect.

Just four months later, on a warm summer evening, that perfect world, the only one we knew, was wiped out and the nightmare began.

That afternoon, Tuesday 15 July, we had arrived home from school and raced out to play. Several of us had our bikes out and were racing each other up and down the road. We could ride at full tilt, then put our feet straight over the handlebars in front of us, kept upright by the sheer speed we had picked up. Then we could put our hands behind our heads, guiding the bike with our legs. Of course, you were already losing momentum, so you had to gauge the split second where your hands had to come down to the handlebars and your legs had to swing down and find the pedals again. Otherwise the bike just threw you off at a vicious angle, with the wheels skidding underneath you, before it landed on top of you. We had been playing this game for a time, waiting to be called in for tea.

Daddy was on an evening shift, so he was doing the cooking, as he usually did when he was there for meal-times. He was being helped, or hindered, by Nana. She had come for the weekend and hadn't yet gone, but had decided to go home while it was still light and early. She would catch the bus at the top of the road to Penny Lane, where she would change route. Mummy said that she would accompany her as far as Penny Lane, then get a bus going in the opposite direction, along Menlove Avenue. She was going to Mimi's house to see Mimi and John. Jackie and I would have tea with Daddy, and Mummy would be back before he had to leave for work.

I went outside, picked up my bike from the garden and manoeuvred it through the gate and on to the pavement. It was a glorious afternoon and now it was going to stretch out on elastic heaven time, even if it was only until Mummy got home. We had hours ahead of us, to do we didn't know what. Precious play. There weren't many of the girl gang out again yet and I was just about to wheel the bike over the road to call for Clare, to hurry her up, when I saw Mummy and Nana coming out.

I waited for them to come through the front garden gate. We kissed and hugged each other. She wouldn't be too long. Look out for Jackie. Be good for Daddy.

I stood still and watched them go up the road, walking and talking. When they arrived at the small crossroad at the top, where they had to turn right to get to the bus stop, Mummy turned round to wave for the last time.

The very last time.

A sense of almost electric terror hit the whole of me.

As she turned round, I had a crystal clear vision of her. From the gate, I could see her clearly, smell her and feel the hug we'd had the minute before. She smiled at me, her beautiful, wide smile, framed by her dark red hair. The hug tightened. I was being seized by that hug.

My heart hammered. I was in a state of wild panic.

I couldn't get the bike wheel untwisted, to ride. It wouldn't unwrap. I flung it down on the pavement and took to my heels. I don't know how I got to the top of the road without crashing headlong to the ground.

I turned right and saw the bus stop and the back of Mummy getting on the bus. She was already disappearing upstairs.

I screamed, but nothing came out. Nothing. Not a thing.

The bus started off and I ran again. I was heaving. It had gone and she hadn't looked back. She hadn't seen me nearly pitching into the road. She would have made the bus stop. Any mother would.

A while later John arrived. I was back in the house, reading and trying to quell a thumping chest. I had always been talked of as 'highly strung'. Well, the strings were tight then.

John said that Mummy wouldn't be long. He had already seen her at Mendips. He had something to eat and then he and Daddy sat watching television until Daddy took us to bed, telling us Mummy would come up when she got back. We could read in bed.

School tomorrow.

Jackie and I fell asleep and were next woken by the sounds of voices downstairs. We sat on the stairs, huddling. We knew a policeman had come to the house. We crawled back into my big bed, under the covers. There were people downstairs and we were confused and too frightened to go down. It must have been hours later when Nana arrived and climbed into bed with us, held us, one on either side, and hushed us, 'shh . . . sshh . . .' She told us Mummy had had an accident and was in hospital.

Our father howled in the next room and Nana went in to comfort him. She went backwards and forwards, from us to him and back again.

I clung to the thought that Mummy had been in the hospital before, when we were fostered, and had come home again. But I was terrified. Everything was all wrong, even Nana hugging us in the bed – she didn't normally do that. And why was Daddy crying so much? He didn't do that last time. I lay, rigid with fear, wanting everything to go back to normal, and sensing that it never would.

The next morning I woke to hear the birds singing. I could hear Daddy and Nana in the kitchen, mumbling. I went down and they both tried to brighten up when they saw me. Nana made tea and gave me breakfast, but the sense that something terrible had happened was still there.

We were taken to school, where the headmaster took us straight into his office. The one where Mummy's prize painting of the boat on the sea still hung on the wall. I stared at it, looking for help. Teachers were coming in and hugging us. We were crying and we didn't know why.

The headmaster repeated that our Mummy had been in an accident and that she was in hospital.

Then we were taken home. Another shock. Stanley's mother and stepfather, Mater and Bert, were in the kitchen, where Mummy should have been.

'What's the matter? What's the matter?' Jackie and I were crying and resisting. We hardly knew them.

'You girls are coming up to Scotland for a holiday with us, Isn't that lovely? Mummy is very ill. You won't be allowed to visit her just yet.'

Nana had gone home, and Daddy was running around the house getting things together and telling us we'd love Scotland.

We were ushered out of our home, for the last time, although we didn't know it.

25: *Eye-witness Accounts*

It was a long, long time before I learned the details of what had happened to her, from two people who were present on that awful, life-changing evening. Nigel Walley was John's good friend and the last person to talk to our mother. This is the account he gave me:

July 15 was a date I would sadly remember for the rest of my life. Late in the afternoon I had left my house in Vale Road and cut through the stile at the side of the house which led to Menlove Avenue, turning right towards John's house, which was about 500 yards away. In the distance I could see a silhouette, leaning against the front gate of Mendips. A few moments later I could see John's mum, Julia, and she was chatting to Mimi and about to leave for the bus stop 200 yards away. We stood chatting for a while and then Julia, turned to me and said, 'John isn't in, so you can escort me down to the bus stop.' 'My pleasure,' I said and we continued down Menlove Avenue. When we reached the junction with Vale Road and Menlove Avenue, Julia and I parted and I turned into Vale Road. I heard a car being driven at high speed and then breaking very hard. I heard a loud thump. I turned round and to my horror, saw Julia flying through the air, before landing with a sickening thud in the road. I immediately rushed over to her, but could see that she had been killed instantly. Her reddish hair was fluttering in the light summer breeze, over her face.

If only I had said a few more words to her, how different

things might have been. The driver of the car that killed Julia, an off-duty policeman who was a learner driver with no licence and no insurance, was put on a manslaughter charge. He eventually stood trial, but was acquitted. With the verdict pronounced, Mimi stood up and rushed to the dock, threatening the defendant with her walking stick. She was pulled away by the court ushers and collapsed on a chair, weeping.

Michael Fishwick, Mimi's lodger and lover, gave me this account:

From Saturday, 12 July to Wednesday 16 July, I was on leave from the Officer Cadet Course on the Isle of Man. Staying at Mendips gave me the opportunity to visit the University and give instructions for the final proof-reading of my thesis, to be corrected and bound. This was completed on the Monday, and Tuesday being a free day and my last in Liverpool, I spent the whole day at Mendips.

Julia arrived in the afternoon, for a visit. John was present, together with some of his friends. Towards the end of the afternoon, John decided to go 'walkabout' in Woolton and was expected to arrive later at Springwood. The rest of his friends drifted off, leaving Julia, Mimi and me. After a short while, Julia realised that it was time to depart as Bobby was on evening shift and she had to be back with the children before he left for work. Mimi walked with her as far as the front gate and then returned to the house.

Mimi and I were in the kitchen, chatting, when there was a screech of tyres and a bang. We said nothing. Just looked at each other for a split second and then ran out of the house and across the road. Julia was lying on her back just on the pavement. There did not appear to be an obvious injury and she looked quite peaceful, but was either unconscious or in a coma. A close look revealed a small pool of blood at the back of her head, masked by her red hair.

There was a small group of onlookers standing back, and one said that an ambulance had been called. I did not notice Nigel Walley, but he might well have been one of the group. Nor did I notice the car or the driver.

Shortly before the ambulance arrived, Julia uttered a loud gasp. I firmly believe that this was the moment of her death.

Mimi climbed into the ambulance, still in her slippers and I went back to the house to collect a pair of shoes and her handbag and to lock up the house. On arrival at the hospital, I was met on the front steps by Mimi and asked to make a phone call to her sister Anne – Nanny. Why me? At a moment like that, you don't ask – you just do what you can to help. Mimi did explain, but I'm not altogether sure of what she said. I think that Harriet, the obvious person to phone, did not have a house phone. The main reason for the phone call, apart from informing Nanny of Julia's accident, was to get some adults to Springwood before the police called. Mimi was aware that Bobby might have gone to work if John was there, as he was quite capable of looking after Julia and Jackie. I made the call, (with great difficulty) and returned to the hospital.

Mimi and I went to whichever part of the hospital Julia was in and Mimi disappeared, leaving me in the waiting room for what seemed like hours, and probably was. What occurred during that time is a complete blank to me. John and Bobby must have arrived at some stage and then departed. I've no idea of whether we met or not.

We eventually left the hospital and took a taxi to Springwood. Both of us were, by now, traumatised. I remember that Mimi's hands were like ice during the taxi ride. It was dark when we arrived, even though it was a July evening. We went in and through to the main room, which seemed crowded with people.

There can't have been that many of the family there, the others must have been friends and neighbours. I beat a quick retreat into what appeared to be the kitchen/dining room, as it contained a large table and chairs. Two men were there – one was Norman, Harriet's husband, the other probably Bobby, as men are not generally good at public demonstrations of emotion as expressed in the other room.

Norman was very efficient (in his welfare officer mode) and promptly supplied me with a very large whisky. He must have seen how shocked I was. Soon after, he took me home in his car.

Neither John, nor Mimi, put in an appearance the following morning. I left them a note on the breakfast room table and caught the midday ferry to the Isle of Man. We were not to meet again until October.

John gave his own account of that evening in a later interview:

An hour or so after it happened a copper came to the door to let us know about the accident. It was awful, like some dreadful film, where they ask if you're the victim's son and all that. Well, I was and I can tell you, it was absolutely the worst night of my entire life.

I lost my mother twice. Once as a child of five and then again at seventeen. It made me very, very bitter inside. I had just begun to establish a relationship with her when she was killed. We'd caught up on so much in just a few years. We could communicate. We got on. Deep down I thought, sod it, I've no real responsibilities to anyone now.

Anyway, Bobby and I got a cab over to Sefton General Hospital, where she was lying dead. I remember rabbiting on hysterically to the cabbie all the way there. Of course, there was no way I could ever bear to look at her. Bobby went in to see her for a few minutes, but it turned out to be too much for him and he finally broke down in my arms out in the lobby. I couldn't seem to cry, not then anyway. I suppose I was just frozen inside.

26: *The End of Life as We Knew It*

By the time our mother was buried, three days later, Jackie and I were at Mater's home in Edinburgh.

Liela was at the funeral. She was studying medicine at Edinburgh, but had been working in Butlins as a holiday job. She had received a telegram: 'Judy. Car accident. Died Tuesday. Funeral Friday.'

I set off for home immediately. I remember John and I going to the funeral in a complete daze. There seemed to be lots of people but I didn't recognise many. I couldn't stand it. I hated the funeral and everybody there. It was impossible to believe it was Julia in that box. I could only think of Julia at home, happy and laughing, as she always was.

Anyway, afterwards, we all went back to my home, The Cottage, and John and I just sat there on the couch, him with his head on my lap. I never said a word. I can't even recall telling him I was sorry. There was nothing you could say. We were both numb with anguish.

Meanwhile Jackie and I were told nothing. We didn't know we hadn't got a mother. John called it the conspiracy of silence that speaks much louder than words. We were shunted into an exclusion zone, by our aunts, the instant they knew we had no mother.

From Edinburgh we were taken to Bert's childhood home in Sutherland in the extreme worth of Scotland. We stayed there for a month, then came back to Edinburgh.

We lay awake at night, in strange houses, whispering about Mummy. We were terrified to think the worst, so we wouldn't let ourselves say what we might be thinking. We had been put away before and Mummy had come home.

I prayed to God to make her better for us. We dreamed of her and talked about it, we sang her songs and talked her talk. We went out after breakfast and stayed out all day long, in caves, on beaches, hanging off cliff tops, doing dangerous things, waiting to be called back to Mummy.

When she was already watching us from heaven, trying to save us from her sisters.

No one asked us, even one time, whether we were all right, or whether we were anything at all. Mummy was already taboo. Her sisters had created a life with no questions, which allowed them to give no answers. They had set the scene for our new life. Shut up and put up.

It was now the first week in September, seven weeks after Mummy had died, and we still had no idea what had happened. We just wanted to go home.

Stan finally brought us back to Liverpool during that first week in September. It didn't feel like coming home. We recognised our city, of course, but had only just been told that we weren't going back to Springwood.

Not today.

Instead we arrived at The Cottage, Harriet's house, in Woolton. This was the same cottage where Mummy and John had lived with Alf Lennon for a short period of time. We were told that this was where we would be staying now. Why? For how long?

We didn't know that while we were in Scotland with Mater, the three remaining sisters, Mimi, Harrie and Nanny, had had us made wards of court. Our father was deemed by the court unfit to keep us, because he and our mother were never married. There may have been other reasons, we will never know. It was decided that we would live with Harrie, Norman and David in The Cottage, just around the corner from Mendips.

Our father would pay maintenance for us, but we couldn't live with him.

They just forgot to tell Jackie and me. I was only told about the court order when I was 21, when the court wrote to me and asked me to attend an appointment to verify its closure.

Our father had left Springwood. He never wanted to spend another night there after we had been taken away. He stayed with Nana, until he could find another place to live.

Whether he tried to keep us, I don't know. He was grief-stricken, and in addition it would have been almost impossible for him to work in his existing job and look after us. He knew nothing else, and very few men brought up families alone in those days. So I imagine that, reluctantly and still in a state of shock, he conceded that we would have to go to our aunts.

Harriet and her second husband, Norman, David's father, rented The Cottage from Mimi, and from the new owners after Mimi sold it.

Liela was 21 years old and had left home to study medicine in Edinburgh. David was eleven months my junior, which was very important in the hierarchy. At least, I thought it was, even if he tried to ignore it.

This was a two-bedroom cottage and I am puzzled to this day as to why we went to live in the most unsuitable house. Nanny had Ardmore, that roomy mansion in huge gardens, over the water, but she plainly didn't want us. And she didn't hesitate to let us know that we were no part of 'this family'. She had her one child and wasn't going to increase her family threefold overnight.

Mater and Bert had a sprawling home in Edinburgh, but having housed us for almost two months, they had also made their decision. We certainly weren't taken to Scotland with the idea of staying there, but equally certainly, they weren't willing to consider it. We had been taken as far as possible to keep us out of the way. So that the sisters wouldn't have to deal with us. Job done.

I wonder if they thought we would evaporate into the nothingness they thought we were.

Mimi, who had been zealous in her go-gettingness of John, was equally zealous in her not-gettingness of her sister's other children. The truly lost ones. She also repeated the 'those-girls-are-not-in-this-family-they-never-have-been-in-this-family-and-they-never-will-be-in-this-family' mantra. You could hear it in your sleep. Sometimes the voice was Mimi's and sometimes it was Nanny's.

As for John, just as he had been about to come to live with us full time, he found himself stuck at Mimi's and banned from even telling us about Mummy. He had to watch as we were sent from pillar to post. Mimi told him that he need never bother with us again. That we were nothing to do with him. He told me this when we talked about it years later, at a time when he was obviously doing some serious soul-searching.

John wrote a letter to Mater, seventeen years later, in July 1975, talking about how he had tried to be with us and help us. The first part of the letter refers to the time after our mother's death, when he tried to persuade Mimi to keep us all together as a family. In the letter he said, 'Mimi wouldn't take them . . . tho I wanted it, apart from Mummy . . . for COMPANY . . .'

Looking back I can see that, given the sisters' attitude to us – that we were Julia's illegitimate offspring and not part of the family – the problem of what to do with us was a moral dilemma and, for all of them, a nightmare. They wanted us somewhere – anywhere– else.

But at the same time as not wanting us, they obviously felt they couldn't actually abandon us. One of them had to step in. I don't know how much our father had to do with our being made wards of court, or in allowing Harrie and Norman, an uncle we had met only once or twice in our lives, to be our legal guardians. We were, after all, on the northernmost coast of Scotland, while our futures were being carved out back in Liverpool. I wonder if a promise by Harrie of speedy baptism and official church membership may have swayed the court. However things got to be the way they got to be, Daddy told me later that 'those women just took over' and that he was powerless.

But Harrie was the one who, however reluctantly – and who *would* want to triple their family overnight? – agreed to take us, so we were in The Cottage. And deafened by the silence.

Jackie and I were still whispering, when we could. It was more difficult now to get time together on our own. We were sharing a bedroom with David.

We still didn't even know where our Mummy was and why we hadn't gone home to Springwood. And where was our father? No one talked about him either.

I was having regular nightmares about Mummy being in a dreadful state of black brokenness in hospital. My father must be sleeping beside her bed, to make sure she didn't die. I didn't dare ask, but my head was breaking up and I was 'being chesty'.

I couldn't breathe.

They told us that Daddy was working away. He had done this before. But he wasn't working away – he told me so later. He had been told he was not to see us or tell us. *His daughters*. He had been told not to come until we had settled in.

He had avoided this once before by having us fostered, to be sure of getting us back. Now, he was caught in the teeth of the tigresses with nothing and no one on his side.

27: *Looking for John*

The only communication we had in that first week, with our new family that we didn't know was our new family, was that we had to go quickly to Horne Brothers, the uniform shop in town, to have me fitted out for the start of the school year. My first term at the grammar school that Mummy had chosen for me. Jackie was still in primary school, so her school clothes only needed freshening up, but I had to have the whole lot, from inner wear to games wear to outer wear.

Earlier that year, all the children in the last term at primary school, all over the country, had taken the eleven plus exam. We sat our papers at a Grammar School in Aigburth, a district in South Liverpool, near the banks of the River Mersey. The first day, my mother had woken me up really early and she had cooked for me the same thing for breakfast that I'd had for the previous night's tea. Fish! It was well-known that fish was the key to open wide your brain.

We caught the bus to Garston and then another bus to Aigburth High School, arriving early enough for Mummy to show me where she would be waiting when I finished my exam. She would be sitting on a bench on Otterspool Promenade, enjoying the sea breeze and thinking of me. We would have a special treat afterwards, before we went home.

'Think what you're doing, lovey. Read everything through at least twice. Don't be rushing. Check it all. I'll be here. I'll be wishing the best for the best girl in ten streets.' That was her name for me, when I did the shopping and helped out with Jackie.

She walked me across to the school entrance, where the staff took over, leading us into the gigantic hall where there were long rows of single seats, all facing the front, and many faces we had never seen before. They allotted us each our own seat, which we were to keep for the next three days. Then, when everyone was in the right place, according to the list, we were given our instructions. When to start writing. When to stop. Absolutely no talking. And the usual advice about reading it twice and checking for mistakes. We had been doing this every Friday morning all year long, in the Scholarship Factory.

A good 95% or more children passed the eleven plus that summer, gaining places in various grammar schools around the city. I had applied to the new, two-year-old girls' grammar, New Heys, which already had quite a prestigious reputation. And it was a local school. Local to Springwood, that is. Mummy was thrilled when I got in.

Now it was to become a life-saver for me, being in that school. Being near Springwood. Letting me melt into the ghost of my mother to keep her close.

The very day we heard that I was going to New Heys, by the morning post, Mummy met me from school that afternoon and we walked up there. It took ten minutes and we stood together, hugging and smiling, and watched all the girls coming out. They wore brightly contrasting uniforms, with maroon blazers, pale blue, or maroon and white striped shirts, maroon and blue ties and heavy leather satchels swung nonchalantly over one shoulder. So chic. And I was going to join them. Mummy and I were tingling with excitement.

We walked together to see the school one Saturday. We had found the shortest way to walk directly from home and timed it, to help us decide what time I needed to leave in the morning. This was a bit further than Springwood Primary, which had been two minutes' run, five minutes' walk from the garden gate. This was a good fifteen-minute walk and we had been joking about getting up with the sun, instead of the moon. We walked right up to it this time, alongside the vast playing fields, as the place was deserted. We climbed over the wall as the double gates were locked and saw the Tweedledum and Tweedledee stone mascot on the entrance wall. We read the large school sign: 'New Heys High School for Girls. Headmistress: Joyce Harland.' We speculated about what she would look like.

I was coming to Mallory Towers, no matter what the school thought it was called. We looked in through the ground-floor classroom windows, oohing and aahing at the size of the full-length windows, which let in lots of light, and the fresh white paint on the walls which were hung with brightly coloured display work, posters and timetables. Our primary school had been in an old Victorian building, with dark green and brown tiles and yellow paint. This was so modern. From dark to bright. We looked through the bars in the whole wall of glass that was the gymnasium, with its beautiful wooden floor, waiting for bare feet, and then peered into the long assembly hall, with its rows and rows of wooden seats. The whole building was resting for the weekend, lying in wait for the Monday girls. We wandered around the back of the building, and came across the tennis courts.

Behind the courts was a large old mansion building and we could hear children playing in the gardens over the high wall. My mother explained to me that it was an orphanage, with the same name as the school, New Heys Children's Home. She told me it had been there a long time before the school and they were there on Saturday because that's where they lived, as they had no parents. And to be kind to them, if we met up. They were younger than we were.

Now here I was, arranging to go and buy the new uniform that Mummy and I had discussed, with someone else, who didn't even know where the school was. We had only been back from Scotland for a week and I was frightened of life.

I didn't know where Daddy was, but I knew where John was, if he wasn't in Springwood. I got up early, crept out of the house and ran round to Mendips, five minutes' worth of running, with my chest tight.

I rushed in through the gate and, just as I was going through the trellis gate to the side garden and the back door, I saw Mimi in the morning room window at the side of the house. She looked very cross. I hadn't spoken to her yet, but she was already cross with me. She knocked her knuckles on the glass, sharply, to knock-knock me away, back wherever I had come from. I hadn't even spoken.

'No. John isn't here. Go home. Now.'

That was all I wanted to do. Go home. Now.

I try to be Mimi, on the other side of the morning room window. She sees Julia running up to Mendips, looking for John. Desperate Julia. It must have been a haunting. No. John's not here (for you, Julia). Go away. Now. It set the tone for the relationship between me and Mimi, one that was never to change. I always knew it but only recently understood it.

When Mimi saw me, she saw my mother and faced her demons.

Later that afternoon, Jackie and I were in the front garden of The Cottage, looking over the gate. I was probably formulating an escape plan for us, to hunt for Mummy, to get past Mimi to get to John.

Suddenly, as if in a dream, Mr and Mrs Starkey were standing there, on the pavement. A vision from Springwood.

We always knew they had gone for walks, to Woolton and beyond, but of course we had never been there at the same time. It was wonderful to see them. My insides felt warmed. She would tell us the truth. I had been seeking a pathway and here was Hannah.

Mrs Starkey leaned over and opened the gate to The Cottage and brought us out. She was hugging us and her face was wet. 'When are you coming to see us?' We didn't have a chance to go further.

Just as suddenly, Harrie was right there. She pulled me back and told us to go in the house. 'Go on. Now.' Everything was now. No questions asked. Just do it, now.

Harrie said something to them, shut the gate, followed us in and shut the door. I went straight through to the front room, to see if I could still see them through the window, but they had gone. Nana was also turned away at the door several times. Our grandmother! We were to cut these unsuitable ties with our old life and get on with the new.

Years went by before Mrs Starkey had a chance to tell me that they had been told that we were living there now and 'don't come up here trying to see them again'. It never occurred to Harrie that they could have just been out walking. They had come interfering, as far as she was concerned, and they were told off, put in their place. Jackie and I were upset that evening and were sent to bed early. At dawn, the following morning, I was in a deep sleep, when someone shook my shoulder and told me to get up, quietly. It was Norman. He had been quiet until that point, a man who mostly stayed out of the way while his strong-willed wife ruled the house. He managed a garage and came and went like a shadow. Later I would come to know him better, and to recognise that he could be kind and witty. But at this stage Jackie and I still barely knew him.

He got Jackie up too, shushing us both, so as not to disturb David. We crept downstairs and went straight through into the front living-room.

He sat us down and stood over us.

'Your mother has died and gone to Heaven. You won't see her again.'

So, there we had it. At last.

We screamed. I mean, we really, truly screamed. We jumped up together and screamed until we went hoarse.

Harrie flung herself into the room. 'What's going on here? What have you done?'

'They had to know. You were wrong, you should have told them. Somebody had to tell them.'

Jackie and I had collapsed into a wailing heap, while the argument between Harrie and Norman about whether or not we should have known, who should have told us and then when, raged on. I don't think they even saw us go back upstairs. We went to huddle in my bed, until it was time to get up.

Later, that afternoon, I went back to Mendips. This time, I got right down the side garden and through the kitchen door. John was there. We went to the Tip, where the boys played cricket, at the far end of Mimi's row of houses. There were lots of low, scrubby bushes and we walked in a bit and sat down. John told me that he had expected us to live with him and Mimi at Mendips and he wasn't even told when we arrived back in Liverpool. When he heard that we were back, he was told he wasn't to come and see us. I think that he was so wild and grief-ridden inside that he didn't understand what was going on any more than we did.

That day we talked of our mother and cried, in a snatched moment in time – before anyone found out we were together.

28: *Life after Mummy*

Even after we had been told the truth, no one in the family talked about Julia, Judy, Mummy, the mother of three grieving children. The mother who had gone. The mother who wasn't coming back. As far as her sisters were concerned, she wasn't to be mentioned again. That was how this family coped with loss.

Jackie and I went to school, ostensibly as if we had simply been on a family holiday and then moved house. Jackie went back to Springwood Primary and I started at New Heys High School.

I was allowed to go to Mendips once I knew the truth about Mummy, but I always had to face Mimi's sour expression so I didn't go often. When I did, John and I would go to the Tip to talk about Mummy and cry for the lack of her.

The three of us were completely devastated and we each found our own ways of coping. Jackie and I, eleven and eight, were living a regimented life, organised around school. I also had home-work to do, for the first time, which occupied time after school and thankfully demanded some of my headspace.

Bedtime plummeted from Springwood time, elastic time, to six p.m. Prompt. Even on the hot, light summer evenings. We were learning a new life, dreaming of our lost and gone-for-ever life. Young children already clinging to ghosts. 'Get on' and 'now' were the unspoken orders of every day for us.

John was rising eighteen, however, and was able to channel his loss and desperation in a freer way. He got wildly drunk for a year, getting himself into trouble for both his words and actions. The steady, if silent, support of his friends helped him to plough through those first months, if not unscathed, at least still in the land of the living.

Several of John's friends remember that time well. I've talked to them since, and asked them for their memories of John's relationship with our mother and how he coped in the months after her death. These testimonies from friends who had been so close to John helped me put together the pieces of that time.

It was especially poignant for Paul McCartney, who had lost his own mother only eighteen months earlier. It gave him and John a special connection:

I know that John absolutely adored Julia. Obviously on the level that she was his Mum. He was just totally bonded to her for that reason. But also because she was in all ways a very beautiful woman and a very spirited woman. She was very lively. I remember her long, red hair. I remember her being very good-looking and so full of life – and she could play the banjo. I mean, this was something else. It was always the men.

She was very ahead of her time.

When I look back on Julia's death, all I can see is the word TRAGEDY, written in big, black letters. The only way I could help John was to empathise, as I'd had the same thing happen to me. There wasn't anything I could say that would magically patch him up. That kind of hurt goes far too deep for words.

About a year after, a rather funny or, more accurately, a rather cruel incident happened. John was just beginning to get his act back together again. That is, he could bluff it out a bit better than before. He and I were out together and we met someone who asked me how my mother was getting on.

'Well, actually, she died three years ago,' I said. He didn't know where to look.

'Awfully sorry, son. Oh, my God.'

Then he turned to John and asked him the same question,

only to be told precisely the same thing. As young lads, we both found his deep embarrassment rather amusing. Laughing about it was a wonderful way of masking our true feelings and gave us a bond.

Colin Hanton, who was the Quarry Men's original drummer, had this to say:

I first met John's Mum, Julia, when I went up to Mendips to see John. He was just leaving the house and after our hellos he asked if I wanted to see his Mum at Springwood. Julia was very pleased to see John and invited us in. We sat and talked. John had his guitar and his Mum sat and played it, talking chords. There was a lot of affection between John and Julia.

We did a gig at the Vespa scooter club somewhere around Penny Lane. Julia came along to watch us and, at the end of each song, clapped very loudly. She was obviously very pleased to see John perform.

When I heard of her death. I was shocked and didn't see John for some weeks. When we did meet, we just stood and looked at each other, eye to eye, and said nothing. John knew that my own Mum had died some years before.

David Ashton had been a friend of John's since their primary school days. He wrote to me with his take on John's family life:

I know the problems that John had. John loved his Mum very much. I was sometimes at Aunt Mimi's after school, when John's Mum was there and know how different the atmosphere was. I was not really welcome. John's Mum was very tactile and would give me a kiss, but I had to go back home. I know what Mendips was like with Mimi and John. Mimi had her own name for Mendips. She called it 'The House of Correction.' The house where things were put into order. Where wrong was made right.

I left home myself at fifteen, to work in Northop in North Wales, on a farm. The landlady had also 'adopted' her sister's boy. I left the job and came back to Woolton to work, as it was too much like what I had known with John.

John's mother and you, his sisters Julia and Jackie were always a part of his life. You always existed in his life. I went many times to the house in Springwood. John and I had various footpaths to get there, without Mimi's knowledge. One particular time, my Mum sent John and me to tidy up my grandfather's grave, as part of Bob-a-Job week. My grandfather was buried in Allerton Cemetery, and we set off on our bicycles. As soon as we got there, John rode off, over the road, to see his mother. It was a secret. I think we were about ten then. Another time, we all had a day off school to greet one of the Royal family, waving flags at the roadside. John and I went straight to Springwood and spent the day there. Later, Mimi asked John what the Queen, or her sister, was wearing and John invented the whole scene!

When I worked on Newstead Farm in Quarry Street, Woolton, with the Lewis family, we had a black and white Friesian cow. We milked and made cheeses and butter. John used to come across to the farm from Vale Road, via Strawberry Field, and that Friesian cow got to be called 'Julia'. Yes Julia! I think Gilbert Scott, the farm manager, called her that, as John was always talking about his mother and his sister, both Julia. I personally loved that cow very much. At that time, I knew more about the cow than I did about girls!

Nigel Walley was the manager of the Quarry Men and was with our mother seconds before she died:

John, needless to say, took his mother's death very hard. He had already lost his Uncle George and then to lose his mother, whom he loved so very much, before he was eighteen. John could hardly face the funeral. He didn't want anyone to see him crying. For many months after his mother's death he wore black in her memory.

John had a tendency not to show his emotions outwardly. His feelings were a mixed bag of guilt and frustration at not having a normal life, like the rest of the gang.

Later in his life he named his young son Julian, after his mother, and wrote a number of songs dedicated to her, including my own favourite, 'Julia'. None of us could have imagined how short John's own life would be and how tragically it would end.

29: *Ghost Hunting*

Jackie and I were only a mile from Springwood, but in another universe. Mummy was taboo in The Cottage. It was strange that they tried to wipe out her existence, when they had her children. Children are, however, by their very nature and basic need to survive, mutable creatures and we learned to cope – outwardly. It was very soon after we moved in to The Cottage that I learned not to mention my mother. Harrie had been in the kitchen, at the back of the house and I went into the front living-room. I was suddenly overwhelmed by grief and angst and burst out crying. Immediately, Harrie was there, shouting, 'What's the matter with you?' I said that I was thinking about Mummy and she turned round immediately and left the room. I know that she couldn't cope with the trauma that our mother's death had caused for her. Apart from the grief of losing her sister, her life had changed drastically, as had ours. But she had no inkling of how to help us in our desperate emotional need. So, we learned quickly never, ever to show our grief openly in that house, or indeed anywhere in the family. Mummy was taboo. More rules. Matters of the heart, were always to be ruled by the head.

I found another way to grieve, and to make a link with the lost life. The path to my school, down Blackgates Lane, took me back to Springwood. My umbilical cord. There was actually another, shorter and more sociable way of getting to school. If I went by bus down the side of Allerton Towers parkland, I could join other pupils from the outlying areas, making arriving at school a 'people' occasion. I only did this if I was very late, or sometimes if the bus was arriving as I left the house.

I much preferred the longer walk down Blackgates Lane, by the side of the golf course. Even in the pouring rain. I would imagine that my mother was waiting for me, to dry me and hug me. This was the lane that Stan and John had walked to find us at Springwood, eight years earlier. The same lane our mother had walked us along to Woolton. The same lane where John and I had spied out stray golf balls and had found nuns and horses.

The journey to school became my new lifeline, taking me back into air that I could breathe and a ghost life I could communicate with. And after school it was a short distance over to Springwood. Although I was meant to be back at the Cottage by four-thirty, I often turned in the opposite direction at the sound of the final school bell.

The first time I went hunting/haunting for my mother I was playing truant. I emerged at the bottom of the lane in school uniform with my satchel and just carried on walking. I hadn't planned it, it just happened. I stopped at the bottom of the lane and sat in the blackberry bushes, waiting for everyone to go through the school gates.

I walked along first to Springwood Primary School, the Scholarship Factory, remembering the day that my mother and I had walked the route together, chatting with animation about my new school. When I got there the bell had gone, and the playground was deserted. I hung on the iron railings, being my mother, looking for me and my sister in the empty playground. Crying, of course.

I moved on, before a teacher spotted me through a window and came out. I crossed the road and walked slowly. The two-minute race was a fifteen-minute haul. This was my own funeral walk. Nothing had changed. The beautiful elm trees were full and green. The pavements echoed as I placed each step in my heavy school shoes. The gardens were the same. Life is so cruel and yet so kind. I turned into my road and found myself at Hannah Starkey's front gate. I couldn't bring myself to be on the other side of the road, where I might have seen Mummy in the garden and believed it. I was torn apart but couldn't leave. Eventually, I walked round to the back kitchen and tapped on Mrs Starkey's door. She brought me in, without a word, and I let go, unrestricted, for the first time. I howled like a wolf. She hugged and rocked me until I went quiet.

I stayed there all day.

'Don't tell Harrie.'

'Of course not. Don't be daft. Come tomorrow.'

I made some sort of decision that I couldn't come here every day to stand in the road, looking, hunting, haunting. I joined after-school clubs and didn't always go. I played school games on some Saturdays, and joined the gym club, but went straight to Springwood afterwards. That meant that I could spend time with Ann and Clare, my friends, and feel like I still belonged to real people for a short time. My family fix. They were on the 'disapproved' list, like Nana. Just like Mr and Mrs Starkey, Nana had been told never to come to The Cottage again, after she had tried to see us several times. They were 'common' (openly kind and loving and said what they meant) and lived in a council house (as Jackie and I had, until our mother died). I knew better than to mention that I had ever been there. I spent huge amounts of time running up and down Blackgates Lane, in all weathers, with schoolbags and games and gym equipment, so that I could be in Mummy space. It was my sanity valve, to enable me to get through the rest.

Daddy's visits were the other lifeline. He had been allowed to visit us once or twice a week, once we had 'settled down'. That meant once we had all three of us learned that our mother was a no-go subject and that we were to get on with our lives, without upsetting people with our own upset. He would come and see us for an hour or so, under Harrie's watchful eye. Enough time for a quick cuddle, a chat about school, what we were up to. We wanted to talk about Mummy – and I'm sure he did too – but that was impossible in The Cottage, with its listening walls. And we weren't allowed to leave with him. I longed to swing on his arm or help him bake a cake, but at Harrie's he was a different Daddy – quiet and restrained and self-conscious.

When I went to see her, Hannah Starkey told me that Daddy had exchanged houses with a family who lived half a mile away, on the other side of Woolton Woods. It was only five minutes' walk from The Cottage. The furniture that had been in our bedrooms was now installed in two of the bedrooms in his new house, waiting for the day when we would be allowed to visit, maybe to stay. The beds, the books, the curtains, the rugs. They were all there. A sad, strange echo from eleven years back, when the furniture from Penny Lane, including John's bed, knitted patchwork and a teddy bear, went with love and heartbreak to Springwood, to wait for him.

Once we knew this, we found Daddy quickly, by going through the woods and knocking on doors. When he opened his the first time, and found us on the doorstep, he was first astonished, then thrilled. The sisters thought we were as empty-headed as they needed us to be. But we didn't care. We had found Daddy and we were able to make secret visits to him, though they always had to be cut short so that we could race back to The Cottage, our secret safe.

Life with Rules was stifling. But there is always a smooth handle to everything, as Aunt Izzie used to say in *Little Women*. A rough handle and a smooth handle. You've just got to look for it.

Well, out of all the trauma, both silent and deafening, we got David. We already had Liela, Harrie's daughter. She had been in our family unit at Springwood for as long as I could remember. She was like an elder sister, who stayed often. Who loved to be with Judy. Our Mummy.

David was eleven years younger than Liela, so we had only seen him when he was brought over or we all met up at Nanny's house. But when we moved into his home, David turned out to be a gift to Jackie and me.

I often wonder about David's life and how we changed it. We robbed him of his personal space, of his mother's sole attention, which he'd had since Liela had left home for Edinburgh. He had to learn to share everything he had, to live with sisters who squabbled and made up as a way of life, who giggled uncontrollably, at the drop of a hat, like witches, and who were dressed identically. One older than him and one younger. I have asked him about this, dreading a negative reply. Of course, he only said positive things. He is too lovely a person to even think otherwise. We have absorbed David into our sisterhood. In fact, he is our honorary brother. We are certainly honoured to have him.

As 1958 rolled into 1959 we were all getting used to the great sea change we had been through. We had had Jackie's ninth birthday and John's eighteenth, both in October, with no great fuss. We spent our first Mummyless Christmas and survived to see in 1959. We saw Daddy, but not always on the actual day of a birthday or Christmas, just for a brief meeting, so that he could give us a present, sometimes a few days later.

I was mentally marking time. 'First Christmas without Mummy. How many more?' My own first Mummyless birthday was still to come, and with early pre-teen angst in full spate, as well as fruitless longing, I didn't think I would get through it. I calculated my grandmother's age, and wondered how she had survived, as her own mother had died in her twenties. I thought I would die in my sleep, rather than have one birthday without my mother. And I wouldn't have minded either, because at that time I thought I would be joining her.

I was living in a nether world of 'hunt my Mummy', following red-headed women around the shops, knowing they weren't her. I jumped late off a bus, chasing after one lady with a vague resemblance from the back. My legs had to race against the fast flying concrete, to stop myself hurtling face forward at great speed to meet it, with the bus conductor shouting at me, from the platform. How could I tell him I was chasing the ghost of my mother?

30: *New Love*

There were two new people who played a vital role in John's rehabilitation, and he met both of them at art college. One was to become his wife and mother to his first-born son, Julian. The other was a fine artist in the making, with whom John formed a deep friendship from the start. They were of course, Cynthia Powell, Miss Prim and Proper from across-the-water Hoylake, and Stuart Sutcliffe, fellow student about to become flat-mate.

We heard a lot about la Cynthia before we met her. John had been attending classes with her from the beginning of the autumn term of 1958. Our mother had died three months earlier, and it surprised me a little that John went back to college at all. If you were to believe in karma, however, then of course he had to go, to meet Cyn and Stuart, in order to continue the slow healing process.

This was a time when John had dual fancies for his *femme fatale*. One dream fantasy for him, as for most other boys, including Paul McCartney, was the fantabulous blonde sex kitten, Brigitte Bardot. The other was her diametric opposite in complexion, the sultry Juliette Greco. John had posters of both women. I can imagine him lying on his bed deciding which one to have for himself! Brigitte won the day and Cynthia, a natural beauty anyway, duly transformed her long fair hair into a dazzling shade of blonde.

The love that John and Cynthia grew together was a prime factor in his recovery. Although they had become an item before Christmas in 1958, we first met her in the spring of 1959, when John brought her round to The Cottage to introduce her to the family. It was a sunny, weekday afternoon and we came home from school to find John in the front living-room, sitting as close as he could to a beautiful, smiling girlfriend. And she knew just how to talk to young sisters and heard me out, talking about school, before prising Jackie's school day out of her too. We all had tea and biscuits and chatted, meaning we asked them lots of silly questions, before they left, hand in hand. She was given the thumbs up. And not just by those present. Mummy would have loved her and the adoring way she was with John.

I came upon them necking in the long grass on the edge of Woolton Woods in the early, early days. This time John told me to 'sod off', without paying!

One day, not long after we had first met Cyn, I was at Mendips with John and he told me that Cyn was coming from town on the bus. I was twelve then and I was looking forward to seeing her again, wondering what arty, studenty clothes she would be wearing. Mendips is right on the main road, which meant that you could see the bus stop if you looked through the upstairs windows, which is why John ran up and down the stairs to his bedroom whenever he thought he heard a bus engine. You could hear whether or not the bus stopped to let passengers on or off. When the bus did indeed deposit Cynthia on the pavement, John shouted 'Yes!' and then flung himself downstairs to watch for her coming through the gate. Then he sauntered through the kitchen, as if he didn't even know she was coming and he was bumping into her in his own garden by sheer good luck! I couldn't believe his cool. I loved it! Cynthia was dressed in black from head to toe, just like John. A couple of art students, in love and looking like art students . . . in love. It was tangible.

When Cynthia moved into Mendips three years later, while they were waiting for Julian's arrival, a similar thing happened, only it was John on the bus and Cynthia in Mendips. This time, I was fifteen. I was chatting to Cyn in the morning room as she was putting on her lipstick, and she was making all those faces you make when trying to have luscious lips. I was staring so intently that she gave me the lipstick as a present, although it was a new one. My first lipstick! Then she brushed her long blonde hair over her shoulders, moving it this way and that. She was waiting for John. We heard the wooden gate latch click open and shut. Suddenly, Cyn, after peeping through the window to check, sat down in the armchair and leaned back, spreading her hair over her shoulders, and closed her eyes. I watched her closely, then switched my gaze to John as he walked in from the kitchen. He was mesmerised! He grunted at me and made straight for the model posing in the chair. A bizarre moment of reversal.

In 1959 John moved out of Mendips and into Stuart Sutcliffe's flat in a student bedsit area of town, Gambier Terrace, over-looking the Anglican Cathedral. John wanted this new-found freedom and space, both for himself and, of course, for trysts with Cynthia.

John and Stuart both admired and influenced each other. Stuart was an incredibly talented artist who encouraged John to maintain and widen his interest in the art world, while John introduced Stuart to the world of rock and roll, teaching him to play the bass guitar. As Quarry Bank High School was now irrelevant, the group renamed themselves the Silver Beatles, a reflection of John's admiration for Buddy Holly and the Crickets.

Stuart became the latest member, voted in as John's new best friend. They were now sharing a large part of their lives together and John saw no reason why, with a little private coaching from him, Stuart could not be included in the group. They acquired a bass guitar and got to work. From scratch. It wasn't long before Stuart could join in with the few chords that he had mastered. He was set to become a Beatle. He joined them on stage, demon-strating his newly acquired skills as a bass guitarist. But he was never a natural musician and his inclusion in the group upset Paul, who was a musician and a perfectionist. He thought that

Stuart's lack of musical ability in music in general and on the bass guitar in particular was going to have an adverse effect on the group and his ambitions for its future.

31: *School Lane*

By the summer of 1959, when John was in Stuart's flat, developing a love for Stuart as a friend and being madly in love and lust with Cynthia, our mother had been gone for a year and Jackie and I were seeing Daddy regularly. He was allowed to visit us in The Cottage, and at last we were officially allowed to visit him in the new house, in School Lane, on the other side of the woods.

It had been a hard year. Now Jackie and I had to face questions from other people, about why we lived with our aunt when our father was a ten-minute walk away. Just as John had been asked why he lived with an aunt and not his mother, a ten-minute walk away. And, just like John, we had no answers. I hated the questioning and the not knowing what to say.

At school, there were questions from the headmistress, the teachers and other pupils. Questions that reinforced my new feelings of inadequacy and unworthiness, lowering even further my battered self-esteem. Questions that were adroitly avoided by those adults who may have had the answers, yet which plagued the children who had none. I learned how to build defences, becoming at once very timid and wary while at the same time constructing the most aggressive suit of armour. Unset jelly inside, bolshy git outside. Whatever cloaked the shame of having no mother, an absent father and no answers.

Then the summer holidays arrived, and after spending the first week in The Cottage, we were told that we were going to stay with Daddy for a week or so. We were ecstatic – a whole week with Daddy. And with Nana, who had moved in to look after us. We had only seen her once since our mother had died, when she had come to see us and been turned away from The Cottage – another connection with our old life that Harrie didn't want. She had tried again to call at The Cottage, arriving in the daytime, when we were at school, to try to sort things out. She was turned away at the door. We didn't see her at all that time.

Daddy was as thrilled as we were. He had always wanted us to stay. Much later he told me that 'they wouldn't let me have you'. I'm not sure whether he meant the court, the aunts or a combination of the two. He said there had been talk of an orphanage but he had been apoplectic about it. I imagine that the court order and Daddy's maintenance payment to Harrie were some sort of solution, mutually agreed by Daddy, Harrie and Norman and the court.

That summer Nana was not as well as she had been, seeming smaller and weaker. She must only have been in her mid-sixties, although I thought she was a hundred! She smoked a lot, as many people did then, and her chest wheezed. Instead of sharing with me, this time, she slept in Jackie's single bed, and Jackie moved in with me in my double bed.

After the week was up, no one said anything or came to collect us, so we stayed with Daddy and Nana for what turned out to be the whole summer. And it was lovely. Why Harrie and the other sisters agreed to this, having previously been so determined not to let Daddy have us, I don't know. Perhaps Harrie had found it impossible, having two small bereft girls in her home, and was ready to hand us over. Perhaps the intrusion of our presence, which she had never wanted, was just too much.

Whatever the reason, we were glad. It was a long, hot summer. We saw little of Daddy really, as his job kept him away for long hours. But we were free of constricting rules and disapproving looks, and that was bliss.

Time became elastic again. Six o'clock bed quickly became a memory. We stayed out until it got too dark to see, until we were hungry or until the parkie came to shut the gates into the wood opposite the house. We made friends with children who lived in the surrounding houses, and were in and out of each other's kitchens and gardens.

Although she was no longer in the best of health, Nana did her best to look after us, mainly by being in the house for us. She was doing the washing and ironing, but Daddy tended to do the cooking in the evening, bringing back sides of meat to be cut cold, for daytime food, until he had his days off. We were a family unit again, though a different one. Deprived of its most important member, Mummy, but a family unit nevertheless.

With Daddy and Nana we could grieve for Mummy a little more openly. Sometimes we talked about her, though not often because it was as hard for Daddy as it was for us and he often became tearful at the mention of her. My father still had Mummy's dresses hanging in the wardrobe – the pink spangly one, the black jersey one and the navy polka-dot one. He would open the wardrobe just to look and to touch, reaching out for the breath of the dress. We crept in there too, to bask lovingly in the contents of the wardrobe. I remember being frightened to touch the dresses and desperate to touch them. To wrap myself in them and to wet them with tears of painful longing.

When summer came to a close there was still no summons back to The Cottage. We could hardly believe it. Was Harrie going to let us stay with Daddy for good now? We hardly dared to hope.

The autumn school term started again for both of us and Nana got our uniforms ready and saw us off. We had the extra walk, through the woods, to get the bus down to Springwood, but we didn't mind.

This time, I caught the bus with Jackie, as we travelled together in the morning, and sometimes, but not often, Daddy could pick us up in the late afternoon. We waited at the bus stop directly opposite The Cottage. From inside you could see everyone standing at the bus stop if you looked out of the window, but there was never an acknowledgement. At first I dreaded Harrie coming out, but I soon realised that she was never going to appear. Maybe nobody saw us. Certainly, no one came to see how we were. The only person we saw from The Cottage was David, when we met him by chance from time to time playing in the woods. It seemed that Harrie had handed us back to our father and considered us dispensed with.

John came round to see us, to see if we were all right. He stayed and played about a bit, ate with us if we were eating. Sometimes Daddy was there, sometimes not. John was working for Daddy part-time in a restaurant and cocktail bar in the town centre, the New Bear's Paw. All the tips were collected in one jar and my father somehow arranged it so that they were all handed over to John at the end of the evening. I don't know how long he was there, but when I had the job myself and received the tips in the same way, the Christmas after I turned eighteen, the older staff remembered John being there. He had entertained them with his wit and had left an impression.

John and Bobby had formed a relationship which survived our mother's death. Bobby was very fond of John and did his best to help him. And John liked Bobby, although he didn't really see him as a father figure.

John also brought Paul to the house, and he too got on well with Bobby. John and Paul used to play records for hours, slowing them down so that they could write out the words to songs. Sometimes they came when we were there, and sometimes when we weren't. Like Springwood, this was a 'back door' house. It was never locked. In fact, it was hardly ever closed, even over night. You didn't need a key.

In October Jackie's tenth birthday was approaching, her second motherless birthday. I wanted so much to make it special for her, because there was no Mummy to take her home to any more.

I had always felt very protective of my younger sister, even if I wasn't very good at it. When we were still living with our mother, Jackie had come into the girly gang as soon as she was able. If we were going adventuring, even to the Oak Tree Den, round the corner from the house, Jackie came along. If she got too tired, or hungry, I would take her home and leave her with Mummy. I was definitively 'the eldest' and watched over her, helped by the gang boss, Ann. Whenever Jackie was with us, I was expected to see that she was all right. It was the same with all younger siblings. We looked up to the older children and looked after the younger ones. We had no problem with the natural pecking order.

After Mummy died I felt even more protective of Jackie. We were always close, but we became closer, because for so much of the time we only had each other. Her birthday was due to fall on half-term, so we didn't have to invent an excuse for not going to school. Daddy went to work in the morning, promising a birthday tea that evening, and left us in Nana's care. We were out of the house before she was even up. I had thought long and hard about what we could do to make it a special birthday. Daddy had given me some money and there was a small newspaper shop in the lane, so we went there first. It was too small to offer much choice and we ended up buying a couple of bags of mixed sweets and a packet of Oxo cubes. Nana used to make a delicious drink with Oxo cubes, melting a whole one into a cup of hot water and breaking bread into it, until it couldn't absorb any more. She sat you right back in an armchair and gave it to you with a spoon. A drink you could sip and eat and savour all at the same time. I hadn't thought through how we were going to achieve this, when I bought them. But I wanted us to spend the whole day in the woods and the next nearest shops would have taken us right into the village, wasting our precious birthday time.

So, we stuffed our party stash into our pockets and went into the field in front of the woods. I organised races for two, forwards and backwards. We skipped without a rope and jumped over sticks held higher and higher. We played hide-and-seek and I didn't even hide very well, as it was a birthday. I thought I would have a go at the Swipe with Jackie, but abandoned that idea when I realised we were almost the same height. We played wheelbarrows and toss-ups and aeroplanes and making up stories. We swung on a tree with low branches. We found the largest oak tree and gave ourselves the challenge of climbing up the great, broad trunk, so that we could sit on the wide branches and pretend we had a tree house. Or do ship ahoy. And when we had finished the sweets we licked the Oxo cubes. When we were on the way back to the house, hours later, hoping Daddy would be back, I asked Jackie if she had had a good birthday.

She said, 'It was lovely. Thank you, Ju. But I want Mummy.'

Nana had made the jellies. Daddy had brought the cake and the candles and the presents, all wrapped up, and we had the birthday tea, going to bed extra, extra late.

Our time in the School Lane house stretched on and on, and we were beginning to hope that we might stay there for ever. In March 1960 I had my thirteenth birthday and survived. Daddy had obviously enlisted the help of a mother somewhere. He had bought me dresses, a frilly underskirt and hair things. Out of school I lived in trousers or jeans, with my hair tied back. This was clearly his effort to encourage the girly side of me. Not that he had a lot of success. But I was touched.

32: *Back to The Cottage*

We stayed in School Lane for almost the entire school year, without any contact with our maternal family, apart from John, of course. Not one aunt got in touch. This sounds astonishing, given that we had been living with one of them for the previous year, but it signifies the reluctance with which they had accepted us at all and, I suspect, the relief with which they handed us back to our father.

Then, just before the summer holidays of 1960, we arrived back from school one afternoon and were told by Daddy that we were going back to Harrie for the holidays, as Nana had to go back to her own house. He said that she wasn't very well, and he couldn't take all that time off work. It was a terrible blow.

Looking back, I can see how difficult it must have been for our father. Nana was getting too frail and wasn't well enough to cope with the day-to-day supervision that was about to be needed during the long summer holidays, and Daddy's job kept him out of the house at all the wrong times. He could provide us with love and material care, but not the time we needed as growing girls. The next-door neighbours at The Cottage had family who lived directly opposite Daddy's house, right on the edge of the woods. I sometimes wonder whether they reported that Jackie and I were out and about, without much restraint.

Daddy wanted us to stay, of that there is no doubt. But he knew he couldn't ask his mother to cope for much longer, and what alternative did he have? What Harrie's thinking was, I have no idea. She must have thought we had settled with Daddy and Nana and that her job was done. However it happened, we went back. Unlike the previous summer, it was not a happy time. David and our other cousin, Michael, went to Scotland for the whole summer, but we were never sent on these trips. Instead Jackie and I were left on our own with Harrie and Norman. We did go to see Daddy quite often, and occasionally we stayed the night, and that made the long summer weeks pass more easily.

But our shells were toughening all the time. We knew now that we would be staying at The Cottage for the next few years – Nana's health, and Daddy's situation, weren't likely to change.

I was now a teenager, but I was still treated like a small child, with strict rules, early bedtimes and no asking questions or answering back. Of course the teenage years then were very different from now – still seen as an extension of childhood, rather than a transition to adulthood. Nonetheless other teenagers I knew were allowed many more freedoms than I ever had, and I looked on with a certain amount of envy, dreaming of adulthood and freedom.

John wasn't around that summer. He had left art college, after failing his exams in July, and gone to Hamburg with his group, who had now dropped the 'Silver' and simply called themselves the Beatles.

By this time new groups were appearing weekly in Liverpool. Rory Storm and the Hurricanes and Gerry and the Pacemakers already had devoted followings. Every teenage boy in the city was in a group.

The budding Beatles had got some gigs in a new club, the Casbah, owned by Mona Best. They'd had a vacancy for a drummer since Colin Hanton had left, so Mona's son, Pete, stepped in just before they left for Germany.

The boys' first manager, Nigel Walley, was now pursuing a serious career as a professional golfer, and this tour had been organised by their new manager, Allan Williams, who drove them across to Hamburg in his own van. The line-up for this first of five Hamburg tours was John, Paul, George, Stuart and Pete. Everyone seems to be in agreement that, despite the hardships they endured there, Hamburg was the making of the Beatles. It was, as Paul put it, 'the 800-hour long rehearsal'. After being forced to play on stage for endless hours and sometimes even sleep there too, often drunk and drugged, they couldn't wait to get back to Liverpool, where suddenly everything seemed easy.

By the time they got back Stuart had met the girl of his dreams, Astrid Kirchherr, a photographer's assistant who hung out with Hamburg's middle-class existentialist crowd, known as 'The Exxies'. She and her friends recognised potential in the Beatles, beyond the down-and-out clubs where they were contracted to play. They took many photographs of them and wore the black leather gear that was to become the non-uniform uniform.

This initial trip, however, ended prematurely. It was discovered that young George was just that, too young at seventeen to be performing in German night clubs. As soon as his real age was exposed, he was promptly deported. Paul and Pete soon followed, after starting an accidental fire in their lodgings. Astrid paid for Stuart to fly home, leaving John to make his own way back. His first wanderings alone in foreign parts.

That first trip from Liverpool to Hamburg was the catalyst that produced the explosion that shook the world. When he got back John told me about the Reeperbahn, the red-light district of Hamburg, and the seedy clubs there. He called them strip clubs. I was agog. I thought that such an underworld only existed in Paris. John was careful to cut the worst excesses out of his stories, telling us that the hardest part was getting no sleep and having no time to eat. I didn't understand about the drug scene, but I knew that their trip must have been wild and drunken.

Allan Williams soon acquired work permits for a second trip to Hamburg, this time with an eighteen-year-old George. John took Cynthia with him for part of this second trip, over the Easter holiday in 1961. He had been bragging so much about it at home, that the really had no choice but to take her along. I'm sure that Cynthia would have heard about the girl groupies from the others and from general gossip and excitement that surrounded the group, and that this probably strengthened her determination to be at John's side during the next trip. Tables were turned, however, with a singular incident, in Hamburg's Top Ten Club, when someone in the audience tried to attach himself to Cyn, while she was watching John play. In the middle of a number, John leapt right off the stage to hit the chat-up man who was trying to get close to his girl.

He must have been wearing his glasses!

During their three-month engagement at the Top Ten they were introduced to Tony Sheridan, a British singer who was also performing in Hamburg. They were invited to back him on a recording of 'My Bonnie'. John brought a copy home for us. We thought he was already famous. After all, he had made a real record, which was on sale for real money in real shops.

It was also during their second Hamburg trip that Stuart came to his decision to stay there. He and Astrid were madly in love and planning to marry. He was going to follow his true talent and study painting.

So the Beatles returned to Liverpool without Stuart. And by this time they were professionals, primed and ready to go. They'd got a new, distinctive style, wearing black leather trousers and jackets with the collars turned up. And they'd switched their DA haircuts for a softer, combed-down look that was later to be christened the 'mop-top'. At a time when all the groups back home were wearing matching outfits, suits and ties, and doing little dance routines, like the Shadows, the Beatles were totally different. And the fans loved them.

In October 1961 John turned 21. That was the big birthday then. Mater came down from Scotland to celebrate this special day with the family at Mendips. I remember her fussing over John, ruffling his hair and saying how wonderful he was. Her present was a gift of £100, which she told John was 'from Mummy'. I had the same myself, on my 21st, and used it for a deposit on a house. John spent his on a trip to Paris with Paul. They meant to hitch-hike to Spain, but only got as far as Paris. They wore leather jackets and bowler hats to hitch rides, as a gimmick, to show people they weren't ruffians. It worked. They got rides and had a wild, drunken time for ten days.

Stuart and John wrote to each other all that winter. I never really knew Stuart, but I knew he was John's best friend and that John was looking forward to seeing him again when the Beatles went back to Hamburg in the spring. However, tragedy loomed. Stuart had been complaining of headaches for some time and he died of a brain haemorrhage the day before John and the others arrived. He was only 22.

I heard about his death and knew it would have a profound effect on John, who had already endured so much grief. I didn't see him for the next couple of months because he was in Hamburg, but I ached for him and hoped that his relationship with Cynthia would give him the love and support he so badly needed.

33: *Famous Brother*

You may think of 1962 as the year that Brian Epstein got Nigel Walley's old job . . . or when Pete Best was sacked and Richard Starkey became the replacement drummer for the group . . . or when John and Cynthia married . . . or when their first single, 'Love Me Do', was released.

Well that's all true, of course, but I have additional memories of the burgeoning of the Beatles.

Our brother had overtaken other brothers in the success stakes now and Jackie and I were beginning to feel the effects of John and his growing fame. At school we talked about it a lot among ourselves and there was even a notice-board where pictures of the Beatles, cut out of the *Liverpool Echo*, were displayed. Teachers would ask about him and I was implored, or rather instructed, by fellow pupils to sidetrack the teachers from time to time with Beatles gossip, when we hadn't done our homework or we wanted some illicit classroom chill-out time.

The downside for me was that now everyone knew that John, my brother, had been living with our aunt, round the corner from The Cottage, and not with us. And that I was only visiting my father, and not living with him. And of course they all wanted to know why. Once again I felt as John had felt, but had less opportunity to avoid the grilling. Everyone wanted to know about him. And the irony was that it was John's life that was forcing the issue, not mine. It had become unavoidable and I felt a simultaneous mixture of pride and anger.

Where was my mother? Was she killed in the car crash? Why didn't I live with my father? My brother? I hadn't even told any of my friends, except for one, that I had lived with my father for a nearly a year – because I hardly believed it myself and had almost known it would come to an end. I learned to rebuff the questioning by various means. Staring them out. Turning away. Talking gibberish. Being sarcastic. Laughing.

Leave me alone. Teachers included.

So, although I loved to boast about John and to bask in the reflected glory, I dreaded the questioning that accompanied it. Only Ray, my school soulmate, who had been with me from the Scholarship Factory right through to New Heys, knew the truth. She had been round to our house in Springwood and met my mother, she knew about my family and she hauled me through this acute and ongoing embarrassment as best she could, by just being there and understanding. We would go right down to the bottom of the school field and lie on the grass, often in silence. Because she knew that I didn't know the answers and that was fine. She unwittingly defused many a tense situation. She understood that I was in turmoil and that she didn't need to examine it, or me.

If the night-long gigs in the clubs of Hamburg were the 800-hour rehearsal for the group, then the Cavern was the platform that introduced them to the world. They had already played there as the Quarry Men, in 1957, but their debut there as the Beatles came on 21 March 1961, just after my fourteenth birthday.

The Cavern was – and still is – situated in the depths of Liverpool's old warehouse basements, in Mathew Street, right in the city centre. The frequent underground trains roaring from Central Station as down to James Street station, prior to crossing the Mersey in the tunnel on its riverbed, make their own contribution to the volume in the Cavern. No matter how thunderous the performance in the club, the whole place reverberates to the deep growling of these trains.

It consists of three cavernous tunnels, with stone arches, and in those days the middle one boasted a rough stage. The rest of the space was for sitting or dancing. The walls dripped with sweat. There was no ban on smoking back then, and that included the groups on stage, but no alcohol was served. Most of the punters drank Coca-Cola, to ward off dehydration, served by cloakroom assistant Cilla Black.

None of the other clubs in town had the raw atmosphere of the Cavern, and when the Beatles played there they were as rough and uninhibited as their surroundings. They wore black leather jackets and jeans, had scruffy hair, jammed as they felt like it, ad-libbed and joked with one another and the audience and grew in popularity with every appearance. It wasn't long before a ticket to see the Beatles play at the Cavern was like gold dust.

John hosted their Cavern appearances, almost fifteen years later, to the Sex Pistols bursting on to the music scene and turning the music establishment on its head. 'That's how we used to behave at the Cavern before Brain Epstein told us to stop throwing up and eating on stage and swearing. We were absolutely "au naturel".'

I went to the Cavern several times and was turned away more than several times. You were meant to be eighteen, or at least look the part, which was a problem for me! I never looked my age at that time, let alone eighteen, and no amount of black eye make-up, black polo necks and dyed black jeans à la Cathy McGowan convinced most of the doormen to let me in, even though my friends sailed past them. I used to pray that they would be preoccupied when it was my turn and I could sidle past and down into the dark abyss.

On those occasions when I did manage to get in I saw the Hideaways, the Big Three, the Searchers and many others. But no, I never saw the Beatles play there. I went in secret, initially, as we weren't allowed out into town in the evening. House rules. When John was playing at the Cavern and other places in the city centre, there was no point in asking him for a ticket as I would never have been allowed to go, despite being fifteen or even sixteen.

Somebody who did see them was Brian Epstein, manager of the NEMS (North End Music Stores) record shop. He popped into the Cavern out of curiosity after several customers had asked for 'My Bonnie', the record the Beatles had made with Tony Sheridan. He recognised that they had something special and soon afterwards he took over as their manager. Allan Williams was only too thankful to be rid of the troublesome gang and warned Brian that they were very difficult and unreliable. In one of the major misses of the business world at that time, he let them go for free!

Brian took over the management of the Beatles in December 1961 and they signed a contract on 24 January 1962. He started to exert his influence on them very quickly. The leather jackets and jeans were ditched. The boys were reluctant, but went along with it because they knew they'd never appeal to a mass audience in their rough gear. They began wearing jumpers and then suits.

I remember Brian coming to Mendips and chatting to Mimi. I can see him leaning back on the table in the morning room, with his arms folded, talking in a quiet voice. Another time, he had his elbow on the mantelpiece. Not an easy feat, as it was quite high. I tried it out myself, but couldn't get near it. He was always unfailingly polite and charming, and Mimi thought he was lovely, which undoubtedly helped her to come to terms with the metamorphosis from John to Beatle.

John had the greatest love and respect for Brian and for what he had done for the group. He would tell Cyn, 'Brian's given us a future. He's our light at the end of the tunnel.'

Brian worked hard. While getting the boys as many bookings as possible and changing their image, he was going down to London, hard-selling them to record companies. Most said no. But in May 1962 he finally secured a recording contract with a small subsidiary company of the renowned EMI, Parlophone Records, whose musical director and general Man Friday was

George Martin. Contracts were signed in June and they were scheduled to make their first single in September.

Paul and George were thrilled to have a contract, but they had a problem, and that was Pete Best. They were unhappy with Pete's style of drumming and felt he didn't fit into the group, but they lacked the courage to do anything about it. So Brian sacked Pete and took the brunt of the flak following the abrupt dismissal. It took a while for the dust to settle. Pete was good-looking and had his own fans, who were understandably furious.

Meanwhile Paul's brother Mike had told him about an amazing drummer who played with Rory Storm and the Hurricanes, Ringo Starr. The boys had met him in Hamburg, when both groups were working there. They didn't know him especially well, but he was the one they wanted. So by the middle of August 1962 the group had a new line-up: John, Paul, George – and Ringo.

34: *A Wedding and a Record*

Something else happened just before that first recording. John and Cynthia got married.

Cynthia was pregnant and disapproval ran high in the family. John was urged not to get married, despite the pregnancy. Mimi demanded that Cynthia go back to her mother to have the baby, despite the fact that Cynthia's mother was living in Canada at that time and the family home in Hoylake had been rented out, as Mimi knew well.

In the end, all John's aunts boycotted the wedding entirely, meaning that we couldn't go either. No one from the family attended. The wedding guests were Cynthia's brother Tony and his wife Marjorie, and Brian, Paul and George. The ceremony, on 23 August, was held in Mount Pleasant register office, the same one where Mummy and Alf Lennon had married 24 years earlier.

Once Cynthia discovered she was pregnant the wedding was organised within a couple of weeks. I went round to Mendips one afternoon a few days before the big day and Nanny was there, as well as John and Mimi. There was tension in the air and I was banished to the kitchen to make tea, but the door was always open into the morning room, so I could have heard everything, even if they hadn't been shouting, which they were. It was all about John's getting married. Or rather, it was more about all the reasons for him not to get married. He was too young. He didn't have a proper job. He had no money. He didn't have a home of his own. He didn't know what he was doing. He didn't have to marry Cynthia, even if she was having his baby. She could live with her mother. John became increasingly upset and ended up shouting, 'For Christ's sake! I want to marry her. I love her! What's the matter with you? We are getting married!'

The week that John and Cynthia were getting married, Mimi was round at The Cottage, talking about it with Harrie. How awful it was. I asked if we were going to the wedding. I wanted to go. My brother was getting married and I wanted to go. Harrie immediately turned to me angrily and told me not to be so stupid, and Mimi's response was to get up and leave without another word, slamming the front door behind her, making it echo down the long hallway.

The next day I went to see Hannah Starkey after school and told her that John was getting married, and she laughed and said, 'Your mother should be there. She would love it! And give that lad all the best wishes from us when you see him.'

Their wedding day was grey and cloudy, and a pneumatic drill outside the register office window meant they could hardly hear themselves taking their vows.

Afterwards Brian took them to Reece's café where they had the set meal of soup, chicken and trifle, washed down with water, as the café had no licence.

It was a rocky start to married life, but John and Cyn were happy. They had each other. And Brian gave them a fantastic wedding gift, the use of his flat in Faulkner Street as a base to start off married life. They needed it – Cyn was living in a bedsit and John was still based at Mimi's, so goodness knows what they'd have done otherwise.

They had only been married for two weeks when the Beatles went to Abbey Road Studios in St John's Wood, London, to record 'Love Me Do', with 'PS, I Love You' on the B side. The very first Lennon and McCartney recording. John brought us round a copy of 'Love Me Do', before it was released. He came running upstairs, waving it in the air like a trophy. He sat on the bed and listened to it with Jackie, David and me. We had never seen a demo disk before, with its plain underside. John was excited and wanted to know what we thought of it.

I was disappointed. I have never really liked 'Love Me Do'. But I said it was great. We all did. For me, without a doubt, the best thing about that record was John on the harmonica.

By late October, 'Love Me Do' had risen to number seventeen in the charts. The Beatles already had a serious fan base in Liverpool, but now their fame was set to spread throughout Great Britain and beyond.

At the time that the group went to London to make the record John hadn't seen any of the family, including Mimi, since the wedding. He found it hard to forgive Mimi's refusal to be there on his special day and kept away from Mendips. It was Cynthia who finally persuaded him that he had suffered enough losses in his life and that this was the time to forgive his family, Mimi in particular. At Cyn's insistence they went to see Mimi one afternoon, unannounced, about three months later and were surprised by the warm welcome they received. Not long before, Cyn had nearly had a miscarriage while John was away, which frightened them both. Luckily her brother had been able to come round, but she was spending a lot of time alone and John was worried. When Mimi heard about the threatened miscarriage, she immediately offered them the downstairs part of Mendips. She would move upstairs. It wasn't right for Cynthia to be on her own so much.

We only knew about all this when Mimi came round and told Harrie. Cyn was rhesus negative and we heard lots about the dangers of that if the baby was rhesus positive, and that it wasn't good for her to be on her own, with her mother being in Canada. We didn't know anything about the near miscarriage, only that Cyn wasn't very well and that John was away a lot, busy being a Beatle.

I was sent to Mimi's on an errand shortly after she'd made her offer to John and Cyn. She was often frosty with me, sending me promptly on my way, but at other times she was kinder, giving me a drink and asking about school. On this occasion she told me John and Cyn were moving in and she said she was going to the flat that day to see them to discuss arrangements. She invited me upstairs and said that she had been thinking of how to split the house. John's small front bedroom was going to be her kitchen, and the large front bedroom, her sitting-room. She would carry on sleeping in the back bedroom. They would all share the upstairs bathroom and the gardens. She bought a Baby Belling cooker and put it where John's bed had been, facing the wall. She would do her washing-up in a bowl, with hot water from the bathroom.

Mimi had always shared Mendips with the students, but we all knew how much against the marriage she had been, and now of course she was offering to move out of her own kitchen and morning room, which can't have been easy. This was a major turn-about and I could only think that Mimi was genuinely concerned and meant to be kind.

Downstairs, John and Cyn were to have the students' sitting-room/study as their bedroom. We had rarely been allowed into that room, next to the morning room at the back of the house. I remember going round the back of the garden and seeing them lying in bed there, late in the morning, with the French windows wide open on to the garden, still asleep. I brought them tea and toast in bed.

It was never plain sailing, however, and it wasn't long before Mimi was criticising Cynthia. It seemed that everything she did and said was wrong. She took them in because she loved John and wanted to help, but she soon appeared to resent it and made their lives miserable. It was just like what we experienced round the corner in The Cottage with Harrie.

35: *Beatle Baby*

The Beatles had nearly released a slower version of 'Please Please Me' as their first single. In the event, it was set aside in favour of 'Love Me Do', but it was resurrected and revamped at a faster tempo as the second release in November 1962. Already the Beatles were making history. Both recordings were home-grown, Paul was the author of the first song and John of the second. This was both innovative and daring and ultimately a key to their rapid success. Most groups at that time were making records chosen for them by record companies. In fact George Martin had chosen 'How Do You Do What You Do To Me?' as their first single, but they'd insisted on recording their own song and, being the innovator he was, he'd let them. George's choice hadn't been bad, though, as Gerry and the Pacemakers, who also signed with Brian, went on to have a huge hit with it.

The Beatles went off to tour Ireland and Scotland in the New Year, after which they left again immediately to embark on a tour of England. They released their first album, also entitled 'Please Please Me', in March, having famously put it together in just ten days. This was raw rock and roll and as near to a live performance at the Cavern as you can get. Turned up to full volume, John's superb rendition of the Isley Brothers' 'Twist and Shout' is incomparable. How did his throat not burst wide open? You can feel the pounding and you just have to respond to the beat. It rocks!

We saw little of John now. He was away far more than he was at home. But we followed everything he was doing by going round to see Mimi and Cyn for updates.

'Please Please Me' reached number one in February 1963. We

glowed with pride. Then, in April, 'From Me To You' was released and went straight to number one. The Beatles were on Brian Matthews' *Saturday Club* on the radio every week, reading out listeners' cards, belting out rock and roll cover songs and adding their own recordings for good measure. I was in the gym club at school, which necessitated going back to school on Saturday mornings to practise. The dedicated teachers would have had an empty gym if they hadn't allowed us budding gymnasts to listen to 'Pop Go the Beatles'.

For me, listening to John on the radio at school on Saturday mornings was a way of following him and being there. He was out in the world, as all our older brothers were. Some were married, some had families, some had moved away. Mine was a radio star! They hadn't yet moved to London homes or made it to television, but they were down south more and more. I missed him and would wonder what he was doing, so the *Saturday Club* gave me a much-needed link.

I was sixteen in March that year, but I was a young and strictly controlled sixteen. I longed to go out with Ray and the other girls, down to town on a Saturday night, but Harrie didn't approve and more often than not I had to stay at home. I wasn't brave enough yet to break the rules. But I longed for more freedom.

John and Cynthia had stayed at Mendips throughout the winter and spring in their newly created ground-floor flat. Julian was born on 8 April 1963, in Sefton General Hospital, where Jackie and I were both born. The birth was extremely arduous and Cyn was exhausted. Some of the fans had heard about the baby, so she had to be moved to a private ward. Brian wanted the birth, like the wedding, to be a low-key affair.

John couldn't come for a few days, as he was touring in the south of England, but when he did he was thrilled with John Charles Julian, to be known as Julian, for our mother. He picked him up, saying, 'Who's going to be a famous little rocker, like his Dad?' And 'He's bloody marvellous, Cyn!'

We all went round to Mendips to see the new arrival, the day that Cynthia arrived back from the hospital. None of us children had been to the hospital to see the latest member of the family. Mimi went, but no one else. So this was the first time that Jackie and I had seen our nephew. John was there, holding Julian, and so was Nanny. It was a welcome-the-baby gathering. When we arrived, they were all standing in a group by the morning room window, peering at him from this angle and that side. They said they could see John and Cyn in this sleeping bundle.

He was the next new thing!

I went round to Mendips from time to time to see Cynthia when John was away, and she came to The Cottage occasionally on her way to the village shops. If I went to see her, I would chat to her for a short time and then go upstairs to see Mimi, who would have thought it very strange if I hadn't. Often she would be making her favourite tea and toast in John's bedroom-turned-kitchen. She said that Julian was 'a crier'.

He did cry a lot. Round at The Cottage, we sometimes looked after him and I was sent out to wheel him in the pram, to try to get him to sleep. That could take an hour or more, and even then he could wake up just being pushed back into the house.

Mimi was very critical of Cynthia's management of her baby, and Cynthia said that Mimi did little to help out, even when he cried all night. Mimi told Harrie about her sleepless nights, because at times Julian was inconsolable. It had been a difficult pregnancy, a difficult birth and now there was a difficult baby. Cynthia found it hard to cope with Mimi, and the spoken and unspoken criticism when John was away, and knew she would have to move out as soon as she could find alternative accommodation.

John had only one official break since the pressurising build-up of the birth of the Beatles, and this coincided almost exactly with the birth of their baby. When Julian was just three weeks old, John went to Spain for ten days with Brain Epstein. Cynthia was desperately tired and couldn't go, but she agreed, if somewhat reluctantly, to John going without her. She was well aware that John needed time out, having completed thirty engagements, including concerts, radio and television, in April alone.

This was the holiday that was to give rise to the story that John and Brain had a homosexual affair. Bob Wooler, the disc jockey at the Cavern Club, intimated as much at Paul's 21st birthday party not long afterwards. John hit him and had to pay damages to keep it out of court. I was shocked when I heard. Although John always liked to be leader of the gang and in charge, he hated confrontation. I couldn't imagine him hitting anyone. Of course it was under the influence of drink, and I know, from other people's accounts, that John could become aggressive after drinking. But I never saw him drunk, so I didn't see this side of him.

We knew at home, of course, that they had gone to Spain. Cynthia talked about it with Mimi in Mendips and Harrie in The Cottage. We could see how weak Cynthia was and how time-consuming a baby was. We knew that John was working very hard and that he had gone to rest in the sun.

The gossip ran into school after they were back, when the fight with Bob Wooler was both local and national news. I hadn't a clue about homosexuality and didn't want to expose my ignorance, so I defended John for fighting. I put up a vigorous case for nothing being John's fault and almost ended up fighting myself.

My turning sixteen in March 1963, just before Julian was born, had heralded a shift in my relationship with my father. Following the year-long stay at School Lane, he had continued to visit us at The Cottage, and we had gone through the woods to visit him, but now things changed for me. One day, soon after my birthday, Daddy beckoned me outside to the gate as he was leaving.

'Can you get away, Hen?' he asked me. I told him I could offer to walk the dog and he said he would wait for me in his car at the bottom of the road.

Daddy had an old green Jaguar, very distinctive, and his pride and joy. A few minutes later I got in, putting Sophie, our black Labrador, by my feet. We moved off slowly, just chatting, and he took me for a coffee. After that, we did it as often as we could. Daddy would give me a nod as he was leaving and I would take the dog and run down the road to meet him. We'd talk about nothing special, just enjoying being together. He'd ask if I was all right and sometimes give me a bit of extra pocket money. It was our secret and I hugged it to me.

Daddy must have felt that at sixteen I was close to adulthood and could begin to make my own decisions. He wanted to see more of me, and at last he could. I am so glad we had those times, as they brought us closer, after all the years apart.

36: *We Love You, Yeah! Yeah! Yeah!*

The first British Beatles tour was as the opening act for Helen Shapiro, the second was as support to Tommy Roe and Chris Montez. This tour had come to the Liverpool Empire in March. We didn't go to see them, but many of my schoolfriends did. They asked me why we hadn't been there, but we didn't even know it had happened until the next school day. I felt very upset that my brother was playing at the Empire and I hadn't even known it. At home no one mentioned what John was up to. If they knew, they didn't think it necessary to tell me and Jackie.

Then one day, a few weeks later, I went to Mendips on an errand and Brian Epstein was there, telling Mimi all about the Beatles at the Empire. So I said, 'What about us?' Brian laughed and said he didn't know we were fans. I protested that we would all love to go, but the next concert at the Liverpool Empire, in which the Beatles played support to Roy Orbison, was never mentioned at home either and we looked set to miss that one too. It had obviously already been decided that we weren't going. Fortunately, my schoolfriend Ray wanted to see the Beatles on stage and she suggested that we go together, which we did. I had no money, so she bought the tickets. I knew I wasn't supposed to go, but I really wanted to see my brother on stage. I just told Harrie that I was meeting Ray and went.

We went to the theatre and took our seats in the audience. John had left Mendips only hours before us and I'd been over to see him there. I hadn't told him that I would be in the audience, as I knew that if Harrie found out I might end up not being able to go at all and letting down my friend too. When the Beatles came on stage, we couldn't believe what was happening. Girls were screaming and crying and jumping up and down. The Beatles closed the first half of the programme, and then, at the end of the second half, Roy Orbison appeared. He was at the height of his fame then and we expected a great show. But something extraordinary happened. Throughout the whole of Roy Orbison's act, the audience, mainly girls, shouted for the return of the Beatles. We could hardly hear him sing and he must have been relieved to get off the stage.

The whole theatre was adrenalin-soaked in madness. It was a bit scary and very exciting at the same time. We had never seen anything like this in our lives before. The largest crowd we knew about was school assembly, when fidgeting girls could be stilled with a glance!

I had to leave before the end to catch the last bus home. I knew I'd be in terrible trouble if I broke my curfew, but the bus was late and so was I. Harrie was furious, but it was worth the dressing down I got, just to have seen John on stage.

The next time we all went to the Liverpool Empire to see John and friends perform was that December. This time, we were all invited as a family outing because they were the main act. The screaming started as the first curtain went up and carried on until they appeared an hour later, only intensifying as they played. We went to the dressing-room afterwards to see the back-of-house in action. I had only been backstage in the school play before that. Then, the small staff room belonging to the PE teachers doubled up as a dressing-room.

This was the real thing. Mirrors surrounded by many light bulbs, shining too brightly. The counters were full of make-up boxes of powders and paints, and there were bottles of Coca-Cola for us to drink. The atmosphere was one of rowdy banter, with some people sitting down on the counters and chairs and others rushing around trying to organise things. Like how we were going to leave, as the crowds were building up in the side streets all round the theatre. Did we enjoy the show? Did we!

We left from the stage door at the side of the theatre. What a palaver that was! Burly men blockaded us in and kept others out. The door had to be heaved open and we were squashed into waiting cars, with the screaming girls trying to stop us moving. The driver just started the car and moved forward slowly but determinedly, with faces almost squashed against all the car windows, including the windscreen. I thought we were going to run them over.

It was frightening, it was exciting, it was madness – and it had come to Liverpool. I had only ever seen this for Elvis. On film. But he sang and danced and flirted with all the girls. He was Elvis. They say it happened first for Frank Sinatra.

It was a brilliant story for school.

The Beatles were now enjoying unprecedented success. After almost three hundred appearances in the sweatiest dive in Britain, they played their last gig at the Cavern on 3 August, leaving behind the rough performances that had made them into the Beatles. They had grown as performers through close and demanding interaction with the audience and wild excitement both on stage and off, actively cultivating the rough edges. On the bigger stage, they were about to be poured into collarless suits and made to bow low at the end of each performance. The raw essence which had been the very foundation of the rise to fame and of the intense rehearsal period in Hamburg, ended here. Of all the times I didn't get to see them at the Cavern, I really regret not dancing them out.

At the end of August, they released the record that was to become their signature tune, 'She Loves You'. Soon after that came Beatlemania, a term coined by the press after their first appearance at the London Palladium, when the streets around the theatre were blocked by hysterical fans.

We seemed to be living with the song as background music.

It was on the radio every two minutes and they sang it on TV, where they appeared more and more often. No Beatles show, live or televised, was complete without it, and this was to be true from then on, until they stopped playing. The very start of it produced effects on the audience that defied belief. John and Paul, Beatle mops shining, would look at each other, then strike the chord simultaneously. John would start bobbing up and down, grinning and looking at the floor and the screams would erupt.

Our brother was being adopted as the world's property. His presence was in the corner of our living-room . . . and everyone else's in the country. It is still the saddest thing that he never invaded the small screen in Springwood. Mummy would have been dancing for joy.

Yeah, yeah yeah!

37: *After Liverpool, the World*

In August John and Cynthia finally found time for a belated honeymoon. A year late. They went to Paris to enjoy their first time alone and away from the Beatles, fans and family since their wedding. John had been to Paris with Paul to celebrate his 21st birthday two years previously, and now he chose to return with Cyn. He loved the culture there, it was one of his favourite cities. I think that if he hadn't gone to live in New York a few years later, then Paris would have been his next choice.

At Brian's insistence, John's wife and baby had been kept under wraps, a secret that, in Liverpool anyway, wasn't really a secret at all. Cyn was forced to go without her wedding ring and, if the press approached, deny that she knew John, but many of the local fans knew she was John's wife. John never liked the secrecy and denial, and he decided he'd had enough. He never thought, as Brian did, that the fans would turn against him if they knew he was married. And now he was adamant. He was moving Cyn and Julian to London.

In fact the 'secret' came out before the move, when Cyn was caught by a press photographer and the papers 'exposed' John's hidden wife. John and Cyn were relieved and there was no serious backlash from the fans. And a few weeks later they moved into a rented flat in Kensington, to give them time to look around for a permanent home in London.

They left Liverpool in early January 1964. We weren't aware of the exact date of the move – I don't remember John coming to say goodbye – but we knew they had gone. We had been seeing less and less of John as the Beatles grew more and more famous.

The actual move, however, added to the distance between John and his Liverpool family, including Jackie and me, and inevitably we felt sad about it and wondered when we'd see him. We were lucky really that it had taken so long.

Days after the move the Beatles went to Paris on tour, and there heard the news that 'I Want to Hold Your Hand' had reached number one in America. They returned from Paris and went to America two days later. Cynthia got to join John on the trip, while her mother looked after Julian back in London.

This was the real beginning of their world-wide fame. They had achieved what had until then been considered impossible for British artists, by breaking into the American market. Yet when they arrived in the States they had no idea what was waiting for them. They believed that the sound of the wild welcome of the thousands of fans at the airport was engine noise.

As for me and Jackie, we saw it all on TV and were amazed. To us America was what we saw in cowboy films and Elvis movies, we didn't know anyone who had actually *been* there. We thought it took six weeks on a big boat!

I also listened to *Saturday Club*, which they were still recording every week, live from the BBC. The tour of America was interrupting this and I thought they wouldn't be on it again until they came home. Not so.

Brian Matthews started the show as usual on Saturday 7 February, and what did he do, but ring up the Plaza Hotel in central Manhattan. They had just arrived in the middle of the greatest hurly-burly, but there they were, on the end of the line, laughing and chatting to everyone back in Liverpool. Each of them was interviewed in turn, as Brain asked them to explain their reception, although the entire country had, of course, seen it on television. They were calling each other to the telephone, taking it in turns to speak to their fans in Britain. And their humour and humility shone through. There was the world waiting to see them, and they were wild with excitement about seeing the Ronettes and the Isley Brothers.

When asked did he want to say anything to the fans back home, John said: 'Yeah. Tell them not to forget us. We're only away for ten days and we'll be back and we're thinking of them. Well, we're coming back to do the film for seven weeks anyway. We'll try and get you a part, pushing a barrow or something!'

John passed the telephone to Ringo:

'We're fine. The first thing we did when we got to the hotel, we had this big, mass press interview with about a hundred people there. Then we got out of there and we had a Cadillac *each*. Marvellous cars! They asked us all sorts of things. Are we bald, what do we do with our money. The usual things!'

When Brian asked them how they proved that the mop-tops weren't wigs, Ringo replied, 'We took them off!'

When George came on, he said they had six records in the American Top 100, including their first ever record, 'My Bonnie'.

Brian asked them about their plans after the phone-in. They all chipped in at once: 'We'll have a bit of a sun-bathe down in Florida. Miami Beach, Brian. It's amazing that you can hear us, seeing that we're in America now and you're so far away.'

Brian then asked about the proposed film, *A Hard Day's Night*. Paul replied: 'We won't be acting coz we'll just be ourselves, we think. We hope. We'll be singing 'n' all. Suppose you could call it acting really, couldn't you? Who can act? None of us can act, that's the thing.'

Ringo chimed up: 'John can act – the goat!'

John: 'If I wasn't in America, I'd punch him!'

Ringo: 'And when you're big enough, you'll be too old!'

Brian asked them if they were planning a holiday. George replied: 'We're getting three weeks, in a month.'

Brian asked where they were going, and John shouted, 'Somewhere Ringo isn't!'

Ringo: 'I'll just wait till John gets the tickets and I'll go the other way! We're very friendly really!'

As was customary, the boys then read out requests for their

numbers. During the show Brian played a fabulous, pre-recorded version of the Beatles doing Chuck Berry's 'Johnny B. Good'. He was one of John's heroes.

For me, the 66 wild rock/blues covers that they sang live throughout this series of programmes constituted the best that the Beatles ever did. I never saw them perform live at the Cavern and only know them there by reputation. But I know that John loved doing those covers. You can hear it. He was in the footsteps of his idols.

The four boys could have pre-recorded everything for the *Saturday Club*, instead of taking precious time out when they had just set foot in America. But they agreed readily to do the programme as the fans expected. So, while America waited, the boys were laughing and joking in front of the microphone, reading out postcards from young girls listening at home. Postcards that they had obviously brought along in their luggage and had at the ready. George finished the phone-in by shouting, 'See you in two weeks!'

This is who they really were. Fan club Beatles.

And on that day, back in Liverpool, my Saturday gym club ground to a halt.

A couple of days later the Beatles appeared on the enormously popular Ed Sullivan Show. Ed read out a telegram from Elvis, the King himself, congratulating them on their success. Oh to have been a fly on the wall when they heard that! John must have thought of Mummy. He would have been so proud . . . and sad.

We watched the welcome home by the British fans at Heathrow on 22 February. The hundreds of thousands far outdid any welcoming crowd the boys had received in America. They were claiming for themselves the phenomenon that was the Beatles.

38: *Fab Coats and Caps*

The very next day the four Beatles went to a house party. Nothing too unusual in that, you might think. But this was Alma Cogan's party. She was a major star at that time. Our mother had loved her and so did my sister. Jackie was always a girly girl, while right from the start I was a tomboy. Jackie had dolls; I had teddy bears. The one and only doll I ever received, a life-size affair with long blonde hair, came from Nana, when I was six years old. It was the first and last. I cut her hair and prised the limbs off to see how it worked, which I thought far more interesting than playing babies. I did think that I could reassemble her, but no such luck. I hid her and only confessed on being faced with the retrieved parts. My father spent a lot of my teens trying to make me more feminine and buying me dresses, which I mostly refused to wear.

Mummy and Jackie meanwhile would peer at the television set to see what Alma Cogan was wearing. I don't know how interesting they found the songs, but the great, full, flared dresses, with stars and spangles, captivated both of them. The screen was black-and-white, of course, back then, but this didn't seem to detract from the awe in which they held her costumes.

John was to become good friends with Alma, and there were even rumours that they had an affair, though I didn't hear of them at the time. I wonder if John told her about how much Mummy had loved her.

Ironically, there was almost another reminder of our mother around that time. The Beatles very nearly played with Judy Garland, on John's birthday, but in the end it was cancelled. She was another of my mother's favourite stars, but this was different. It wasn't about the dresses. It was about her singing. We saw her many times on television, and her non-glitzy clothes appealed to me far more. I remember the curtain rising on the stage of the London Palladium, to reveal her standing there, wearing a simple black jumper and a straight white skirt.

A month after John got back from America his book, *In His Own Write*, was published. It was a collection of cartoons, drawings, little stories and witticisms that John had produced over the years.

He had been collecting all his things from Mendips on various home visits over the past year or so, and among these were his drawings and writings. John had always been prolific in both. He loved to use the blackest Indian Ink on crisp white paper, producing line sketches, and the first caricature we had seen, although we had never heard it called that.

He had been producing a cartoon comic strip, which he called 'The Daily Howl', for years. I don't know when he started that particular magazine, but Mummy and John had been drawing with pencil, then Indian ink, as long as I can remember. Before he carried a guitar everywhere, he carried his sketch-books, which were usually school exercise books. The writing side had started off as balloons containing the cartoon characters' lines. He would show our mother the drawing and they would then come up with the words. This had developed into short stories. We were all great admirers of *The Goon Show*, and in particular Spike Milligan. John imitated Spike's style, which suited his caustic wit to perfection.

So now these artefacts had been siphoned off to London, to the publisher Jonathan Cape. The result was an instant bestseller.

I bought a copy; it didn't occur to me to ask him to give me one. I loved the humour. I have always been an avid fan of *Alice in Wonderland*, and then of Spike Milligan, starting with *Puckoon* and its opening lines of 'Three metric miles . . .' and now John was joining them!

I was hugely proud, I think the whole family was. To us, though, John's fame hadn't been sudden, it had escalated bit by bit, so at home nobody talked about him any differently from before. In fact Harrie seldom mentioned him. It was at school that I felt more aware of his fame, because a notice-board was devoted to him and teachers would come up and ask if he was really my brother.

March saw the release of 'Can't Buy Me Love', which went straight to the top of the charts. The Beatles were becoming rapidly subsumed into everyday life in Britain. They were becoming part of the national psyche. Here, there and everywhere.

In the spring of 1964 they arrived to perform another series of concerts at the Empire Theatre in Liverpool. John still stayed at Mendips during these visits, and this time he had a treat in store for us.

Although John and Cynthia had abandoned art college for Beatle and baby reasons, some of their contemporaries had finished their courses. One of their friends, Helen Anderson, had studied fashion and design and had recently opened a workshop and cutting room, over a shop in Bold Street in the city centre. This was the same Helen Anderson who had famously leaned forward in an art class in 1958 and affectionately stroked John's hair. Cynthia, watching, had felt jealous and realised at that moment that she was in love with John.

John came to The Cottage and told us that Helen now made clothes and that she was going to make each of us a coat, in the material of our choice, either leather or suede. Even better, we could design them ourselves. This was unbelievable and we were wildly excited. We were all going to the shop together the next Saturday, he said, so start thinking about what we would like.

I went to bed drawing my coat. Jackie and I were awake for hours, changing our minds, but I kept on coming back to my original garment. It was to be blacker than black, in suede, with a black leather collar and matching leather trim on the sleeves and the pocket edges. The coat was to have a red silky lining, in the sleeves as well, and would come to the top of my knees. My not-at-school coats were normally Liela's cast-offs, so the idea of something so glamorous all for me was wonderful.

We went to the workshop the next day, as promised – John, Cynthia, Harrie, David, Jackie and me. Nanny was there with Michael too. There were large tables like school desks, covered in skins, and the leathery smell was powerful. David chose a black leather three-quarter-length coat. Michael chose a grey leather one. Jackie's was lovely dark green leather and knee-length. They all had linings that would match the coats. Then Helen turned to me, standing quietly at the back. I was thinking that my coat would be too difficult to make. I explained what I had designed in my head and showed her a drawing. I expected her to laugh and offer me a black leather coat, but she studied my sketch, turning her head this way and that, grinned and said, 'That's lovely. I think it will have to be antelope.' And so it was.

When the best coats ever made on the planet were ready, there was another surprise. Each coat had with it a matching Beatle cap, just like John's. How cool was that! What a lovely brother.

And while our big brother was caught up in the most frenetic year of his group's meteoric rise to global stardom, our lives of quiet domestic and school routine couldn't have been more of a contrast. We watched John's progress with fascination and pride, and loved it when he came back to Liverpool and we saw him. Those times were increasingly rare, but despite what was happening in his life John never seemed any different. He was just John.

When we did see him we asked what it was like to be famous, and he'd laugh and say it was great. I could see that it was, and that he was having a wonderful time, but I wished it hadn't taken him so far away from us. I loved spending whatever time I could get with John. After Mummy died, he was the only person in the family – apart from Jackie – with whom I could cry and talk about her. He had become a last link with her, and now that he was away so much I really missed him.

In June 1964 the Beatles arrived in Sydney to start a tour of Australia and New Zealand. Knowing that Mimi was in touch with relatives in New Zealand, John had invited her to join him on that leg of the tour. Mimi was delighted. She was going to visit all the members of the family out there and take John to meet them. She had never stopped corresponding with the far-flung members of the family, and some of the younger ones had even visited us in Liverpool. I remember meeting a removed cousin called Jill, who had arrived in London to look for a job in nursing. Liverpool and Mendips were her first port of call, to introduce herself.

While Mimi was away, I found the key to Mendips. Harrie had been left to keep an eye on the house, as we were the closest, living in Woolton, and Mimi must have been gone a week or so when I came across a foreign key while tidying up in The Cottage. I knew it must belong to Mendips, although I had never seen the front-door key before. Mendips, like Springwood and School Lane, was a back-door house. I went to try it out after school one day and, yes, it opened the door.

For me, it was like finding gold. This was the first time I had ever been by myself. I mean, the first time I had had a whole establishment to myself. Rooms and chairs and beds and a bathroom and a garden, all for me. I never lit the fire, and it did get cold there sometimes, in the evening. I wore my coat. There was no electricity, Mimi must have switched it off. But as it was summer, I could read until late by the windows and in the garden. I just loved being alone. I even stayed overnight a few times, telling Harrie that I was staying with my friend Ray – which she allowed, very grudgingly now that I was seventeen. I played mini-golf in the garden, lay in the sun, went to bed to read in fading light until my eyes ached. I slept in John's old room when I did stay, as it was friendlier than the rest of the house.

I loved that time of peace and space. But then Mimi came back from New Zealand and I lost my bolt-hole.

She brought us presents from John, picked up when the boys went to Hong Kong and found time to stroll round a market. David, Michael, Jackie and I each received a watch and a radio-alarm clock, with fake-fur coverings in black and white. We thought they were fab.

39: *Premieres and Shopping Trips*

The first showing of *A Hard Day's Night* was the Royal Charity Premiere, which Princess Margaret and Lord Snowdon attended. It was followed by a reception at the Dorchester Hotel in Central London.

None of the family in Liverpool went to this. We were waiting for the real premiere, which was to take place in Liverpool, of course. It was on Friday, 10 July 1964, with a reception at the Town Hall, followed by the screening of the film at the Liverpool Odeon. And we were all invited.

Mimi, Harrie, Nanny, David, Michael, Jackie and I were picked up from Mendips in shiny limousines and taken into town in grand style. We had said that we would get the bus, but John laughed his head off at this.

We had never seen so many people in the city centre. It took the car a long time to crawl through the crowds and to park. It felt awkward, like a ship on land. We were afraid we were going to be late. We finally got to the Town Hall, a very beautiful building, for the reception. Eat your heart out, Dorchester Hotel. You have nothing on this.

The Town Hall is situated at the top of Castle Street, up from the River Mersey. It has a balcony, overlooking the length of this stretch of mini-mall, and we stood there, astounded by the size of the crowds. There were more than 200,000 people gathered there.

Liverpool hadn't seen scenes like this since the record-breaking days of Dixie Dean, the greatest footballer ever to come out of Liverpool, and a real Scouse hero in the 1920s.

Liverpool was proud of its progeny. The Beatles were welcomed as true heroes and they loved it. Inside the Town Hall, we helped ourselves to the food that seemed to be everywhere. We went to and fro, viewing the crowds from the balcony, peering at the Mayor with his heavy chains, and finding John to laugh with. They hardly had time to eat, because people were constantly asking questions. I gave John a sandwich, but he held it in his hand and eventually gave it back to me. The cars arrived to take us, in shifts, up to the Odeon cinema in London Road, to watch the film. John, Paul, George and Ringo went and we were left waiting for a car. We could have run there in ten minutes or less, but Harrie marshalled us to the foyer to wait.

We were ushered to our seats in the nick of time. John appeared on the stage to welcome the audience, as did all the boys. John peered upwards in the direction he knew our seats were and shouted out, 'Where's me family? I've lost them,' and we shouted back, 'We're all here, John.'

This was to have an echo in a later conversation I had with him, when we spoke after a prolonged period out of contact. 'Where's me family?' he asked me then. The answer was the same. 'We're all here, John. Where are you?'

We watched the film with our film star brother, well, in the same theatre anyway, and munched the complimentary chocolates. We all loved it.

The Beatles dominated the charts, on both sides of the Atlantic. You couldn't go a day without hearing about the boys in the media – where they were, what they said, how they looked.

In July that year John and Cynthia bought Kenwood, a house in Weybridge, Surrey, for £20,000. That's when we knew that John was a millionaire. And despite John's ridiculous schedule, they had been talking about having us – the sisters and the cousins – to visit them in their new home. Harrie wanted to send us all together, but Cynthia and John insisted that Jackie and I went first, followed by David and Michael on a separate visit.

They had been in the house for about six weeks when we arrived, via our first ever flight from Liverpool Airport. Now, this same airport, moved further up the road, has been renamed for John. Liverpool John Lennon Airport. There is a wonderful bronze statue of John, which makes my heart skip a beat whenever I pass it. Which I often do. I think of course of John, and I think of Mummy. How proud she would be of this, and only two miles away from Springwood.

John and Cynthia's new house was in a state of being done up. In fact the work had hardly been started when we arrived. There was no kitchen downstairs, just a gaping hole where it was planned to be. There were no electric gates either, no swimming pool, nor landscape gardens. But John was enormously proud of it, telling us all about the plans and showing off the elegant oak staircase, the large reception rooms and his den, which was red and lined with books. In the absence of a functioning kitchen downstairs, the food we ate was cooked in the housekeeper's flat at the top of the house. John insisted that we sat down as a family to eat, in the oak-panelled dining-room downstairs, around a mahogany table under a chandelier. We sometimes ate roast dinners, but most of the time we had very simple food, like our favourite egg and chips, with two-year-old Julian perched in his high chair beside us.

John and Cyn slept in a huge bedroom with an ensuite bathroom. We couldn't get over the sunken bath, we'd never seen anything like it.

Comedian Eric Sykes lived next door, on the other side of a large, thick hedge. John warned us straight away not to try to explore his garden, as he had been known to take pot shots at intruders!

We went into London several times, in the chauffeur-driven car, taking Julian with us. We bought him his own Beatle outfit, consisting of a miniature black polo-neck jumper, black jeans and shoes. He looked like the little rocker his Dad had predicted.

We trawled Harrods, Harvey Nichols and the King's Road,

with Cynthia's cheque-book at the ready. Everything we liked, she wanted to buy. We had arrived in our best clothes, but renewed everything at least once: coats, dresses, skirts, jumpers, jeans. Every time Cynthia got out her cheque-book and signed 'Cynthia Lennon', she would explain that we were John's sisters. We loved this, especially because our own family, still considering us outsiders, never referred to us as John's sisters.

While we were in Kenwood we saw the fan mail, which was arriving by the sackful every morning. John said that we could open the letters and read them, and even reply if we wanted to. When the Beatles were still in Liverpool, the fan mail had been dealt with in a small office off Dale Street, run by the fan club secretary, Freda Kelly. We went there once with John, and there was a mountain of mail on the desk and climbing up the walls. We were stunned. It certainly hadn't occurred to me that hundreds, if not thousands of (mainly) girls were writing to John and the boys. I couldn't imagine for a minute what they had to say. Now, it seemed to have been transferred to Kenwood, and with no secretary to wade through it all daily, it had truly piled up. So we started reading – it was a chance to find out what the allure was! There were love letters, proposals of marriage, offers of dates and telephone numbers galore. We found it amazing.

John and Cynthia took us to see George, who was living with Pattie Boyd in nearby Esher. There weren't any sofas or chairs and we all sat on huge, embroidered cushions on the floor and had drinks and snacks. It was my first experience of a hippy house and I wanted a home just like theirs.

All four Beatles were now the proud owners of customised, black Mini Coopers, with darkened electric windows. Ringo's had been delivered with an outsize boot, to accommodate his drum kit. John hadn't yet passed his driving test, but still insisted on driving us to have a picnic by the Thames. John, Cynthia, Julian, Jackie and me. He drove right across the golf course in Weybridge, laughing. This time we didn't stop to collect golf balls to sell back to the golfers. The money problem had been resolved.

When we remonstrated with John, laughing, about driving on the greens, he said, 'I'm a Beatle. I can do anything.'

At that time, that was the feeling, everywhere.

40: *Finsbury Park Astoria*

The Beatles were playing at the Finsbury Park Astoria and John had said that we could go. We hung about the dressing-room this time, overawed by the presence of Mick Jagger and Keith Richards. This is the bit they would never believe back at school. Just as you had the natural divide between Elvis fans and Cliff Richard fans (one I never understood), so another loyalty split had occurred. The Beatles or the Rolling Stones. I was always a Stones fan myself, and our heroes were in the dressing-room, with the Beatles. John knew I preferred the Stones' music, and he laughed about it – he didn't mind a bit.

In the dressing-room they were all drinking Coca-Cola. I believed that for years, though in reality of course it was probably liberally laced with alcohol. John and the boys were getting ready to go on stage. The knock came on their door. Five minutes. John said that we would watch the show from the wings. No, we said, we wanted to be in the audience.

When the dressing-room door was opened, the noise from the auditorium was deafening. The Stones had gone, whether to watch in the auditorium or not, I don't know. John had said that we would watch the show from the wings. No! No! I insisted that we wanted to sit out at the front. We shunted words back and forth. Then the boys had the call to go on stage. We all went into the wings, with the fire curtains still down. I looked through them. The first four rows were completely empty. I asked John could we sit down there, and as they were about to go on and you couldn't hear a thing by now, we were helped down from the side of the stage and went to sit in the third row. He was shouting something I couldn't hear. Then he was lost behind the heavy curtains.

When they did open, seconds later, to reveal the boys in position and ready to go, the whole theatre erupted into a cacophony of sound that was surreal. I don't think that the audience heard one single word of the first song – 'She Loves You'. John was straining to out-shout the shouters and bobbing up and down, with a broad grin but with his eyes boring down into the wooden floor of the stage. Many of the pictures of him on stage around this time are the same – John looking down at the floor. The reason was his contact lenses.

He had started wearing them a few months earlier and the stage lights played havoc with his eyes, as he was still building up tolerance. Lenses were still novel then and anyone who has worn the old, hard type will know what I mean. You had to build up gradually the time during which you wore them. An hour a day, then an hour in the morning and an hour later on. Then you increased the time to two hours, three hours, until eventually, the times met in the middle and you were wearing them all your waking hours.

John's late-night, late-day lifestyle didn't lend itself to wearing the contact lenses that existed then. He would put them into his eyes in the dressing-room. The strength of the stage lighting would be too harsh, and the only answer then is to look down, to cover the eye with your eyelid and try to reduce the strain. If you see a picture of John, minus his glasses, looking down, then that is exactly what he is doing. Struggling with contact lenses. As you know, it wasn't too long before he gave up on them and re-adopted his glasses, releasing short-sighted people everywhere to wear their glasses happily. Buddy Holly was supplanted by Mahatma Gandhi, via the National Health.

I had asked John to get me some contact lenses too. We asked the optician, who said that I was still too young and that my eyes need another year or two, to 'settle'. So another one of our shopping trips on that visit had been to Bentalls, a large department store in Kingston-upon-Thames, to buy me some funky glasses. Cynthia and John both had glasses from there and thought that I would like a pair too . . . Yes, please! I came away with one pair to wear every day, for close work, schoolwork – they were fabulous – and another pair as a treat. They had dark green frames and tinted lenses. I couldn't wait to wear them.

Those groovy shades were later broken at a Rolling Stones concert at the Liverpool Empire, when a mad girl fan, waving her arms and leaping about, knocked them off and then landed on them!

A year or so later John did get contact lenses for me, when I was nineteen, just before I went to college. Harrie took me to the optician and John paid the exorbitant sum of £54 – the equivalent of a full term's student grant. I achieved a twenty-year span wearing those hard lenses, losing them in all sorts of places, putting them back in with a bit of spit, wearing two lenses in one eye for a week by mistake. All lens wearers have sorry tales to tell.

Anyway, as John and the boys pounded out 'She Loves You', and Jackie and I watched from the third row, the fans had started to lunge towards the front of the stage, pushing past the security men and shoving us forward. John looked down at us, then shouted into the wings. Suddenly, we were shunted sideways in front of the stage and then hauled, unceremoniously, across the stage floor, back into the safety of the wings.

'I told you so,' John got in, between songs.

After the concert we were sent back to Weybridge with Cynthia in a car, which was waiting for us. John partied all night and came back the next day. He wouldn't have dreamed of drinking in front of us or letting us party with him, which meant, of course, that Cyn had to go home too. We were his little sisters and he considered us far too young to stay out late. Behind the rebel front John could be terribly proper. This was something that John inherited from his aunts, who could be real sticklers for manners and 'correct' behaviour from other people.

By this time I was in the sixth form, doing French, Spanish and English. Before we left Kenwood, John told me to work hard for my A levels and that Mummy would have been proud of me. He told me to work harder than he had done at college, and I told him that it wouldn't be difficult!

A day or two later we went back to Liverpool and school. It had been a wonderful visit. John and Cyn had seemed happy and unchanged, despite the grandness of their house and the money they had.

After the fun and excitement of our visit it was hard to be back in Liverpool, with all the restrictions of our life there. I threw myself into schoolwork – always a retreat from the world for me, and now more so than ever. I had little chance of being a hip teenager, with the right clothes and make-up, but I enjoyed school and could lose myself in the world of lessons and home-work.

41: *Mimi's Move*

There was no respite throughout 1965, only acceleration. Whirling dervishes, Beatles style, and hit after hit.

In June, the Queen's Honours List was published and the Beatles were awarded the MBE and became official establishment. Not everyone was thrilled about this. Within a week, several high-profile medal holders returned their own MBEs in protest at this new, not-yet-understood category. Rock Royalty.

We were all extremely proud of John, for meeting the Queen as much as anything. It was more of the far-out fantasy that was never quite real. At first I thought they were being knighted.

John wasn't the first person to give this medal back when he made the gesture in 1969, in protest at the Vietnam War. I wonder how early the seed of its return, and of John's emergence as a peace campaigner, was planted.

In late June, John's second book, *A Spaniard in the Works*, was published. John was interviewed, sometimes grilled, about this book. In some quarters, it was regarded as lightweight nonsense. In others, it was treated as an intellectual challenge and a philosophical quest.

When one interviewer asked John whether there was a social conscience underlying his writings and scribblings, he replied, 'Oh, I'm not a do-gooder about things. I don't go around marching, I'm not that type, I do it to get laughs.' John was being the class clown on the world stage. It must have amused him enormously that the cartoons he drew at school to infuriate and send up teachers were now 'literature' and merited his appearance at literary events.

He was asked about the influences behind his book, but despite many suggestions he only admitted to one prevailing influence, and that was Lewis Carroll. I also know that John loved Jerome K. Jerome's *Three Men in a Boat*. This book, like several others, including Spike Milligan's *Puckoon*, is a sure-fire guarantee to lift you out of the deepest doldrums. John had given me an old copy of *Three Men in a Boat*, when I had told him that we were studying it at school. I was fifteen then. We could hardly make it through the reading-out-loud in school for laughing, and I would go home and read it again, spluttering hysterically. We all enjoyed it so much that our fabulous English teacher, Mrs Shepherd, got us to write a story of our own, using the same characters and the dog, in another potty adventure. We all submitted chapters over the school year and let the story move in its own way. We chose the best chapters each month and eventually we had compiled a book of about twenty chapters.

I had received a typewriter as my fourteenth birthday present, from my father. I had asked for it specially. It was my second. The first had been a lightweight affair, almost dainty, in pale blue, but this was the real business. It was a heavy-duty, black, solid machine, an old Underwood, with a very messy black and red ribbon. It was so heavy that you needed to put both forearms under it to move it along even an inch or two. It was established on the table in front of the bedroom window, overlooking the trees outside the house. I loved it.

I volunteered to type out our class book, which we elected to call 'Three Men on the Moon'. Every night I had to rush to finish my homework, so that I could get on with tap-tapping. Clackety-clack. I had to press the keys quite hard, well, hammer them really. Then I had to keep checking to see that the type was truly black and that the ribbon hadn't slipped or got caught, leaving a blurred, red glow on a letter or word. I think playing the violin at the time must have helped. My finger tips were like leather and didn't feel the punishment they were taking.

When John was round at The Cottage during this time, he came upstairs to see what I was doing and started to read the typing over my shoulder. He laughed and took the rest of the pages and sat on the bed to read the whole story, laughing all the time. I was thrilled that he found it so funny. It wasn't just our class then! We could hardly write it for laughing, nor read it out loud! He said I should be a writer or a journalist. I wanted to be a vet, though in the end I became a teacher.

The Beatles were on television a lot. Some of these programmes had been pre-recorded and others were live, but you didn't have to attend a concert to see them, they were now regular guests in everybody's living-room. As well as on their bookshelves, in their record collections and in their daily newspapers and entertainment magazines.

In our own small corner of it, that madness was about to promote change. Mendips had become a find-and-knock and even stay-in-the-garden place for fans from all over the country. I'd be sent over to Mimi's with a message and would just gawp at the girls sitting in the front garden or crowding round the door. It was getting too much for Mimi, who thought they were all completely mad. John suggested that she move, and Mimi said she'd like Bournemouth.

Stan went to London, to see the *Help!* premiere. A few days after the show, he went with Mimi, John, Cynthia and Julian on the first visit to view a house in Poole, next to Bournemouth. Mimi loved it and knew that she could make her home there, and John was more than happy to invest in the house for Mimi, as a thank you for everything that she had done for him. There was a condition attached. It was to be a fantastic holiday retreat for the rest of the family, 'in the warm south' as John put it. There was plenty of room.

Mimi sold Mendips and moved to Poole at the beginning of August 1965. I'm sure Harrie missed her, and Nanny too, although she lived further away. Everyone visited.

I didn't have time to find it strange that Mimi was no longer at Mendips, or to miss seeing John there, because I left Liverpool at the same time. Having taken my A levels and left school I went to work in a holiday camp in north Wales with two friends. Liela had worked in the same camp some years before and had encouraged me to go. I was away for the whole summer, tasting real freedom and loving it.

42: *The King*

It was on their second visit to the States, in the summer of 1965, that the Beatles met Elvis. Remember how I wished I'd danced out the final stage show of the Beatles at the Cavern in August 1963? Well, I would swap that for only one other Beatle event – this meeting.

After the Shea Stadium concerts, they were resting in Bel Air, California, where Elvis was living. They went to see him at his home, 525 Perugia Way. I asked one of Elvis's entourage, the original Memphis Mafia, to recount this visit for me. Jerry Schilling was a close friend and confidant of Elvis and, most importantly, he was there. I wanted the full story because of our mother's rapturous feelings about The King. If Mummy had been alive, I don't think John would have thought of going without her.

Jerry says that Elvis met the Beatles at the door. I wonder who knocked! Although there was plenty of room in the house, Elvis preferred the cosy comfort of a small den, which was just off his bedroom. In the den there was a large television, which was always on, mostly with the sound turned down. There was a bar and a good sound system, playing his own and other records. Elvis had taught himself the bass guitar and liked to play along to the music.

This is where Elvis, all four Beatles and others of Elvis's troupe gathered. Elvis sat down and started to play his bass guitar and they all just stared. I can only imagine that they were starstruck. This was Elvis, The King, and they were John, Paul, George and Ringo, four boys from Liverpool who were in the presence of the man who had started it all off for them. The man who had given their music life.

Elvis spoke first, saying, 'Y'know, if you guys are going to sit round and stare at me all night, I'm going to bed.'

In Jerry's words, 'That kicked it off.'

After chatting for an hour or so a roulette table was brought in by Elvis's manager, 'the Colonel'. They all played roulette and pool, and the Beatles left as dawn was breaking. Jerry called it 'a warm meeting'.

I wonder if John told Elvis about Mummy and the records and the dancing in Springwood – and the cat named after him.

John used to spend his relaxing time in his small red den in Kenwood, with the television on, playing records and accompanying them on his guitar. Later he moved across the world and spent more time in the Dakota Building, the luxury New York apartment block where he lived with Yoko, lying around watching television, listening to records and playing his guitar. It must be a Star Thing.

The next day, Jerry went to meet the Beatles in their rented house, as invited. He knew where the house was, as Elvis had himself been interested in leasing it at one time.

John welcomed Jerry and a friend. They went outside, where George and Paul were sitting on a small patio. They had a concert later that night and their freshly washed mop tops were wrapped in head towels.

John asked Jerry to 'do him a favour'. He wanted him to pass on a message to Elvis. Something that he had been too embarrassed to say himself the night before. 'I didn't know how to say this to him last night. The sideburns. I nearly got kicked out of school for having Elvis sideburns. Tell Elvis, if it hadn't been for him, I wouldn't be here.'

Jerry told Elvis. He smiled.

43: *The Nightmare, Part Two*

John's life was becoming more and more restricted. He was a prisoner of his own fame. All four of them were. My life, on the other hand, was loosening up. I floated out, like a bird.

I felt that I was the lucky one.

While working in the holiday camp I met the most handsome and intelligent Irish student and fell madly in love. I spent the summer working hard and playing hard and, after the restrictions of life over the past few years, it was wonderful.

My father, knowing a bit about holiday camp life, came to see me to make sure I was all right. I was, and I was thrilled that he came.

Daddy had married again, a few months earlier. It had come out of the blue for me and Jackie. In the seven years since Mummy had died we'd met only one other girlfriend, and that relationship had soon fizzled out. He had been so distraught after Mummy's death that until I was at least sixteen he couldn't talk about her without weeping. Now suddenly there was someone else, and not just someone – a wife.

Jackie and I had reluctantly met her once or twice, but that was that. We didn't want to know. Although it wasn't in any way unreasonable that Daddy should find someone else, neither Jackie nor I could accept her. Teenagers can be tricky at the best of times, and hurt teenagers are very tricky indeed. Perhaps it was because a part of us still believed that Mummy was alive. Because of the way we'd been told, because for us there had been no funeral, because no one spoke to us about her – for us it was as though there had never really been an ending. I was still looking with hope and despair at red-haired women in the street, thinking I'd seen her. So the idea of Daddy marrying someone else was just too hard to bear.

It was my old soulmate Ray who told me that he had a right to happiness and that I had to accept it. I understood that. So, we made a compromise. I saw him as much as I could but, by unspoken agreement, always by himself. If Daddy had harboured any hopes of us all becoming a family together, they would have been dashed very fast. But in fact I'm sure he didn't, he knew how we felt about Mummy, and that as young adults it was too late for him to try to reform a new family with us and a mother substitute. He accepted the situation, and when he came to the holiday camp he came alone and nothing was said of his wife.

I came back to The Cottage with just enough time to turn around and leave again for college in the north of England, where I was going to study French and Linguistics. I was beginning my own new life.

My only sadness was in leaving Jackie behind. She was now sixteen and had started a hairdressing apprenticeship Woolton the year before. I knew she would soon be off and independent too.

I had only been at college for a week, when I was approached by a reporter from the *Liverpool Echo*. They wanted to interview me, as John's sister. I had no hesitation in refusing. I wrote to the *Echo* and asked them to please leave me alone. I just wanted to be a normal student in the crowd, so I didn't tell anyone that I was John's sister. The same old questions would have come again.

My father came to see me for the first time, after about two weeks. He arrived without announcement one Saturday. Several people had approached me and said that he was looking for me before I saw his old green Jaguar and knew that it was true. He had brought cakes, biscuits and chocolates for the starving students, which we shared with him in my room. He wanted to see everything and everywhere. Where we had lectures, where we ate. I took him along for the tea and biscuits that were available every day at four o'clock. He was the only parent in the place and he chatted to everyone on our table, asking them where they were from and what they were studying.

Nearer Christmas, he came again and asked if I would like to come and work for him over the Christmas holiday on the weekends and occasional evenings. He was offering me John's old job at the New Bear's Paw in the city centre, which Daddy still managed.

I didn't catch the Beatles' show at the Liverpool Empire that year, as it was on 5 December and I was still at college and not due home for another two weeks. It was party time and ever since my summer job, I had been able to stay out all night and come in with the milk if I wanted to. I was going home to strict rules and set bedtime, even though I was eighteen, so I waited until the last minute to go back to Liverpool. When I did go home, I worked for my father for a few days and evenings over Christmas and New Year and then worked during January sales week in Lewis's, a large department store. Allen, my Irish summer love, arrived in Liverpool on the boat from Ireland and came straight there to find me. We had only seen each another once since we'd each left the holiday camp – so we kissed in the middle of the ground floor and I promptly got the sack. What was important for me was that he met my father, who liked him. Daddy was worried that we were too serious too soon, but we were in that madness stage of first love. Daddy and I talked about it when he drove me back to college, to start the new term, in January. He wanted me not to rush things with Allen, and I promised I wouldn't.

A week later the unthinkable happened. I was in a student residence, and lived on the ground floor, with the advantage and disadvantage of having the student telephone right outside my room. There was a seven a.m. call and I rushed to get it, knowing that the hour was unusual, but not knowing that it was for me. If I had known the news it would bring, I might have run in the opposite direction.

I was extremely surprised to hear Nanny's voice. I could hardly take in what she was saying, although it was a simple enough message. Daddy had been driving back from managing a banquet, in the early hours of the morning, when he had crashed the car and been killed.

My father was dead.

Seven and a half years after losing Mummy in a car accident, I had lost Daddy in the same way. It was so utterly, horrifyingly unbelievable that I couldn't take it in. I lay on my bed in a state of bewilderment and pain, willing it not to be true. For the past two years Daddy and I had been growing a lovely relationship, finding a new closeness, talking about all kinds of things, finding where our lives could knit well. We had spent a lot of time together over the Christmas holidays and he had promised to visit me soon. And now he wasn't there.

I went to find a friend who had a car and asked him to take me to Liverpool. We travelled in white silence, and when we arrived in Woolton, I asked him to drop me at the bottom of the road. He was hesitant about leaving me in such a state, but I wanted him to go.

I went to The Cottage and opened the front door. Harrie shouted, 'Who is it?' and when I replied, she immediately shouted, 'You can't mourn here.' I was stunned. Harrie had never liked my father and hated emotional displays, but I had thought she would feel compassion for me at such a terrible time. It seemed not. Horrified by her words, I left without seeing her and ran down the road towards Springwood in a wild and confused state of despair. I had no idea what to do next.

I wanted to see Jackie, but had no idea where she was. I didn't know that she had been allowed to go to work, not knowing that our father had died. Did Harrie think that no one would tell her? She was told the news by her astounded employer, who sent her straight home. But by that time I had already been and gone. Jackie was sixteen and just starting to see more of Daddy, as I had at the same age. Now she had lost him before they had truly found each other again.

I stopped short of Springwood and sat in a field, trying to put my head in some sort of order. Mendips was empty. John had gone. There was no one to run to. Nowhere.

I walked to the nearest telephone and asked my friend, who had gone home, to please come back and get me. He was astonished but must have driven like a lunatic to rescue me. I asked him to take me back to college. I had no other thought in my head but to be safe and alone, and no place to grieve but my college room. After Harrie's rejection I couldn't brave Liverpool for a minute longer, not even for Jackie.

Back in college I went to bed with the covers over my head for a week.

Not a single person from the family contacted me. My mother's sisters had long since dismissed my father as insignificant and probably had no concept of the terrible loss and grief I felt.

The next week I went to see Nana. We rocked and cried together in her old brown leather armchair. I had missed the funeral, but I couldn't have faced it anyway.

Odd as it seems, I didn't think to contact John and let him know that Daddy had died. I assumed he had been told, and when I didn't hear from him I felt that he too didn't care. And of course I felt very hurt. It only cemented the feeling that Jackie and I didn't belong in the family, or matter to anyone.

Even if I'd wanted to contact John, I had no way to. I'd never had a phone number for him and Cyn. Our visit to Kenwood had been arranged by Cyn with Harrie, as we were still treated like children. We'd always been kept out of the loop, everything being arranged over our heads or behind our backs.

In fact John didn't hear about Daddy's death for several months. No one thought to tell him. It was only Bobby, and we were only the girls. As far as they were concerned, none of us were anything to do with John.

I went back to The Cottage at Easter and knew everything had changed, irrevocably, and I couldn't be there any longer. I packed some things and spent two weeks with Ray, going to see Jackie at work during the day. I knew I would be fine, I would work at the holiday camp in the summer, but I worried about Jackie, who was still living at The Cottage.

A year later, Jackie came to live with me at college. The student with whom I shared a room agreed to smuggle her in with us until we found her a cheap room nearby, and she travelled back to work every day from there. Eventually, worn out by all the time spent to-ing and fro-ing, Jackie found a place of her own in Liverpool.

It was Mater who finally told John that our father had been killed. But even then he didn't contact us. I think in truth, that he couldn't face us with Daddy's death, after our mother's death. We were all thinking we were recovering from the first trauma, but it was never far from the surface in all three of us – me, John and Jackie. None of us could cope and we muddled on, dragging death with us through our lives, bearing it by burying it, in our own different ways.

John chose to show he cared by doing something practical. Nothing was discussed with us, as we were considered too young. Nothing new there. But Cynthia later told me that they talked at length about our situation and what would be the best way to help us. And they settled on a plan. John would buy a house, as a 'nest egg' for us.

I was living in halls of residence and Jackie was a very young sixteen and still living at home, in The Cottage, when they were first discussing the house. Harrie and Norman, as our guardians, were to be allotted a budget for a house, where we would have more room. It was assumed that we would all have a base in the house, as long as we needed it.

Jackie and I had no understanding of the whole matter of the house at that time. We just knew that Harrie and Norman were moving into a newer, bigger house that John was buying it for us all. It was only much later that he told me it had always been meant for me and Jackie. He was quite clear. And it became a symbol for me of John's love for us.

Harrie looked at several houses in the Liverpool suburbs, before deciding to move on to a new estate, about two miles away from The Cottage. Ringo had bought his family a house there in the summer of 1966, and Harrie and Norman had been invited to go and see it. Harrie chose a three-bedroom, detached house, when it was still only at the foundations stage. This process took some time to get under way. I think it was early the following year, 1967, by the time things were settled and we watched the house grow. I saw it very occasionally, but Harrie must have been counting the bricks.

44: *Psychedelic Waves*

When John said the Beatles were more popular than Christ and that Christianity would eventually vanish, thousands of people across America were highly offended, and there began what was almost a witch-hunt. Soon we were all afraid for John, as he was for himself.

Radio stations denounced the Beatles, and their records, books and pictures were publicly burned. And they were about to start a tour of the States. No one, including the Beatles, knew that it would be their last. It was the total stress of this tour that prompted their decision never to tour again.

Although John apologised, on landing, for the comment and tried to explain what he had really meant, he was frightened for his safety during that trip. He was being threatened almost everywhere they went.

The final straw for all of them was the Candlestick Park concert in San Francisco, in August 1966. Rumour has it that the mass hysteria was so overwhelming that at one point, as an experiment, the boys opened their mouths but didn't actually sing – to see if anyone could tell the difference! I don't know whether or not this is true, but the pointlessness of these big tours was as stark as it could be. It had to stop.

John summed it up in his own words when they got back, 'There'll be no more 'She Loves You's.'

While John and America were storming each other that summer, my friends and I returned to the holiday camp, to work and play, and Allen came back from Ireland. Although we had been apart more than we had been together, a year on our romance

John in relaxed mode in 1963, wearing the uniform of the revamped Beatles.

This was probably taken in about 1961. Harrie is tidying up Mater's hair, with Paul looking on in the background, wondering if he was next!

This is Nanny, in the early 1990s, telling me all the family stories.

Stan took this photo when his wife Jan came to meet the family at Mendips in 1959. Norman is sitting on the arm of the chair, Mimi is on the pouf on the right, Harrie and Jan (in the foreground) are on the sofa.

This is the family gathered for the premiere of the film *A Hard Day's Night*, in 1964. Back, L-R: Norman, Michael, David, me and Jackie. Front, L-R: Mater, Harrie and Mimi.

The Quarry Men played on a lorry at the Rosebery Street celebration of the 750th anniversary of the granting of Liverpool's charter. John is in the centre, it was the 22nd of June 1957.

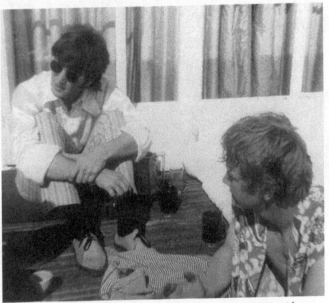

A fully-fledged Beatle here, in 1966 with our cousin David on the balcony at Mimi's house in Sandbanks.

John and George taking a break from touring, in the Bahamas in 1964.
Cynthia took this shot.

I love this photo of John and George en route to London in 1964.

This was taken in 1967 outside the house in Weybridge. John looks a little gaunt and world weary.

This snap of John was taken in New York in the early 70s by a fan and sent to Mimi. Note the Elvis badge!

Mimi on the riverside steps at Sandbanks, some time in the late 60s.

This is me and Jackie in Ireland at Christmas, 1969. I sent this photo to John in New York in 1975.

Me and Jackie again, in 1985, in Mathew Street Liverpool,
outside the Cavern Club.

was as real and passionate as ever. Loving him, and being loved by him, gave me something solid and wonderful, a gain after all my losses. Allen understood and listened, he was utterly loyal, and no matter who came and went in my life he was there for me.

I was following my brother's progress through the media, like everyone else. I was glad for his success, and at the same time sad because we had lost him. After our lack of contact following my father's death I knew that he was pursuing his path, and I mine. And although they appeared to be very different, in many ways they were leading to the same place – both of us were developing a powerful social conscience and feeling the need to do something to right the wrongs of the world.

My own wider awareness was kick-started into life that winter in Caen in France, where I had moved as part of my university course, to study French literature, history and geography, from September 1966 to Easter 1967. Although it had been terribly hard to say goodbye to Allen at the end of the summer – when he went back to his university course in Ireland and I to mine – I was excited about living and studying in France. Most of the students there were taking an active part in the political arena. I marched in Paris with hundreds of thousands of anti-Vietnam protesters and was active in the beginnings of the feminist movement, led by my heroine, Simone de Beauvoir.

I was so proud of John the following year when he publicly denounced the war in Vietnam, raising the profile of this war madness. He was using his position on the world stage to say out loud what he had been thinking for some time. He and George had made a conscious decision to break the silence that Brian Epstein had always insisted on. They couldn't go on having the ear and eye of the public and pretending to be blind, deaf, dumb and ignorant.

When Allen came to visit me in France at the end of term, I met him in Paris. We explored the city together before travelling across France to Germany, where we stayed with Liela and her husband and children. She had gone to live in Germany after finishing her studies and was practising as an anaesthetist in a hospital in Saarbrücken.

Back in France, students were flocking to see Georges Brassens and Jacques Brel, both revolutionary singers, artists and poets. We were looking for answers. The world, including us, was in an existential state. We demanded to be here and now, not there and then.

While I was being politicised across the Channel, in November 1966 John met Yoko, at an exhibition of her radical conceptual art. But none of us heard anything about it until some time later.

Meanwhile in February 1967 French radio had a manic devotion to the Troggs and 'Wild Thing'. The manufactured Monkees were very popular there too. In England the double-sided single 'Strawberry Fields Forever' and 'Penny Lane' had just been released. In order to listen to English radio in my room I had to put the small transistor radio I had brought with me on to the bottom pipe of the radiator, in the corner, so that it would echo. I still couldn't get a decent volume. I would be at my desk, writing never-ending essays, with half an ear to the music. When something came on that I wanted to hear better, I would squash myself down in the corner and put my ear right on to the speaker. Of course, I was listening out for 'Strawberry Fields' and 'Penny Lane'. It was so bizarre hearing about those places in France – I don't know if it gave me homesickness or cured it.

The psychedelic movement gathered momentum. John, tripping on LSD by this time, had sent his white Rolls-Royce to be painted in the whirls and swirls of every discotheque in the country. The anomaly here, for me, is that John seemed to be craving peace and anonymity, yet he declared himself at every turn, still the class performer who couldn't resist the limelight.

The Beatles were a backdrop to everyone's lives during this time. The records just kept on coming. *Sergeant Pepper's* changed the world as it plunged us ever deeper into psychedelia and encouraged us all to throw off restraints, hitherto unquestioned. We travelled the country at the drop of a hat to see the big groups playing live, and we danced all night to the music, wild and abandoned, in our ever-shrinking mini-skirts. The funky, groovy black walls, which had made for dense, dark dives, had given way to walls, ceilings and floors swirling with brightly coloured ink blots and flashing lights that made your head spin. We would find anywhere that gave us a scrap of floor space and collapse in a heap, to talk about life and the universe. We were preparing to be street politicians, without knowing it. And the Beatles had done this – aided and abetted by Jimi Hendrix, of course.

I had returned from France, at Easter, to finish off my college year, but Allen and I went back for the summer months. We found jobs with a French student organisation in the Haute Savoie, not far from Geneva. We hitch-hiked down there and whiled away the hot summer months clearing the wasteland around an old château, only returning when we absolutely had to, in mid-September. Back in Paris, we found that there was an air of expectation, even urgency. We were breathing the fumes of freedom, striding out to we didn't know where, looking for answers to the why.

The psychedelic experience had helped to break the conservative, post-war mould and mood in Britain. People everywhere were questioning the system. The war in Vietnam became an issue, first in America and then in Europe, and a focal point for street politics. Make Love Not War was the New World Order, while women's lives were being radically changed by the advent of the women's liberation movement and the contraceptive pill.

That summer, Pattie Harrison developed an interest in Transcendental Meditation. Her enthusiasm was to take the Beatles to Bangor, in North Wales, to hang out with the Maharishi, who would give them a mantra and a meditative hotline to peace, in exchange for some fruit and a week's salary.

The Beatles had only been in Bangor for two days when the news came through that Brian Epstein had died of a drug overdose. We were still in France when Brian died, on 27 August 1967, and saw snippets of John and the other Beatles talking on television. The inquest verdict was accidental death. It was so sad, and made sadder by the understanding we have now of Brian's struggle with being Jewish and gay, and his isolation. Things would have been so different now.

45: *Marriage*

I started my last year at college in October 1967 and had a lot of work to complete before Finals the following June. Four of us shared a house, and the table, floors, chairs and beds were paper-laden as we realised how much we still had to do. Too little, too late. If only we had started this earlier. No doubt the same thing was happening in colleges and universities around the country.

In mid-February my brother went to India with Cynthia. I heard it on the news. Part way through the two-month stay John became disillusioned with the Maharishi and they came home. Soon afterwards John and Yoko were seen out together in public.

My head was in another space. I had been swotting like mad, then celebrating in the same way. We didn't have a television and we listened to music rather than the news. When I did finally learn that John and Cynthia were parting I was terribly sad. Cyn had been a part of our lives for so many years, and a friend to me and Jackie. I knew how hard it must have been for her, and I felt so sorry for Julian, who was only five.

In those days Jackie and I and the rest of the family knew nothing of John's extra-marital flings, of groupies and drugs. We were the most naïve people on the planet. Rock and roll stardom was an alien place and its secrets unknown until John fell in love with Yoko, when he had to declare himself – and Yoko – to the world. We were as astonished as everyone else. Yoko was a complete surprise, and a strange one at that.

I finished my degree and moved to Ireland. Allen was at university in Belfast, where he came from, studying psychology and archeology, so if we wanted to be together, that was where we had to be.

We got married on 16 August 1968, in Belfast register office. I was 21 and Allen was 19. I didn't invite any of my family. We saw it as a formality, so that we could live together openly in Ireland, without upsetting his family. But despite this I cried all the way through the ceremony. I wished more than anything that my parents could have been there, Daddy to give me away and Mummy to be happy and proud of me. I was sure she would be. Allen was my first love.

Allen's parents had tried to dissuade us, saying that we were too young, but in the end they accepted that we wanted to be together and very kindly paid for the wedding and the honeymoon. His sister Kay and her husband Terry were the witnesses. We went to the West of Ireland on our honeymoon, where we stayed in a hotel by the sea.

Allen's father had given us his old car as a wedding present. It was an Austin Westminster. Neither of us had passed our test at the time, so we had to assure him that of course, we wouldn't be driving it until we had at least one legal licence between us. Actually, we couldn't wait for him to finish his tea and go, so that we could drive somewhere, anywhere. We were almost behind his taxi as my new father-in-law drove away.

We spent the summer exploring Ireland and being newly married, before Allen went back to university.

I had found a new family.

And I had breathing space.

The only person I contacted was Jackie, who had left home by then. I wrote to her and gave her our address. About a week later, very early one morning, we were woken by her voice in the garden saying to her friend, 'Yes, this is the place. There's Julia's knickers on the line.' They were shrieking with laughter, despite the hour! We had a ground-floor flat, so they came in through the window and stayed for a week.

I didn't try to contact John – I still had no way to – but I wasn't worried, I thought we had all the time in the world. We were each living our lives and I was sure we'd be in touch again when we had both settled in our new relationships. We were both madly in love, and I felt that we had much in common, both of us marrying our chosen loves (John and Yoko a few months after me and Allen), though he had a little more publicly!

About six weeks after I had married, I came back to Liverpool for a visit. Jackie had told me that Harrie and Norman had finally moved out of The Cottage and into the new house. After years of being overcrowded in the two-bedroom Cottage, they had moved into a spacious new home on their own. Jackie was now sharing a flat in Liverpool with friends, and David had moved south. He had lived with Mimi for a year, while studying the new computer science in Bournemouth.

I felt a strange sadness at not having the familiar Cottage to return to, even though I had really left home in the summer of 1965, as students do. It was small, but a real country cottage in every sense of the word. It was also in a beautiful place, with the immense green grounds of the nurses' training home directly opposite and Woolton Woods right next to that.

I found my way to the new house and was greeted by Harrie at the front door. There was a frosted glass porch, with lots of plants and wood-block floors downstairs. There was a large, L-shaped living-room, overlooking the garden, which was still full of rubble from the building work, and a fitted kitchen. The deep, plum-red carpet from Mendips was on the stairs. We walked around the downstairs, then we went up to see the three bedrooms.

'This is Norman's room. This is my room. And this is David's room. Is that clear?'

I was absolutely stunned, but what was I supposed to say? As usual, nobody had thought to explain anything.

I said, 'I understand.' I slept in David's room.

That November John and Cyn's divorce came through, and

three weeks later John and Yoko released the *Two Virgins* album, probably best remembered for the two non-virgins on the cover.

At one of Yoko's avant-garde shows, when she and John had barely met, one of the exhibits had been a suggestion to climb into a black bin-bag, to help achieve An Experience. Now the black bag had evolved into a white sack, in their joint performance, 'Alchemical Wedding', at the Royal Albert Hall, just before Christmas. We saw it, along with the rest of the planet.

For me Ireland was an escape hatch. I was grateful to be away from the furore surrounding John. No one in Ireland knew he was my brother, apart from Allen's family, who very discreetly never mentioned his public antics.

46: *The Unreal Peace Show*

New Year of 1969 saw the release of the *Yellow Submarine* album. Allen and I gave this a miss and stuck with the wonderfully creative and addictive *The Beatles*, known affectionately to all as 'The White Album', singing along with every word. The Beatles also gave their last performance, on the roof of the Apple building in London, in a wind-blown session that was to become an all-time classic. We watched, with everyone else, on the small screen.

We weren't invited to John's wedding, on 20 March, but it was well-nigh impossible to avoid the reception. The newlyweds had their honeymoon in Paris and then headed straight for Amsterdam, where they went to bed, as a wedding present for the world's media, for you and for me.

I was living in another country, but you'd have to have been on Mars to escape my brother's post-marriage celebrations. And a lot of the time, that's just where I wished myself. I was so pleased that I was away from home, where people might have known me. I was in a place where I didn't have to try to explain or justify John's weird behaviour.

John had managed to turn his naughty, rip-taking schoolbooks, whose content had almost resulted in his being expelled, into best-sellers. Now he was going one further. It was as if he was on the main platform in the school assembly hall, with the headmaster and teachers seated in the front row – and the audience was forbidden to leave until the show was over.

John had always loved being the centre of attention as a child – what child doesn't? He'd always put on all kinds of performances for us; he and Mummy used to mimic voices from the radio and make each other laugh. At school he'd been the class clown. And he was still doing it. His marriage/interview/peace bed was pure performance theatre. And it resulted in the exaltation rather than the expulsion of the main players. It could have been a late, private showing for Mr Pobjoy, the headmaster, and his staff. It was at once comical and embarrassing. It was unreal, and how on earth did they get away with it?

John liked to chronicle his life in his work, and this was no exception. His protest. His marriage. When he rose from the peace bed, he and Paul rustled up 'The Ballad of John and Yoko'. In the recording, John portrayed himself and Yoko as hapless victims in their attempt to marry as quickly as possible, and their eventual Amsterdam bed-in as a mini-concert for peace.

For me, the cringe-provoking bed-ins were redeemed only by the creation of 'Give Peace a Chance', recorded during the second honeymoon bed-in, in Montreal, Canada. The song said it all. We are all composed of the good, the bad and the peacemakers. Let's give peace a chance. It was and is wonderful, and it has become one of the staples of peace politics. It was sung by half a million protesters at the November Peace March of 1969 at the Washington Monument, led by Pete Seeger. This was the largest anti-war rally to date, and I felt so proud that John's song was such a vital part of it.

My madcap, introvert-playing-extrovert brother was almost forgiven. Total admiration swept everyone away, and I was no exception.

At the time I shrank back, but now I can see that there was far more to what John was doing than pure exhibitionism. All his adult life John had been fleeing his demons. The grief and loss he had suffered as a child had been transformed into a desperate craving for love and attention. He wanted to be loved by everyone – the whole world. And he pretty well was! But of course that didn't do the trick, it didn't make the ghosts of the past – his father's loss, Mummy's loss, Mimi's coldness – go away. So he just kept trying harder, and doing more. Perhaps every child who has been abandoned by their parents – through parting or death, struggles with feeling unlovable. I did, Jackie did, and John did. It was almost as though John's over-achieving, 'look at me' stance was an attempt to prove that he really was lovable after all.

John was also an idealist. His hero was Gandhi, hence the peaceful protests. And he had the world's eyes on him, so he was able to make his point – about world peace – very powerfully. His family may have found it embarrassing: Stanley called him 'a bloody idiot' and most of us agreed. But at the same time there was a naïvety about what John did that was touching.

One thing I feel sure of – while the aunts and even some of the rest of us found his antics hugely distracting, Mummy would have laughed, hugged him and encouraged him to go on being daring, brave and bold. She would have loved his creativity and his idealism. He brought politics and pop together, like Bob Geldof and Bono more recently, and she would have applauded him for it.

While John was attracting the world's attention, our cousin Liela had returned from Germany, where she had been living and practising medicine since she had qualified seven years previously. She got a job as an anaesthetist at the Royal Ear Nose and Throat Hospital in London and I often went over to help her out with her three children.

Liela had contacted John on her return to England and had been to visit him and Yoko. John offered her the use of the Beatles' flat in Sloane Street. So although I hadn't yet seen John, we had the flat and his presence was there.

The wardrobe in the main bedroom took up the whole of one wall, with sliding doors reaching from floor to ceiling. It was stuffed with Beatles gear and stage outfits: collarless suits and leather and velvet jackets and trousers. I wore different jackets daily. The smallest ones belonged to George and so fitted me best, and I just loved his style.

231

One day, when Liela had gone to work and I was looking after Robert, her youngest son, I decided that we would go to see John. I wore one of the wilder, bright velvet jackets and set off with the pushchair. I had no idea whether or not he was actually in the building, but I went to Apple, in Savile Row, and introduced myself at the desk. The receptionist sat back in her chair and said, 'Oh yeah?' when I told her that I was John's sister. I was so taken aback that I was instantly hugely embarrassed and I faltered. A man came across and said, 'Well, whoever you are, John Lennon isn't here, so you'd better leave.' I almost fell through the door, dragging the pushchair after me, anxious to get out of the place as quickly as possible. It was one the most humiliating experiences I've ever had and I didn't try again.

47: *A Call from John*

I had been in Belfast for almost a year when John telephoned me, from Harrie's new house in Liverpool. He was visiting with Yoko. I was both surprised and thrilled to hear from him. If I'd known that this was to be the last time I would speak to my brother for four years, I would have gone straight to the dock and on to the ferry to see him. As it was, when John said, 'Can you get over here? We're here for a day or two', I told him that Allen and I were just leaving for our second honeymoon in Italy. I promised to come and see him when we got back.

John expressed his sorrow at my father's death. He said, 'I'm so sorry. I didn't know at the time, nobody told me.' I was shocked.

This was huge news to me. I had thought he knew, and didn't want to be involved in our loss. So it was consoling to realise he was ignorant of it.

We asked each other about married life – were we happy? The answer in both cases was 'yes'. I told John about trying to see him in the Apple offices in London and he said he probably had been there and that, in any case, I should have just walked past the receptionist and the man, up the stairs. He would have loved to see me. He said repeatedly, 'I can't believe that.' I had been angry with myself already for not marching on in and finding him, and to hear John say it too made me even more sad that I hadn't done it.

Soon afterwards, a cheque from John for £100 arrived in the post, as a wedding present. It came in the nick of time, as we had to pay for a new set of gates for our driveway. After Allen's father had given us the car we had both taken our driving tests. Norman had been passionate about cars and had given David and me many lessons, so I'd had a head start. But then we moved into a house that had wrought-iron gates hung between gateposts that were too close together. We hit the gates more than once, swinging into the driveway and backing out of it, denting them. We'd been wondering how to afford replacements, so John's money was a blessing.

After the visit to Harrie and Norman, John carried on up to Scotland to introduce Yoko to Mater, Bert and Stan. John was driving, in an Austin Maxi, and they took Julian and Yoko's daughter Kyoko, both then six, with them. With both Mater and Harrie, Yoko declined the proffered dinner – roast in Harrie's case – in favour of preparing macrobiotic food in the kitchen for herself and John. John, apparently, ate the roast as well as the macrobiotic food.

A day or two later he crashed the car in Golspie in Scotland. He always was an appalling driver and he went off the road, landing himself and Yoko in hospital. The children were unhurt and John and Yoko weren't badly injured – a few stitches – but the car was a write-off.

By this time John and Yoko had bought Tittenhurst Park, an enormous mansion in Sunningdale, near Ascot, with 73 acres of land. The Maxi was taken back there and displayed on a plinth in the garden. Stan went to stay with them soon afterwards. Stan looked at the wreck and said, 'What's that?' and Yoko said, 'It's a happening.' She had turned the accident into a piece of art, and I wonder what John must have thought. Having lost his mother in a road accident, crashing himself would have shaken him badly. Who knows, perhaps turning the result into art had a healing element.

Stan couldn't understand why they had gone in the Maxi in the first place. 'You've got a Rolls, a Porsche and a Ferrari,' he said to John. 'Why didn't you take one of those?' I think the answer was that John wasn't comfortable driving powerful cars; he probably felt much more at home in the Maxi.

The final comic moment of Stan's stay came when he suggested, to John's delight, that they have sausage, bacon, egg and chips for dinner, which they did. Yoko, ever mindful about health, sent the chauffeur to London for sushi.

In late September, John announced that he was leaving the Beatles. They all had to move on, if they were to grow as individual people. I was pleased for John.

These events were markers on John's runway, while he was flying away from us. It had been a long journey already: from Mummy, to Mimi, to Cynthia. Contact between John and his family had been diminishing over the past few years for many reasons, but mainly practical ones – as he was living in London and working around the world. When he met Yoko, the distance became more a distance of the mind. He was consumed by love and longing to be with Yoko, and the abandonment of his first family was a fast process. He was still in England at this point, but already disappearing over the horizon.

I had been hoping all through this time that John and I would be able to get together when the dust had settled. The dust from the break-up of the Beatles and of his marriage to Cynthia. I was waiting, patiently, unaware that time was running out. And my plans to visit him after our trip to Italy were put on hold when I discovered that I was expecting a child.

My first son, Nicolas, was born in April 1970. I had a wonderful family-in-law, who went out of their way to help us, both financially and emotionally. He could not have been a more loved baby. But I really, really missed my mother. I wanted her to be there.

John and Yoko had lost two babies when Yoko had miscarriages in November 1968 and again in October 1969. I was very sad for them, as I knew the happiness a baby brings.

Belfast was a city in strife by this time and we came to a

difficult decision. Difficult because of the support we would be missing, but easier when we thought of our son. We returned to Liverpool and rented a flat right opposite the Cathedral, not far from Berkeley Street, where Mummy and her sisters had lived for so long. Allen got a job working for a small financial services company in the town centre, while I stayed at home with Nicolas.

In the event, we didn't leave all that help behind either. Five-pound notes arrived in envelopes from Ireland, to make sure that we were eating well. And when, in the spring of 1971, we told Allen's family that we were having another baby and moving house – from the flat around the corner from Berkeley Street to a house across the water – they sent for me straight away, so that I could rest while Allen organised the move.

I was so fortunate in the kindness I had from my new Irish family. We had met a mixed reception from my own family. Harrie demanded to know immediately why I had come back to Liverpool. She thought I had settled in Ireland, so what was I doing here? I was definitely upsetting things, without knowing how. She telephoned Mater in Edinburgh to tell her what was happening, probably thinking that Mater would write me a letter, demanding to know what I was up to. Instead, however, Mater arrived on our doorstep, with a bag of food and one hundred pound notes.

Mater explained the money as my mother's legacy. The same as the hundred pounds John had been given nine years earlier, and had used to take Paul to Paris. Mater said mine was to be used for a house deposit, on behalf of my mother. She told me that my son was the image of Mummy and that she would have been so proud of me and of him.

We found a house very quickly, in a fairly run-down area on the Wirral, across the River Mersey. It was a shabby old Victorian four-bedroom house, within walking distance of the ferryboats, which meant that I could still use Liverpool as my shopping base. Back in Belfast, Allen's grandmother, known to all as Granny Aggie, was worried that we didn't have enough furniture, and she set to work. We opened the front door one day, not long after we had moved in, to find a ship's container blocking the road. Granny Aggie had completely emptied her best parlour of all its furniture, including a Parker Knoll suite, the Axminster carpet, a large wool rug, long brocade curtains, the familiar coffee table and the piano. I am still lost for words.

My mother-in-law came to stay in September 1971, while I gave birth to my daughter Sara. Life soon became a round of feeding and nappies. We had little money, but we were very happy with our family life.

I took my new baby over to see my grandmother, Nana, as I had with my son when we arrived back in Liverpool. She adored both babies and was always delighted to see me, as I was to see her. She was my one remaining link with Daddy.

Not long after that, Liela moved out of London and settled in Manchester with her family. I was so glad that she was nearer, meaning I could see her more often. It had been difficult travelling see her in London with a small baby. I still helped her out with the children, but I needed no forcing. I loved to be with her. When she had some time off, she came across to see us with her three children, the dog and the parrot. The first time she came to our new house she decided that I needed a car. She bought me an old green Mini Cooper S for £70, to make my life with two babies easier. Freedom! We saw a lot of each other.

The month my daughter was born, John and Yoko moved to New York, and I wasn't even aware of it until they had gone. He, too, was in the process of establishing a new family life. I kept thinking he would be back soon. I had never heard of the Green Card. I didn't know he had emigrated out of our lives.

48: *Little Boy Lost*

Harrie had been ill sporadically for a long time, but none of us had been aware how serious it had become. She had had gallstones removed in the summer of 1966, when I was working for my second season at Butlins. Nanny had rung to tell me that Harrie had been rushed into hospital and I caught the train back to Liverpool and went straight to see her. It was obvious that Harrie was very sick, and I did my best, along with everyone else, to raise her spirits. She made an excellent recovery from that bout of illness, and we thought that she had beaten it. Her determination to get better was strong, and she was soon back at home. But late in 1971 she had started to feel ill again and was undergoing many tests. Harrie had always been thin, but now she seemed to be losing even more weight.

Throughout 1972 she became steadily weaker, and in November she went into hospital again, with hepatitis. By early December, Nanny was always at her bedside, Mimi had arrived from Poole, and Mater had arrived from Edinburgh. Liela and David were both there.

I had paid her a visit and she showed remarkable strength. Liela had warned me to stand by in case she needed blood, as we were both Group O. After Mater had visited I took her back to Harrie's house, where she was staying. We stayed up nearly all night, drinking tea and talking, and I returned home as dawn was breaking. We were very hopeful that Harrie's sheer will would win the day.

I was getting ready to visit her the next afternoon, when Mater arrived. Harrie had died an hour before. The baby of her family, she was only 56.

I was very, very sad. Harrie and I had had our moments – many of them – and I had found it hard to forgive her for the rejection after my father's death, but in her own way she had attempted to step into our mother's shoes and I have to concede that this was an impossible task. Her idea of mothering – formal, strict and emotionally distant – was a world away from my own, but I did love her. Whatever had happened, she had taken in two bereft children and although she knew nothing about dealing with our bereavement, we had lived with her and her unreason-able, unfathomable, unquestionable rules for seven years.

I think the problem stemmed from the fact that none of us – neither her sisters nor her children – ever got over the death of our mother. We were there, Jackie and I, needing love, when love seemed to have died with Mummy.

John was trying to get his Green Card in America, so he couldn't leave. He telephoned Norman and sent flowers.

Cynthia came to the funeral, with her mother, the first time we had seen her in about five years. We talked and she left us her telephone number. It felt good to have re-established contact. I saw that Mimi and Cynthia were talking together, but it was only later that Cynthia told me what they were talking about. Mimi was expressing dismay at Cynthia and John's divorce and telling her they should have stuck together and that everything would have worked out! Cynthia had given up too easily!

That same year brought another death. Nana died unexpect-edly, and I was deeply shocked at her loss. I had hoped she would be there to see my children – her great-grandchildren – grow up, or at least for a little longer. I missed her.

We had moved again, at the beginning of 1973, to a large old house, with a bigger garden, nearer the park. This time, it had already been renovated, which was a pleasure, after having walked on planks across the kitchen in the first house, while Allen and his brother cemented floors and plastered walls. I had become adept at managing two babies on the bendy boards.

Mater and Mimi came to visit. Mater lived in a wonderfully roomy terrace in Murrayfield, in Edinburgh, a most desirable residence in a most desirable area. The one thing our homes did have in common, however, were the huge bay windows. Mater advised us to invest in beautiful carpets and curtains and just sit on the floor! As they were leaving, she mused that she had been thinking of new curtains for Murrayfield for some time now. The very next week, a colossal parcel arrived by special delivery. Mater had sent me her beautiful, rich deep navy curtains as soon as she returned to Scotland. They transformed the house.

Another year went by. Allen was working very hard building up a business, so we were comfortable, if not wealthy. I was at home with the children and I loved that time in my life, waking up with the day stretching ahead, free to go adventuring with my little ones. Allen had awarded himself a company car, and had handed it over it to me and the children. We were mobile, which opened up all sorts of possibilities. We lived near a wonderful promenade, which looked across at Liverpool. There was a fantastic open-air swimming pool up the road, where we spent whole days with Allen's sister and her children. Just beyond that were the sand dunes. We didn't have to go far to have an exciting day out.

In October we saw on the news that John had left Yoko. I was shocked. John had turned whole worlds upside down to be with her, abandoning us all in the process, and now the Romeo and Juliet of rock and roll were fed up with each other, after just a few short years!

He was apparently in Los Angeles with a replacement love, who Yoko reportedly considered an ideal companion for his trip. May Pang was a young girl who had worked for the couple. I thought that John had now taken leave of any sense he had left. He had climbed into those bags as an intelligent, creative member of the human race and had emerged a nutcase. Now, he seemed to be in free fall and I dreamed about him often. I dreamed that we were back in Springwood, sometimes we were all children again and sometimes we were all grown up, but always with Mummy as she was in our childhood. I still have those dreams and wake up either sad or glad.

Eliott Mintz, friend to John and Yoko, long ago christened John's fifteen months in Los Angeles his 'lost weekend'. John had been catapulted into freedom, probably for the first time in his entire life. He behaved like a wild and turbulent teenager, Mimi-less and Yoko-less, revelling in the dark side, the result of which we watched on television and read in the newspapers. We saw and read about fights and arrests. It seemed that reporters were on standby for the moments when he slipped, and he didn't disappoint them.

His reported behaviour seemed to be the adult equivalent of his behaviour on the streets of Woolton village, after he was moved to Mendips. Out of control. I wanted to hug him, he seemed so small and vulnerable, despite all the noise. Behind the scenes, however, other things were happening. He took responsibility as a father for the first time since he had gone to America. Encouraged by May Pang, he invited Julian and Cynthia to visit, re-establishing a relationship with his son. I hoped he would go a step further, and arrive in England to see us all. But that wasn't to be.

It has been reported that Yoko was in constant touch, during this 'away' time, in one way or another – letter, telephone, telepathy? – and that he was drawn back to her in some nefarious way. I have my own opinion about that. John was an adult, even if he had been playing the part of a child-man. He made his own decisions at the end of the day. He made the decision to return to Yoko, because that's where he felt safe. Yoko was more than willing to organise his life, not only with John's consent, but with his full approval. He wasn't happy, cut loose and far away. John needed a mother figure running his life. He was still lost without Mummy. He was unhappy and he knew the answer. For him, happiness lay in the security that Yoko offered, so when he had woken up from the nightmare of unstructured freedom, he went home. In a way he went back to the warm kitchen in Springwood, to his mother, where he was happy, even when he was unhappy. Little boy lost. That's how I understand it.

At home, I too was seeking a mother figure. I was going to see Nanny, spending a lot of time there, sitting in her garden with the children. Nicolas was just about walking, and it was Nanny who followed him around the garden, rescuing him from stone paths and rose thorns, and who sat me in a garden chair and brought me drinks and good food while I nursed Sara. She never gave up on criticising me, and sometimes I went home very upset. I needed a mother figure, however, and Nanny's red hair – though not the same red – always reminded me of Mummy. Nanny would have found it well nigh impossible to get rid of me.

Yes. I understood John.

49: *Renewed Contact*

Sometime in early 1975, Mater telephoned me. She was laughing and said straight away, 'You'll never guess who's just phoned me!' Well, no, I would never have guessed. 'John's looking for you. He's asked me where he can find the girls.'

My instant response was, 'Wonderful! When? Now? Can I ring now?' Mater gave me the number and I couldn't wait for her to get off the phone, so that I could phone him in New York.

John was back in New York after the 'lost weekend', during which he had started to rebuild his relationship with his son, Julian. He had woken up to what he was losing. I believe that, for John, this was the most important bridge he had to build, but that it was followed by his need to re-establish contact with the rest of the family. So here was the reach-out. And we reached right back to meet John.

I had to exercise patience. There is a five-hour time gap between England and America, and Mater told me to phone at midnight, British time, to get John at seven p.m., his time. That was a long evening, let me tell you. I went through the mechanics of putting the children to bed and I paced the floor. I couldn't even ring Jackie in Liverpool, as she wasn't on the phone. The hour arrived and I dialled the number. John didn't answer the call himself, which was disconcerting. A woman answered and started asking me who I was and what I wanted. After five minutes of answering her questions, I was becoming embarrassed and said to her that I just wanted to speak to my brother and that maybe he didn't want to speak to me.

She said, 'Please, just one more question. What was your father's middle name?'

I replied, 'Albert' and then said, 'I'm going now.' John cut in immediately, shouting, 'Don't go! It's you. It's really you, Julia. I'm sorry about the inquisition. I had to be sure.' What sort of world was he living in?

We talked and talked. The essence of that first phone call and, really, all the others was Mummy. Remember this? Remember that? Springwood. Can you remember her laugh? Can you see her face? Can you hear her voice? Yes, yes, yes. We could both remember that. We both said that we dreamed of her and I told him about the Magic Mirror. He said he could see us. We laughed and we cried. He said he wanted to help Jackie and me financially, but I said not to talk about money. We had plenty of time for that. Contact was the most vital thing. We must keep in contact. He asked me to get on a plane now. He would send the money for the ticket. I said that I couldn't go while the children were in school. Stupid, of course, but I didn't know then that I should have dropped everything and just gone.

One of the outstanding lyrics of John's music encapsulates my feelings about that now. 'Life is what happens to you while you're busy making other plans'. If we have something we want to do, we must do it and not prevaricate. I so wish I had.

I had phoned John the first time, and he said, as we were finally able to end that conversation, that I was to 'call Colette' next time. He was telling me to call 'collect', meaning that the telephone bill would be his, not mine. However, not understanding what John meant, I replied that if Colette was the woman who had picked the phone up a couple of hours earlier, then I didn't want to speak to her again. John was hysterical with laughter and told me that he meant to say 'reverse the charges'. He even used the expression 'I guess', which sounded strange coming from him. He was acquiring an American style.

The laughter was a good way to break off that first call. I lay awake all night reliving the conversation over and over again.

John phoned again within the week, and this time conversation flowed easily from the start. I felt as if it was a phone call following a visit, as if we'd met the week before. We were both more relaxed and we both had so much to say that we talked across each other. We settled into a 'your go', 'my go' routine and I just loved talking with him. He asked all about the children and was delighted that Nikki had Mummy's red hair and hazel brown eyes. He asked me to describe him and Sara in detail. He wanted to know if I talked to them about him, if they knew who he was. Yes, they knew Uncle John. He apologised again and again for the lack of contact and said that his life was now back on track and that he wanted contact with all of us. He had suffered a madness, he told me, with drink and drugs, but he had put insanity behind him and was looking ahead, to the future. And he wanted us in there. He was going to write to everyone as well as telephone.

His intentions were wonderful, and I am sure he meant every word. I accepted his yearning for his English family, all of us, as a resumption of John as John. John, our brother, our cousin, our uncle. I have never seen him as an icon on the world stage. To me, John was my brother, who was in the same spiritual life space as me and Jackie, with the same deep longing for our mother. A traumatised genius. Traumatised for exactly the same reason as we, the girls, his sisters, were. Mummy gone.

Now he seemed to have found some happiness. He was in contact with Julian and was having a baby with Yoko. I reassured him that none of us had gone away. We were all thrilled to have him back, if only by voice and pen.

Welcome home, John.

In another call, he asked me where we were living and, when I told him, he said that we ought to get to 'the posh side' of the Wirral. He knew that, of course, because it was where

Cynthia had lived. I said that we would, in time. He asked me to describe the house and the rooms, starting with the bedrooms and working down. When I got to the dining-room, where I was sitting by the fire, he asked me to describe the room in detail.

Allen was a keen amateur photographer and developed his films by turning the bathroom into a makeshift dark-room, hanging the negatives to dry on lines strung across the room. Some years before, Harrie had given him several family photographs and negatives and asked him to make large prints. He had done this for her, and then, for me, he had enlarged pictures of Mummy. The prize picture was so large that it consisted of four A4 size prints put together to make a picture of her, which was hanging on the wall, along with other photographs of Jackie and me. There are very few photographs of my mother, and this one, my favourite, was the one where she had her arms around the young John, taken in Nanny's garden in the summer of 1949, when she was pregnant with Jackie. I had asked Allen to make me a large print, without John, so that it could be just Mummy. I looked up at it and told John about it.

Before I had finished describing this image, smiling down at me, John demanded the photograph and any others on the wall. I objected that they were the only enlarged pictures I had and that they had been done especially for me. John replied that he had nothing! And that I could have them done again.

The next day, I carefully peeled the Blu-Tack from the walls and sent him all the photographs. Although I had all the normal-size prints, I never again had those photographs enlarged.

It must have been about this time that John also asked for various other items, including his Quarry Bank school tie and, somewhat surprisingly, Mimi's clock, which was engraved 'George Toogood Smith', and had always been in Mendips. John was nest-making for his yet-to-be-born son Sean, and Mummy was to be a part of their lives, alongside Jackie and me and other 'home' souvenirs. Sean would have an impression of John's first family. John in Liverpool, where he grew up and spent the first 23 years of his life. John in the city that moulded him.

50: *Looking for Julian*

Yet another call brought an unusual request from John. He had been trying to get in touch with Julian, in Hoylake, about ten miles away, on the other side of the Wirral. Cynthia had returned to her home ground and had bought a bungalow near the sea. John gave me the address and asked me to go and see them. I asked him for Cynthia's telephone number, but he said, 'If I give you that, you won't go and I want you to see Julian and report back to me.'

John said that he was looking forward to being an uncle to my children and to Jackie's, and that he wanted me to be an auntie to Julian. He wanted him to know me again and for me to take him out and about and introduce him to my children. John and I had always been close to our cousins, and he wanted the same for our children. Julian, now twelve, was 'a cracking lad', John said, and he wanted to keep close contact with him. He said he had found Julian again and now he wanted to build on the relationship. He told me that he knew he had neglected Julian and felt guilty about it, that he loved him and didn't want to mess up his life, as his own father had done. He wanted as good a relationship as he could manage, given the physical distance between them.

I know that John didn't follow through on this. He saw Julian again a handful of times, but after Sean was born he became so focused on the new baby that his good intentions with regard to Julian were lost. John had an inherent weakness and lacked a true sense of worth – something that all our mother's children have suffered from. In the end it was this that let him and his son down. But at this moment John had every intention of rebuilding a good father-son relationship with Julian. He said that Julian hadn't phoned recently and he wanted to know why. 'His mother must have a cob on' with him he said, meaning that he thought that Cynthia was upset with John for having returned to Yoko and that she was preventing Julian from phoning.

John had also written me some letters by now, and he stressed in these, too, that he really wanted me to go and find the young Julian and let him know what was happening and tell him to get in touch with his father straight away. I was to tell him face to face that John was waiting to hear from him.

I was reticent, even though I had agreed. I hadn't seen Cynthia since Harrie's funeral, just over two years before. She had made a general comment as she was leaving that we must get together, but we had made no specific plans. What on earth would she think if I just turned up, asking to see Julian? I put it off until, eventually, Allen said that I had to go. We drove with the children to Hoylake, one Sunday afternoon, found the bungalow and knocked on the door. I was nervous as this was uninvited and unexpected. Cynthia opened the door and was clearly shocked to see me. My timing had been unfortunate, I could see she had a guest and was thrown by my sudden appearance. She said that I had just missed Julian, he was out with his friends and that she didn't know when he would be back. I said that John had sent me, that I would love to see Julian and that he was to phone his dad as soon as possible.

I turned and fled and reported back to John that Julian was out.

John told Liela in a letter that he had sent me to see Julian, without success. I was truly sorry to have let John down and to have missed the opportunity to get to know Julian. But I felt too embarrassed to turn up on Cynthia's doorstep again. In another call, John reverted to the subject of our house and where it was. He knew the area and pointed out that it was on the 'shoddy' side of the Wirral. He had a suggestion to make. Well, he had two, actually. The first was that, since I was married to an Irishman, which seemed to please him no end, would we like to go and live on a little island he had bought off the west coast of Ireland, called Dornish? There was a small snag, however. There was no fresh water on this paradise in the Atlantic ocean, but it could be brought in by rowing boat. I turned this down flat. Being a hippie had its limits!

The next suggestion was better, but I refused it nevertheless. John, like the rest of the family, loved North Wales. We had all spent happy childhood time there. Anyone who is familiar with that wild, mountainous terrain will appreciate that, once experienced, it is never forgotten. It seeps right into your system and you are hooked.

John said that he had dreamed of this so special place. He said that he would buy a farmhouse in North Wales and that Jackie and I could live in it with our families, my two children and Jackie's son. He was thinking of a big place, with land. I could choose it myself. And he could visit. He had always thought of buying there, he said. I asked would the house belong to Jackie and me. The answer was no, that it would belong to Apple and not to worry about that, he would see that everything was all right. I said to John that I couldn't possibly consider that, thank you so, so much, but to put the proposition to Jackie when he next spoke to her. Allen and I had a large mortgage, but we were living in our own house and we couldn't leave it to live in a house owned by a company. If he could give it to us, however, we would find something fantastic for us and for him without delay. He said that wasn't possible, that he didn't have that kind of ready cash to spend (it would have cost between £15,000 and £20,000, depending on the land) and that I should think about it.

It seemed strange that my super-rich brother apparently had less actual spending power than I did. I was free to spend whatever we had, without question. And here was John telling me he couldn't do that! The price of wealth and fame seemed very high.

This led us to talk about the house in Woolton, that he had bought with Jackie and me in mind, back in 1967, after he heard of our father's death. Uncle Norman was still living in the house, and our understanding was that we would have the house, or be able to realise the money from the house, when he died. It was Norman's home. John saw things differently. He said that he never intended Norman to have the house, but that he didn't know what to do about it. And that I, Julia, should ask Norman to leave. John the coward! I told him not to be so silly and, if he really thought that, to tell Norman himself. John repeated, in a letter to me, that I should 'put Norman out' and move in with Jackie. But apart from anything else, it was a three-bedroom house, far too small for us all to share. It didn't seem to occur to him that we had partners and three children between us. And dogs and cats.

John then asked if I would like him to send some money. This time I said yes immediately. He asked me how much and I pulled a sum out of the air that I thought would help us out, without being greedy. I asked would three thousand pounds be all right, thinking that it would indeed be a fortune for Jackie and me to share. He laughed and said, 'Is that all?' I said we would be rich with such an amount and it arrived by return of post, with a request for a receipt for the tax man, who 'is always after me'.

I laughed and laughed when the postman, who obviously had no idea who it was from, or what it contained, pointed out that there was no stamp on the envelope and I had to pay triple the postage to get the envelope from him.

John wrote a note to accompany the cheque. He said to enjoy the money. And don't tell Mimi. He said it and he wrote it. He told Mater he had given us the money and they both agreed it would be disastrous to tell her.

I didn't tell Mimi. There was no reason to. I knew that would mean trouble for all of us. Some things never change.

But Yoko rang Mimi and told her that John had given the girls some money. Mimi told Liela, and Liela told me. As usual, Mimi's reaction was an extreme one. She was mad with us all. John, Julia and Jackie. In fact, she was incandescent.

By this time John had got in touch with several family members. He was writing to me, Jackie, Norman, Liela, David, Stan and Mater, and at one point wrote, 'I've got so many letters I can hardly remember which I answered.'

In a letter to Liela he wrote about the fifteen months he'd spent apart from Yoko having his hellraising stint: 'I'm no big drinker normally, last year was . . . er . . . special . . . this year I'm clean as a whistle.' He said he was still stuck in America (i.e. didn't have his Green Card) and didn't think that would change before the 1976 election.

In another letter, to Mater, written before Sean's birth, he said, 'I couldn't deal with Mimi till after the birth.'

When John phoned me, I was always there. When I phoned him, however, I wasn't always able to speak to him. Yoko usually answered. And as time went by and John's calls to us ceased, we found it impossible to reach him. Every time I tried, I got Yoko. In fact, I wondered, did John ever pick up the phone in his own house, or did Yoko walk around with it in her pocket? She seemed to me to be monitoring his life and equally he seemed to be allowing it.

'John is asleep. You don't understand his life.' 'No, I can't wake him up.' 'John is out. Yes, I'll tell him you called.' I felt that she was impatient with me and probably fed up with all of us, back in Britain. It seemed to us at the time that it was John who was backing off, but now I'm not so sure. Whether or not John ever knew that I was still trying to make contact, I will never know.

Julian was experiencing the same thing. He and John had re-established contact in Los Angeles but, as I learned later, now

Julian couldn't call him up without going through Yoko either, who often told him John was unavailable.

I realise that Yoko had no idea how important it was for Jackie and me to resurrect a relationship with John. To be our mother's children again. But, surely, she must have known how important it was to encourage John to speak to his son.

Sean was born on John's 35th birthday, 9 October 1975, and I sent him a welcoming card. I think that most of the family sent a card. And John did continue to write. He wrote to me, describing the stay in hospital after Sean's birth: 'It was pretty ruff the last few weeks before hospital . . . and ruffer in there. I stayed the whole two weeks, sleeping on the floor . . . feeding the baby every four hours . . . he was under "intensive care", i.e. TORTURE . . . for the first week it was an effing NIGHTMARE.' He went on: 'I'll send some pics of Sean as soon as we get a chance to breathe, he'll be five by then the way we're feeling! But he's a blessing and we're thrilled . . . we might get over there early next year (spring)? If the visa comes thru ok (touch woodworm).'

In a letter to Liela he said, 'When I told her [Mimi] the name of the baby [Sean] . . . she said "Oh John, don't BRAND him," which I thought was hilarious . . . Brand him an Irishman? Like his father?'

After a short while John's letters tailed off too. He and Yoko had a new baby and all their efforts went into that baby. I understand that, after their previous sad losses. But it seemed that after the series of calls and letters from John in 1975, Jackie and I were written out of his life at a stroke. Why did John surrender to this state of affairs so readily? If we couldn't get through on the phone, why wasn't he phoning us? After all, it was he, John, who had telephoned Mater, looking for us. Eighteen months later, it seemed that he had tired of us. It was crushing. Trying to reach him had become a humiliating experience, and within a few months we gave up.

It seemed to me that John was like a child, submitting to the will of the strong woman. Yoko/Mimi had metamorphosed into mother and resumed control. I can't say that John gave up. Or gave in. Nor can I say why he didn't keep up contact of his own accord. John was naturally consumed with love for his new son and devoted to Yoko and his care of them. We saw it all on television and read of his 'baby' life. He wrote from time to time to different family members, seemingly wanting to encourage us to keep the lines of communication open, but the closeness was short-lived and he didn't contact Jackie and me again directly. And yes, it hurt.

However it happened, silence resumed.

51: *Chester*

Even though I wasn't able to speak to John again, I wondered how I could repay him for his kindness in sending us money. After much thought, I had a brainwave. We all knew that he was being a house husband. Our mother and her sisters had been adept at sewing and embroidery and he had seen that. She had taught Jackie and me basic stitching, and Mater had encouraged us to embroider tray cloths of country cottages and wildflower gardens when we were in Scotland. I went to a specialist shop and bought an Irish linen tablecloth and a whole array of embroidery silks. I was very ambitious, I have to admit. The cloth would be worthy of a state banquet! I had young, time-demanding children, so it was a slow process, as I was only able to concentrate on such a task when they were in bed. I wanted to make a beautiful finish, so I was filling it all in, rather than just embroidering the outline. It was a labour of love, from me and Mummy to John.

Some months after we had first spoken with John on the phone, in 1975, Mater became very ill. She had suffered from arthritis for many years now, which had affected her hands, and she found it painful to walk in extremely cold weather, but I had no idea that there was anything else wrong. In fact there was, though at that stage no one knew what it was. She had been attending doctors and hospitals in Edinburgh, in the summer of 1975, without a diagnosis, when Liela invited her to come to Manchester, where she could arrange for Mater to see some specialists. Mater was admitted to the Withington Hospital in Manchester and, as Liela was working on the wards and in theatre there, she asked me to go and spend some time with her.

I sat on Mater's bed for several days, and we talked about life and love. We talked about my mother, and she commended me on my children and said how proud Mummy would have been to know them. She gave me advice on cooking for dinner parties and what to concentrate on in the home. We talked about how different all our lives would have been if Mummy had not died when she did. She apologised for the way things had turned out for all three of us. She said that she was truly sorry that Jackie and I had been treated as outsiders by some of our own family. That it should never have happened. She wanted to see us happy. I wonder if she knew she was dying.

Soon afterwards, Mater returned to Edinburgh. Within a very short time she became desperately ill, and Liela, David and I drove up to see her. Sadly, she died the very next day, of pancreatic cancer, a devastating disease that had taken just three months to overpower her. She was 64, and we felt her loss deeply.

John was still having problems with the Green Card. If he had returned for the funeral, he would not have been allowed to go back to America.

He sent flowers.

I became pregnant with my third child and, just as John had done, I became ever more absorbed in family life. We had been considering moving house for some time now and soon after David was born, in April 1979, we put the house on the market, expecting that we would move in the autumn. It was sold within a week, however, which took us by surprise. David was just twelve weeks old when the sale was finalised and we hadn't recovered enough to go house-hunting. If we didn't want to let the sale go, we had to do something quickly.

I rang Uncle Norman at the house in Liverpool. Could we please move in with him until we had more time to go house-hunting? There wasn't a second's hesitation. 'When are you coming? I'll start making room straight away.'

I started to clear out the house. We had a book collection

which numbered in the thousands. I filtered them into the 'must-haves' and the 'definite re-reads' – and kept them all. Much of our furniture would be stored in Norman's garage and at friends' houses. I burned letters, including John's, on the fire. I know it sounds unsentimental, and that some people keep all their old letters, but I never have – I've always been a clear-out-the-clutter type. Only two of John's letters escaped the flames, and even that was an oversight. I found them years later, between the leaves of books, where I have a habit of storing things, including money, for a rainy day. In fact, I found several lots of ten-pound notes as I was going through the books, packing them into tea chests.

I spoke to Yoko on the phone twenty years later, to put our case for the same house that we were about to move into, and I told her, when she demanded evidence of John's words, that I had burned his letters. Yoko was astounded. 'No one destroys John Lennon's letters,' she said.

But to me they weren't 'John Lennon's letters'. They were letters from my brother and they had to be cleared out for the move, along with all the others. It didn't even occur to me to keep them.

We went to live with Uncle Norman towards the end of the summer term, in 1979. We expected to stay with him for just a few months, giving us time to find a house, but after being gazumped on the first one we found it took us months to find another and we ended up staying with him for almost a year.

We had been visiting Norman a lot since Harrie died, but this was the first time I had actually lived in the house. I thought it might be too much for him, with a new baby and two enquiring children of eight and nine, and had been worried about his space and time being invaded. In fact the opposite turned out to be true. I hadn't known Norman well when I was a child. When Harrie was alive he was a shadowy figure to us, very much in the background. But now we got to know him well and he was delightful. He loved having the children there and became involved in their lives, collecting them from school, talking with them, taking them out and spoiling them. He told me that he had thought my mother was wonderful, and that he had taught my father to drive, which I had never known.

Norman was on a pension by this time, so we proposed that we would pay all the bills and buy all the food, which allowed him to save up for a newer car and have some money in his pocket. This was a satisfactory arrangement all round. During the week Norman and I spent hours playing chess and reading and walking David in the park in the summer, and we all got on very well.

Early in 1980 we found a house in Chester and were having the survey done, when Norman said that he had begun to think that we should stay. In fact, why didn't we stay? He had been working out how we could do it. As the house was quite small for all of us, he suggested that we use our house deposit to build another room over the garage, as had been done with many of the houses in the road. He would move in there, leaving us the whole house. He said that it was my house really, mine and Jackie's, and that he shouldn't be living there on his own. It would be better if we stayed.

Allen and I talked it over and decided that no matter how kind Norman had been, we needed to have our own house. We had a young family and, although there was no mortgage to pay with Norman, we were unsure of our position. We thanked Norman for his kind offer and moved out in April.

We arrived in our new home just in time for David's first birthday. Chester is an old walled Roman city, with the River Dee running through it. I knew that my grandmother had been born there, and in some ways it felt like a homecoming. It is only twenty miles from Liverpool, and we'd shopped there with Mummy as small children and had taken boats out on the river. We were now making a new home for our family, in the very place that had been the departure point for Liverpool fifty years previously.

I was still visiting Nanny, as before. I would arrive, with David in tow, in time for lunch and leave in time to collect Nicolas and Sara from school. After we had been in Chester about six months, Nanny told me that Mimi was coming to stay with her and had expressed an interest in a move back north, possibly to Chester, a city for which she had always had a fondness. I invited them to come and see the house and use it as a base for house-hunting, as it was in the town centre.

Nanny had never visited me in Chester, so I didn't expect that I would see them. But I was wrong. They not only turned up – they came every day for a week.

Mimi seemed serious about moving to Chester, nearer to her last remaining sister. I sent them written directions, as we had no telephone, and they would arrive each morning at the house, straight from the station. I would have David in the high pram and we would set off for the town centre.

On the first day Mimi went right into the first estate agent's office we came across, marched up to the desk and announced that she was John Lennon's aunt and wanted a house for seventy thousand pounds. I was very embarrassed and reversed out with the pram – not an easy manoeuvre. I waited outside while Mimi and Nanny went into the second office, a few doors away, and within a minute Nanny came out to join me muttering, 'Well, I'm not doing that again.' Nanny and I waited together outside the next one. Mimi had accumulated many glossy property leaflets in the three offices, so we found a café where we could look at what she had. I then pointed her in the direction of other estate agents, while Nanny and I stayed put.

Despite the many brochures there didn't seem to be a house that was quite right. On the last day we went down to have tea at a riverside café, and there it was – the house of Mimi's dreams. It was directly across the river from the café, with a large conservatory overlooking the water. And it was obviously lived in and not for sale. Mimi waved her hands about, to 'put the fluence on it'. We all laughed, including the people at the next table. I really expected her to haul us all over the bridge, to find the front of the house and knock on the door, although Nanny and I would have been hovering further down the road. I said to Mimi that she could move in with us if she was really serious about living in Chester, to give her the time she needed for such a move, but in the event, the move never materialised.

We were making improvements to the house and exploring Chester, settling in, bringing old friends to stay and meeting new people. Summer rolled into autumn and autumn into an early winter. Nanny's 68th birthday was on 17 November and I went to see her with a present a few days later. Anything to do with cats was most welcome, and over the years nearly all her birthday cards, from everyone, were of cats.

When I arrived at her house Nanny said that she had had a wonderful surprise. John had telephoned from New York to wish her a happy birthday! She was so pleased. He had really good news, too. He told Nanny that he was coming home in the New Year. He said that we would all have to go to Nanny's house, Ardmore, as it was the only house large enough to hold us all, and he would come to us. He wrote the same thing to Liela. Nanny repeated this news over and over. She said that John had told her, 'I've made everything over to Yoko, it's about time I saw to my own family.'

We were all so excited about John's imminent return that we could hardly wait until the New Year. It seemed like forever away. He was within reach, at last. Other people started to talk about it, making it more real. I hadn't spoken to him myself, but I knew it was true. I panicked and started to stitch the tablecloth furiously, determined to get it finished for him. I couldn't wait for him to meet my children. Uncle John, who had been invisible, was about to become real. I had always talked about John to them, and now they would be able to build their own relationship with him.

I was pleased that we had four bedrooms. He could stay.

52: *8 December 1980*

As we didn't have a telephone, I had given close family the number of my new friend Sylvia, who lived directly across the road, in case of emergency. In the eight months that we'd lived in Chester, they'd rarely had occasion to use it. When Sylvia came to knock on the front door, early on the morning of 9 December, it was still winter dark and very cold. Allen had just left for work and I was giving the children breakfast and getting the older two ready for school.

Sylvia said that Liela was on the phone and wanted to speak to me. I thought immediately that something had happened to one of her children and raced across the road. As Liela relayed the devastating news that John had been shot a few hours earlier, my mind went black. Liela said she was coming straight away.

I ran back to my own house. No. No. Please God. No. No. Not again. Not John.

Sylvia didn't know I was related to John and I didn't feel able to explain, and she was left wondering what on earth the telephone call could have been. But she could see it was serious and she followed me home and took over organising the children for school, then took David across to her house, while I sat, turning into stone, waiting for Liela. I was so cold. I felt there was a band of icy steel tightening around my head and chest until I was a ghost.

Liela arrived an hour after the call and we spent the day together, hugging and crying. I don't know how she drove back to Manchester. Sylvia saw her leaving and came over. She later told me that she had been hearing the news of John's death all day and was wondering if there was a connection. She busied herself with the children when they came in from school, and as soon as Allen came home, I went to bed and howled all night.

Mummy, Daddy – and now John. How much more?

I didn't get invited to the funeral. Jackie didn't get invited to the funeral. No one in John's English family, apart from Julian, was invited to the funeral. We were not contacted or informed of anything. And I felt there was no way I could phone Yoko, after she had made it so clear before that our calls weren't welcome.

Of course there wasn't a funeral, as such. We now know that John was cremated in secret the day after he died and his ashes were returned to Yoko in a jar. But we didn't know that then.

There were the public vigils, notably the one in New York's Central Park, which the whole world was invited to attend. That spot was subsequently dedicated as a memorial in 1985, and called Strawberry Fields. But we were waiting for the funeral of our brother John. A private ceremony, for those who knew and loved him. Nobody told us there wasn't going to be one. We were left to watch the ceremony in the park on television.

Only I didn't watch television. I didn't read newspapers. I avoided the screen and the news stands. It was too painful to see him everywhere.

Nor did I hear the last radio interview John had recorded with Andy Peebles, for the BBC, only hours before he died, but many listeners have since told me that in it he said 'Hello, Liverpool.' He also talked about how he had been angry for so long about our mother's death, and said that now he was ready to go back home. He said he was sorry that he'd neglected his family and friends and that he was ready to get in touch again. He really had been coming back. I don't think that I could have listened to the interview at the time, but what John was saying has touched and enlightened me.

For months I did only what I had to do for my family life to go on, and then rushed home to sit in a corner, crumbling and hurting.

Think black. Think blank. I was saved from insanity by my children.

53: *Changes*

There had been cracks developing within my marriage for some time, and John's death – and its effect on me – added more stress than it could absorb. A few months later we parted, and Allen returned to Ireland.

Now that I was on my own with the children, I knew that I would have to work, once David went to school. So I signed up for a year's further study, to start in September 1981, to gain an honours degree, moving on from my original French and linguistics to French existentialism and education, and specialising in pastoral care. I only had to attend a few lectures each week and was able to study from home, which kept childcare needs to a minimum.

At this point my head was in a constant state of hammering and panic. I felt close to breakdown and needed to have my mind occupied. Each night as soon as the children had gone to bed I immersed myself in my studies and often stayed up all night reading.

I taught secondary school French and English for two years after that, but I was exhausted, both mentally and physically. Sylvia had been dropping David at nursery school while I went to work, but I wanted to be at home with him. So I made the decision to sell the house and stay at home with the children. In 1984 we moved into one of the old Georgian cloister houses by the Cathedral in the centre of Chester, renting from the Church. It was a beautiful Grade 2 listed house, directly overlooking the Cathedral Green, with a walled garden at the back. I could never have afforded to buy it, even if it was for sale. It was an easy choice to make and we settled in there very quickly.

The first thing I did with the house money was to buy a car that wouldn't need constant attention, and that summer the children and I took off to explore France for six weeks. I let the children dictate the journey, as long as they instructed me in French. 'Tournez à droite! Tournez à gauche! Allez tout droit.' We roared around France, testing every swimming pool and laundrette. The children had their feet out of the windows and we wore out Annie Lennox's 'Sweet Dreams' at full volume on the tape player. It was such a haphazard holiday that we sometimes had to sleep in the car, as we had left it too late to find anywhere to stay. We would offset this by booking into a five-star hotel the next day to clean up and to eat well.

We had been living in the Cathedral cloister for eighteen months, when, on the fifth anniversary of John's death, the BBC put out a programme to commemorate his life. Although I wasn't too keen on watching it, I thought that Nicolas and Sara, now fifteen and fourteen years old, needed to see it. I knew that their friends would probably watch it, with their parents, and that it would be talked about in school.

The programme was horrendous. My mother was portrayed as a disastrous, uncaring and ineffectual parent. Mendips had three flying ducks on the wall. A dark-haired Cynthia married John wearing a headscarf tied under her chin, and there was not even one mention of Julian. I could hardly watch the rest of the programme, I was so upset at the appalling misrepresentation. Right at the end, there was a short interview with Yoko, sitting on a sofa, in New York, with Sean. She said how pleased she was with the programme and that it was a good way for Sean to learn about his father and his father's family. Suffice it to say that Jackie and I weren't mentioned at all. I don't know who supplied the information, but the result was a nonsense.

I telephoned the BBC the next day and was told that John didn't have any sisters. Liela decided to write directly to ten-year-old Sean, with a more accurate version of John's early life, so that Sean would indeed know about his father, from his father's own family. Liela told him about his grandmother, our Mummy.

'I think I ended up writing him about four letters' she told me. 'Unfortunately, there was absolutely no reply. I wonder whether he ever even got them. Personally, I think there's somebody in New York who would be happier if Sean didn't really know about his father's family. If that's so, then all right. There's nothing more I can do about it.'

One day, towards the end of January 1986, I was preparing to collect David from school, when Uncle Norman arrived. We had seen him over the Christmas holiday and he had seemed fine then. He was clearly upset now. He gave me a letter to read, which he had received that morning. It was from a New York law firm acting for Yoko. It said she wanted to offer Norman the opportunity to buy the house he was living in, 'for a mutually agreed price and at mutually agreeable terms', before it was put on the open market. Yoko was doubtless unaware of the fact that Norman was on a pension and had no money. In the circumstances, the lawyer's offer may as well have been a notice to leave the property. He had been asked for a speedy response.

This was an enormous shock. Now for the first time we really understood that the house did not belong to us, but to Yoko. John had bought it through his company, Apple, which owned it, and the house had gone to Yoko after John's death. It seemed that John had not secured it for us, nor had he let Yoko know that he intended it for us.

We went to photocopy the letter straight away. I gave Norman a copy and we talked about what seemed the inevitability of his having to leave the house. After we had left and moved to Chester in the spring of 1981, he had started to take in students from Liverpool University, in order to boost his income. He said that there had been occasional telephone calls from a New York lawyer's office, verifying who was living in the house. As I was separated by this time and only renting the Cathedral house,

Norman suggested that he give the students notice to leave and that I went back with the children to live with him, maintaining that that is what John had intended after all. I turned this down immediately, knowing it would be a financially insecure place to be with my family, and asked him whether he wanted to come and live with me instead. When I gave him a lift to the station later that evening, we had come to some sort of decision. If he had to leave, we would get a place big enough for all of us. I told him not to worry and waved him off.

I went home and rang my cousin David, Norman's son, straight away, having already posted him a copy of the letter. David rang Yoko and remonstrated with her, saying that his father had retired and that the house was not just a bricks and mortar asset, but home to Norman, and had been for fifteen years. I wasn't there for that conversation, but Norman didn't receive any more letters and lived there in peace until his death, four and a half years later.

I carried on visiting with the children, usually for Sunday lunch. We had left various board games there, for cold-weather visits, along with books and drawing materials. Norman and I played chess or cards and read the papers. Family stuff.

I was not in any way surprised when I learned, many years later, that Mimi had been particularly keen to have Norman removed from the house. Mimi had never liked Norman and she bitterly resented his living in the house in Woolton after Harrie had died.

Following the nonsense teledrama, I had to do something about the misrepresentation of John's story, my story and Jackie's story, before I really did have a mental collapse. Our mother had been publicly mauled and no one had defended her. I was incensed at the injustice of it and it slowly dawned on me that I had to speak out. John, the eldest sibling, had gone. I was next in line. The history of my family was being reinvented and sent out across the globe and I had to put it right. I was naïve enough to think that I could sort it out. I had no inkling that this distortion of the truth would become mainstream thinking or that Yoko would later insist that I had hardly known John and that he had hardly known his mother.

I rang the *Liverpool Echo*. Bill Smithies, the features editor, came to see me in Chester. We talked everything through. He explained what the newspaper would want, including photographs. I agreed to a series of interviews and we decided that they would publish the article while I was in France with the children. He said there was bound to be a fuss and that I had to be prepared for it. I wanted the fuss to be about my mother, so that was fine by me.

It wasn't long, however, before I was even more shocked. In the first interview Bill referred to my mother's four children. It was said in a split second, but the look on my face told him that I knew nothing about a fourth child. He apologised profusely, then got up and left. He asked me to ring him when I was ready to resume. I don't know who was more embarrassed. I was 38 years old and a stranger was telling me that I had a sibling I had never heard about.

I got straight in the car and went to see Nanny. It took three visits before she would tell me anything. When she did relent, she told me simply that it was true: my mother had had a baby, after John and before me, and named her Victoria. She said that my mother had known all along that she wasn't going to be able to keep her baby, that Pop wouldn't even discuss it. Nanny and Mimi had both helped to look after John, as my mother was quite ill, both during and after the pregnancy. She was also very depressed, which wasn't surprising as she was being reminded daily that she wouldn't be keeping her baby.

Nanny told me never, ever to mention it again. That she would never talk about my mother's pain again. She went upstairs and I stayed downstairs. We were both crying.

We all knew that my mother's favourite girl's name was Victoria and that when she was growing up, she had even told people that that was her name. A teenage fantasy. Nanny told me that occasionally someone would call at the house and ask for Victoria, only to be told that Victoria didn't live there, but Julia did! So, although the existence of the baby was a profound shock, the name was not.

I don't know whether or not Mummy ever knew her daughter's new name, Ingrid. I can only hope that she didn't, as there was a Norwegian family living at the top of the next road in Springwood. They had two blonde daughters, Astrid and Ingrid. How painful that would have been for her.

After Nanny had confirmed Victoria/Ingrid's birth, I set about trying to make contact with her. I rang the Norwegian Embassy and wrote them a letter, but without luck.

It was to be another twelve years before we discovered where she was. In August 1998 she gave an interview to the *Sun* newspaper. She said that she had found out in her late teens that she was John's, and our, half-sister, but had not wanted to upset her adoptive mother by making contact with us. She had waited until after her mother's death to come forward. The article ended with a question in bold type: Julia and Jackie, where are you?

We were delighted. We had been there, all along, wanting contact with her, and at last she had appeared. We got her phone number and various family members spoke to her on the phone at length, several times. When I talked to her I told her as much as I knew at that time and reassured her that she was in no way given up willingly and that our mother had had no choice. We all gave her an open invitation to come and see us. All at once or one by one, whichever she preferred.

Sadly, despite repeated invitations, she never came.

She had told me on the phone that her adoptive father, who was ill, wanted to return to Norway to live. The family had travelled backwards and forwards over the years and Ingrid had a half-brother in Norway, from her father's first marriage. After her father's death, she moved to France, where she still lives.

I met her just once. On 8 December 2000, there was a ceremony at Mendips in which an English Heritage blue plaque was placed on the outside wall of the house, commemorating the twentieth anniversary of John's death. It was Stan who pointed out to me that Ingrid was hovering outside the house. We spoke to her and I walked up the road with her for a few minutes to talk. We asked her to come with us to the Town Hall, where everyone was meeting up. The cars were waiting and we had to go, but Ingrid and her companion didn't come and sadly we haven't seen her since.

We have always been puzzled about why Ingrid hasn't come to see us. We would truly love to get to know her properly and will welcome her if ever she does choose to come.

In May 1990, Yoko came to the Pier Head in Liverpool to give her 'Come Together' concert. She had sent cousin Michael enough tickets for all of us to attend, which I thought was kind. We saw fifteen-year-old Sean in the flesh for the very first time, singing and running up and down the stage. We would have loved to meet him, talk to him and tell him about his family in England. We had gathered all our offspring together for the occasion – the next generation of seven children, who ranged in age from fourteen to twenty. I'd like to have given him the booklet I'd made about his father and grandmother. But the tickets we'd been sent had 'No Stage Access' stamped on them.

We left without meeting Yoko or Sean.

54: *Norman*

In October 1991, I was about to leave the house to meet a friend one evening, when I had a phone call from Broadgreen Hospital in Liverpool, asking did I know Norman Birch. He'd had an accident and could I come right away. Of course I could.

They assured me that he was all right. The last time he had been in hospital, it was for a minor operation and he'd hated the food. I had smuggled him in his favourite ham, egg and cress sandwiches to encourage him to eat, and this time I almost stopped to buy him fish and chips. As it took so long to get there, however, I decided to see how he was first.

Nothing had prepared me for the shock I received on giving my name at the reception desk. A doctor came out to meet me and guided me to a side room and then said how sorry he was, but that Norman had died. He had been knocked down by a car, almost outside his house. They hadn't wanted to tell me before the twenty-mile drive, and the person who asked me to go there had sounded so normal that I would never have guessed the truth. I was asked to identify him, as David, his son, was in London and I was deemed next of kin. I shall never forget seeing him. The morgue was no colder than I was.

David had had to take in the dreadful news at a distance and immediately walked out into the cold night, in great distress. He and his wife and children had a very close relationship with Norman. It was a big shock for all of us, as it was so totally unexpected. Another family member killed by a car. It was unreal and unbearable.

Within weeks, the lawyers had asked David to clear out the

house in Woolton. David, in a state of shock, arrived in Liverpool with his brother-in-law and emptied the house in a weekend, taking most of the furniture back to London. He hadn't had time to come to terms with his father's death before he was piling all his belongings into a van to cram into his own attic, two hundred miles away. I went across to see them and to take them some food, while they were packing the van. David gave me a chess set, as Norman and I had enjoyed many hours playing chess together during his life, and his long, tweed overcoat, which I am still wearing to shreds.

55: *Mimi*

There was a long-term problem between me and Mimi, which I had always sensed, without understanding what it was. The reality of it had hit home hard after Mummy's death, when I went hunting for John.

With hindsight I believe that Mimi resented my mother almost from birth. Mummy had been the favourite, the happy-go-lucky one, while Mimi was burdened with responsibility, which can't have been easy for her. After Mummy died she must have felt overwhelming guilt. On the night of the accident, in the hospital, she spent a long time, hours, alone with Mummy. No one will ever know what she said to her. With me being her sister's daughter, even bearing the same name, it is possible that every time she looked at me she was reminded of her resentment and her guilt. I went to see her in Poole occasionally, and we could get on for a few days at a time, but there was always an unspoken barrier between us. While I was living in Ireland, back in the early 1970s, Jackie had been invited to live down south with Mimi. She stayed with her for a while, before she went to live in London with friends and then came back to Liverpool, where she met Paul and had her son, John, in 1974. She stayed in Liverpool for the next twelve years, before moving to London in 1986.

Jackie saw a lot of Mimi, much more than I did. I think that maybe Jackie went to see Mimi as I went to see Nanny.

The first time I went to see Mimi after John died, we talked about him. She had been devastated to find that her house belonged to Apple, just like the house in Liverpool. Mimi had believed the house to be hers, just as Jackie and I had believed the Liverpool one to be ours. John had bought both houses to help his family, to give us an inheritance from him. Now Mimi bewailed the fact that John had left her 'beholden to Yoko'. I saw framed photographs of Sean as a baby, as a toddler and as a little boy all over the house. There had been photographs of Julian all over the house the last time I had visited. I asked Mimi where they were and why all the pictures were now of Sean. There wasn't even one photograph of Julian. Mimi was staring through the window, out to sea, so I didn't think she had heard me. I asked her again.

At last Mimi said, 'You never know who is coming.' I couldn't believe what I was hearing. Was she so afraid of losing the house that she felt she had to curry favour with Yoko by putting photos of Sean everywhere? By banishing photographs of another small boy? John's first son? It seemed so.

By the time of Norman's death, Mimi was 85 and in slow decline. We all agreed not to tell her about Norman, as she was so ill herself. She was a smoker and she had always suffered from bronchitis, which contributed to her ill-health. I remember being with her in Poole during a visit from the doctor. She had been smoking when she realised that the doctor had arrived, and to my amazement, she had a final puff and opened the drawer of the beautiful table beside her, stubbed out the cigarette inside and slammed it shut. When the doctor had gone, I cleaned out the drawer and removed many cigarette stubs.

After the death of her long-time housekeeper, Mrs Bailey, who together with her husband had been looking after the house and garden and, increasingly, Mimi herself, a nursing agency was engaged to supply care for Mimi, paid for by Yoko. This was a kindness which continued for two years, until Mimi died.

Whenever I visited Mimi, I would cook all her meals, using fresh ingredients, rather than serve up the tinned and packet food prepared in an instant by the nursing staff. I would also tell the nurse on night duty that she could go home and I would tend Mimi myself. She loved an unrushed, warm, soapy bath, and I would sit on the bathroom floor, letting her soak. Bedtime often entailed drinking tea at any hour throughout the night, something not willingly tolerated by the nursing staff.

I had been travelling down to see Mimi more than I had done before, trying find the handle which would smooth and soothe the rough edges of our relationship. I thought that she might want to talk about her life, about Mummy and about John. Very occasionally, I had the feeling that she wanted to talk to me, particularly with the three a.m. and four a.m. teas. She would be staring at me, almost glaring, her hands plucking at whatever was covering her. Mimi had always had beautiful hands, with manicured, red-painted nails. She had told me years before that when she stopped using nail varnish, she would be giving up on life. Her nails were now unpainted and I offered to do them for her. 'No,' she snapped. Then she looked away. Sometimes, she mouthed silent words. I asked her once to speak up, because I couldn't hear what she was saying, and she said, 'Shut up!' Mostly, at the end of her life, we would drink tea in silence and I would try to make her comfortable and then go to bed, until she called again.

Just weeks before she died Mimi had a hip operation. I couldn't believe that she was about to undergo such a thing in her weakened physical state. When she telephoned me to ask if I would come down to Poole to bring her home after the operation, I agreed immediately.

I expected her to stay in hospital for some time, but very soon after the operation, on a Friday afternoon, the Ward Sister of the hospital in Bournemouth phoned me at school. She said that Mimi was demanding to go home immediately, but that they weren't considering letting her go home until I was there. I promised I would try to be there by the time they got her home.

I asked my head teacher to release me and went to collect

David from his primary school and we set off straight away. Normally we broke the long journey to Poole by staying with friends in Bath or Bristol. This time, however, we went directly to Mimi's.

Even so, she was home by the time we arrived. I was flabbergasted when I saw her. She was lying in a cot bed, a frail, sick patient in a state of distress and, I believe, pain. She was trying to move from side to side. It was very disturbing. I put David to bed and sat with Mimi, talking about the journey, school, the state of the sea at the bottom of the garden. I made her tea that she couldn't drink and felt absolutely helpless. I told the night nurse that she could go home, but she refused. She said that I wouldn't be able to cope with Mimi on my own. David and I stayed until dawn on the Monday morning, when I had to get us both back to school.

Prior to the operation Mimi had slept in her bedroom and spent her days in the living-room. There were two comfortable armchairs, one by the fire and one in front of the window, and Mimi spent her time moving, with increasing difficulty, from one armchair to the other. She would just be settled with a cup of tea in one place, when she would want to move to the other one and would have to be helped across the room.

After the operation she could no longer get up and her bed was brought into the living-room.

I saw Mimi once more, a few weeks later. She was still lying in bed. I sat and talked to her of this and that. I had taken a photograph from her window several years previously, of a spectacularly beautiful sunset. I had it framed and sent it to her. Now I sat with the picture and reminded her of how I had taken it, rushing outside and running down the garden barefoot, Mimi shouting that I was going to miss it. I felt that her mind was still working, even if she could no longer express herself.

In December 1991, Mimi died.

It was only two months since Norman's death. We never did

have that talk. I was sad that I had never had the courage to speak openly to Mimi. I had known for a long time that there were things in her past that were agitating her greatly and I had assumed that it concerned my mother and John, but I hadn't dared ask. I also knew, without knowing why or how, that I agitated her beyond reason and always had done. But even as she was lying helpless in bed, I was still too frightened of her to ask. Now she had gone and I would never know Mimi's truth.

I went with Cynthia to Mimi's funeral. When I realised that Mimi was terminally ill, I had tracked Cynthia down to where she was then living, on the Isle of Man. I thought she had a right to know and I gave her Mimi's phone number, and Cynthia did speak to Mimi, shortly before she died. We took the train to London and stayed in Julian's flat overnight, leaving early the next morning for the journey to Poole.

Most of the family were already in the house by the time we got there, but the door was opened by complete strangers, who told us where to put our coats and where the bathroom was. I was astounded. Who were these people?

It turned out that they were accompanying Yoko and Sean, both of whom we now met for the first time. Sean was a handsome and charming seventeen-year-old. He was immaculately turned out and I complimented him on his beautiful coat. He said that Yoko had brought him via Savile Row, in order to buy him smart clothes, wanting him to look his best. I chatted to him, both in the house and at the hotel where we all went after the service. I told him that John would have been so proud of him. I was sorry that Julian hadn't been able to come. He'd had a relationship with Mimi and stayed with her in Poole, and it would have been wonderful to have both of John's sons with us.

Cynthia approached Yoko in the kitchen and explained to her that John had bought the house in Poole, in the mid 1960s, not only for Mimi as her home, but also as a holiday retreat for the whole family. She suggested that Yoko give us the house, as that was what John had intended. Yoko listened and then, without a word, walked away. In fact, unknown to us, the house had already been sold by Apple's lawyers. The house that John had bought was to be knocked down and a new one erected in its place.

I asked Yoko, that day, why she had been so unhappy about our phone calls to John. She replied that she was 'only protecting John'. I replied, 'What do you mean? From his sisters?' She looked at me, then looked down and replied, 'Well, I didn't know.'

We arrived at the crematorium, to find a wonderful display of flowers, including an array of white blooms from Paul. Seeing Mimi's nurses there, I asked which one of them had been with her when she died. I had so much wanted to be there with her myself. I approached the nurse and we went to the flower garden. I asked her how Mimi had died and had she said anything. Initially, she didn't want to tell me. She said that I wouldn't want to know. She then said that, after all the fighting for life, Mimi's final words had been, 'I'm terrified of dying. I've been so wicked.'

We went straight into the service to join the others and I stood by Yoko. She squeezed my hand for comfort as I cried.

I was crying for so many people.

56: *Moving On*

After many years on my own, bringing up my children, I met Roger Keys, early in 1991 and it wasn't long before we took the decision to move in together. By then Nicolas and Sara were at university, so Roger came to live with me and David, who was twelve.

Since 1986 I had been working part-time with adolescents who suffered problems at school and had been excluded, often more than once. There was, at that time, a growing culture of exclusion, both educationally and socially, for reasons which included misbehaviour, disruption, emotional disturbance and challenging family backgrounds. And, from the top down, no one quite knew what to do with the excluded children.

Twenty years on, it is an extremely well-established educational area, known as EBD (emotional and behavioural difficulties). But at that time there were no official labels, just a lot of 'problem' adolescents.

I went back to study for an MA in Education, focusing on social psychology, in order to understand my job better, after which I increased my hours to full time. I ended up working on my own with some of the most damaged children in Chester, in the heart of a vast estate. Damaged often meant ignored, by family, teachers, 'the system'. Later, I was to add to this by becoming a psychotherapist. Along with all the theory, I drew on my personal life experience in order to execute my job to the very best of my ability.

I understood the anxieties of the teenagers and their parents. No one asked them questions, no one listened to them, very few cared about them. Behind closed doors, decisions were being made daily about their lives that they knew nothing about. I took it upon myself to fight for them, to open the doors to which they had no access, to plead their case, be it in school, in education meetings or in court. I developed a reputation at work for not letting go, if I thought something could and should be done. I was determined that these vulnerable young members of society should have a voice and therefore a choice. If they were allowed to know what was going on, they could be a part of the process of change, instead of being victims subjected to the whims of authority and to the constant political change in the education and social systems.

It was both time-consuming and exhausting, but I really loved my work.

Roger and his business partner Peter owned a local garage. Peter's wife, Pam, had developed a mysterious illness, which, tragically, the hospital didn't diagnose until it was too late. Pam became increasingly sick and died of cancer in 1993. In the aftermath of Peter's burn-out and exhaustion, Roger and Peter decided to let the business go.

Roger and I had been talking for some time about going to India, and we thought that now might be the time. We volunteered to work for Save the Children, as a teacher and an engineer, and subsequently received a phone call from the new director in India, Roy Trivedi. He said to call him when we got to New Delhi.

Apart from Save the Children, we had another connection in India. I had been studying yoga with an Indian teacher for years and she had many friends in the subcontinent. She invited one of them to our home and he said that we would be welcome on their ashram and that there was plenty of work for us to do. All in all, we had many places to go and projects in which we could be involved once we got there. We were very fortunate.

David came with us. He wasn't the most enthusiastic student in school, and my boss, a senior educational psychologist, advised me that the trip would give him time to grow up. He could go to college on our return. This is exactly what happened. I was conscientious enough to take Maths and English textbooks along with us, but I'm afraid that, by common consent, we abandoned them very quickly.

We went out to India in November 1993 and stayed for a year, becoming involved in three charity projects based in schools and an orphanage. As we were entirely self-funding, our money ran out faster than we had thought. I had left my car with Nicolas, my eldest son, to use until we returned, but I phoned him and asked him to sell it and send us the money.

We returned to Chester in November 1994, sad to have left the wonder that is India, but full of the most fantastic memories.

We carried on working for our adopted projects after our return, talking to Ladies' Circles and Round Tables, and relying on the continuing generosity of our friends.

Before our trip I had been on a tour of all the schools in the area and left collection buckets. I invited anyone who was interested to put money in the buckets, 'for India'. Some schools ran raffles and cake-stalls. Everyone we spoke to wanted to help. The money went to buy school uniforms for some of the poorest children in India. On our return, I went back to the schools and left beautiful scarves for the teachers as a thank you from the Indian children. For our friends, who arranged and took part in sponsored walks, even while we were still in India, we brought home white silk scarves, blessed by the Dalai Lama.

On our return we found a house to rent in the middle of Chester and enrolled David into the College of Further Education. I went back to work with my troubled teenagers and Roger went to work with some friends, who had their own garage.

57: *The House*

Soon after our return, on a visit to my family in London, I saw my cousin David, who told me that Liverpool Council had been in touch with him, demanding council tax for Norman's house, almost four years after his death. The Council obviously thought that the house had belonged to Norman and had passed to David. They wanted the previous four years' tax, in arrears. As it was a final tax demand, they would take him to court if it wasn't paid in full, immediately. As none of us had been near the house, nor heard from Yoko about what she was doing with it, this was a shock to David. I promised to find out what I could.

I went to Liverpool at the first opportunity. I was nervous about going to the house after so long. I turned into the road slowly and drove down the hill, past the familiar pristine houses with their well-kept gardens. Then I saw the house. The front garden was like a rubbish tip, overgrown and clogged by weeds. The paint was peeling from the windows and the whole place looked derelict. I parked the car in the driveway and climbed over the side wall. The back garden was in a similar state and weeds had taken over the patio. I couldn't see through the windows as they were covered from the inside with either blinds or curtains.

I'm not sure what I'd expected to find. After Norman's death I had blanked the house from my mind. I knew that it would not, after all, come to me and Jackie, and that, along with Mimi's house, it belonged to Yoko. And I had felt too depressed about Norman's death to put up a fight. Now here it was, ignored and run-down. I left, feeling bewildered.

I returned a week later and this time I went to see the next-door neighbour. We had been friendly when Allen and I had lived there with the children back in 1979–80. He welcomed me and asked what was happening to the house. It had remained empty since Norman's death and the rapid house clearance. The neighbour had known that John had bought the house principally for Jackie and me, as Norman had made no secret of it. So, were we moving back in, and why had we been absent for so long?

Apparently they had tried to find out who was responsible for the house themselves two years back, when the wayward growth of the tree in the front garden had begun to interfere with the neighbouring telephone and cable systems, but to no avail. They eventually had to call out British Telecom to cut down the tree, and even BT couldn't trace ownership.

I told him that the house belonged to John's estate, and that therefore it now belonged to Yoko, and that we had no inkling of how she had disposed of it. That afternoon, I visited about five of the neighbours. The people who lived in the house opposite suggested I go to Strawberry Field, the Salvation Army Childrens' Centre made famous by John's song. I did, and discovered that the house had been handed over to the Salvation Army.

This was later confirmed by the Salvation Army colonel in London. In a letter he advised me that 'the house was gifted to the Salvation Army in the United Kingdom from the estate of John Lennon in the United States . . . transferred on 2nd November 1993 . . . without any restrictive covenants being placed on the premises.' He went on to say that the derelict state of the property was due 'to the inordinate delay' in the transfer. The future use of the premises was 'under active consideration and it is anticipated that it will be occupied in the not too distant future.' In fact, a retired Salvation Army officer was soon living rent-free in the house.

I decided that I needed to speak with Yoko and at least hear why she had given the house away. My cousin Michael, who was in touch with Yoko, talked to her and she agreed that I could call.

The phone call was a disaster. Yoko asked me what I wanted and I explained the situation concerning the house as well as I could. I told her that John had bought the house for Jackie and me, in recognition of the fact that we had lost both parents. Yoko's immediate response was 'You hardly knew John. You hardly ever met him.'

I was astounded. Was this the same phone in the same New York home where I had been talking to John twenty years previously? She clearly hadn't been listening at the time. Had she done so, she would have known how untrue that was.

We ended up shouting at each other, achieving little. I took a deep breath and returned to the point of the call, that John truly intended the house for us, his sisters. Yoko asked me for proof. I was close to tears and angry. I said that John had written both to me and to Mater, mentioning that the house was for Jackie and me. She asked for the letters. But I didn't have them. I had burned mine when we moved house, and at that time I had no idea what had happened to Mater's. Eventually, we agreed that we were both too angry to get anywhere and that I would phone her again the following week, when we had both had time to think more calmly and clearly about the house.

Before the week was out, however, my cousin Michael told me that he'd had a call from New York. I was never to darken Yoko's phone again. The return call, any call, was off. It seemed that there was nothing more I could do.

58: *Back to India*

We had maintained close contact with the projects in India, and we wanted to return and see what progress had been made and where we could go from there. We decided to go back for at least another year, and possibly two.

By the time we left, in February 1996, David was nearly seventeen. He moved into a shared house in Chester.

We visited each of the projects, starting with the Gandhi Ashram for girls, in the Himalayas, where Roger set about refurbishing the essential gardening tools and the supporting pillars of the main room, while I taught the girls English, art and yoga.

The very way of life in the ashram extolled the virtues of family life, of hard work, and of undiminished belief in the Hindu gods, who transmute into every creature and being in the universe. The girls sang to us at every opportunity and, of course, wanted us to sing to them in return. We sang all the songs we could recall, from 'Greensleeves' to 'Michael Row the Boat Ashore'.

Then I had an inspiration. Let's do 'Imagine'. Not only would they soon be able to sing it with us and for us, but the meaning was so right. These girls had no material possessions, but they had everything. They understood life in a way that we in the West never could.

We came unstuck straight away, with the words. We knew the tune, but the words wouldn't come. So by five the next morning we were waiting for the first bus to the nearest town with a telephone. Almora was forty miles away, but the journey was so stunning that it was worth the trip. We went to a telephone office and called a friend, Margaret, back in Chester. 'What are the words to 'Imagine?'

'What?' she shouted down the phone. 'I don't know. You should know.' We laughed a phone bill of ten pounds and eventually she promised to send us the words that day.

Later she told us she'd had to slow the song down over and over to get the lyrics. We received them at the ashram about a fortnight later. The girls loved the song and learned it and are probably still singing it, with dance movements too.

We then returned to the school for the children of temple prostitutes in Andhra Pradesh, Central South India, where the director asked me to write a report for Oxfam detailing the land available for sale in the area. Oxfam would then buy the land and sell it back at the lowest price to the local people, turning them from tenants to landowners overnight. It was a wonderful scheme, which gave the farming community a power over their lives that we take completely for granted.

It took three months to gather all the information and to get it into order. The temperature was regularly 50 degrees centigrade, and we had to choose whether to sleep outside and be eaten alive by huge mosquitoes, or in the huts with lizards racing round the mud walls all night, occasionally dropping right on our heads, and rats' tails hanging down through the bamboo ceiling. It was a close call, but as this was also King Cobra country, and anyone sleeping outside was in danger of a killer snake bite, we mostly opted to swelter inside with the lizards and rats.

Having finished the details of the report, I wondered how to soften it. It seemed like a catalogue of hectares, landlords, panchyats (village councils), crops and numbers of villagers, and I wanted to end it with words as opposed to digits. Then I realised I had the solution. I had the words to John's 'Imagine'.

Perfect. So, at the end of the lengthy report, which had now been typed up and bound and looked like a truly official document, I wrote out the song by hand, with John's name underneath.

The report was going to Norway and London, where they would of course recognise 'Imagine'. But in that part of India they had never heard of the Beatles. Just before the report was due to go, I was called to the main office. They liked the report and hoped it would be successful, but 'What is this here? Who is this John Lennon?' They pronounced it 'Yon Lunoon'.

I replied, 'He's a minor western poet. Please leave it there.'

We then went down to Kerala, to our third project, a Catholic orphanage for girls run by a lovely Swiss couple. They needed to go back to Switzerland to talk to their sponsors and arrange for more money. Could we possibly go and stay in their beautiful flat in the orphanage so that they could go together? Could we? Wow! We stayed there for two months, assisting the fantastic Indian staff. We played with the children, took them to school in crocodile lines, collected them, swam with them in the river and washed mounds of school uniforms, rubbing the clothes with plant soap and laying them out on the hot rocks to dry. We took the children to hospital for immunisation and check-ups and attended mass with them twice weekly. We ate the hottest food on the planet, all heavily laced with lime pickle, while feeding the younger children by hand. Heaven.

After Kerala we had made plans to go to the Himalayas to do some walking, as we had done on the last trip to India. We had already booked our train seats back to New Delhi, a three-day journey through the heartland of India, when I received a letter from Jackie. My sister was in a dark place.

We arrived back in Delhi and I phoned her. She was in a bad depression. The mountains would have to wait. We rearranged the return flights and went home.

We arrived back in Chester in October, and while Roger set about finding work and somewhere for us to live, I went straight to London.

I found Jackie in a terrible way. I had no answers, other than to be there with her. We talked a little, ate a little, sat a little and slept a lot.

I looked around her flat. Not one photograph of Mummy, of John, of me, and none of Jackie. She didn't belong to anyone. Just like me. Just like John. She came from nowhere, wandering aimlessly, with no grip on reality. Lost.

I had brought a bag full of photographs. Photographs of Mummy, the few that we all have, and of John, Jackie and me. Stan had sent them to all the family some years before. Copies of the ones I had sent to John in 1975.

We spent the next few weeks talking, crying and putting photographs on walls. Getting there.

59: *Nanny*

I returned north after three months. I was fifty in March that year, 1997. We had found a cottage and it was in a raw state, but we decided to have my fiftieth birthday party there anyway. Friends and family arrived from all over the country to celebrate with us. After the party, we left and didn't move in until it was fit to live in.

During both our trips to India. I had been afraid that Nanny would die. I was relieved when we arrived back from the first trip and she was still there, as tart as ever, ready with her acid remarks and endless tea.

When we went away for the second time, however, I was fully aware that she was weaker than before. Thankfully, when I returned north after my stay with Jackie, she was still sitting in her high-backed Parker-Knoll armchair, gazing through the large bay window into the giant willow tree and making her pronouncements.

I could see that she was more frail. Michael, her son, came as often as he could to see her, and kept her large garden in good order, and I made a conscious decision to spend as much time with her as I could.

I had resumed my work with my lovely disorientated adolescents, but at least twice a week, and sometimes more, I turned my car east instead of south at home time and went to Rock Ferry. I went so often that Nanny began to expect me, and I felt guilty if I hadn't been for a week.

During the harsh winter months, which she hated, I talked her through her distress at the bareness of the willow tree and we counted the weeks until there would be the slightest sign of a bud, bringing new life. We had been doing this for many winters now. We relished the spring and the unfolding leaves and the summer with the lovely droop of the branches. I sat with her late into the summer evenings, drinking tea, with Nanny stroking her cat Blackie, and my dog Annie, a Newfoundland, lying across our feet. During those months Nanny sat in her chair, reminiscing, telling me all the family stories I had wanted to know. But she wasn't telling me. She was talking to the universe, gazing at the sky. She talked and dozed and I listened and dozed.

Before I left, if it was late, I would walk behind her up the long wide stairs, ever more slowly, and wait until she was in bed. I would bring her a final cup of tea, knowing that she would be rising at four or five in the morning to start the new day. I would go downstairs, shouting 'Goodnight, Nanny. Sleep well. God Bless' all the way until I got no response and I knew that she was falling asleep. I drove all the way home, about forty miles, wondering how soon I could get back to see her.

If I had to leave early, Nanny would wave me off at the gate, wearing her dressing-gown. I always felt sad at leaving her behind and worried about whether she would be all right, knowing at the same time that she would.

Nanny was adamant that she would stay in her own home. She would brook no argument, and as long as she was physically well enough to cope, with a home help, then we all felt that her wishes should prevail.

Her acid tongue never failed to upset me, right to the end, but I gradually learned to become indifferent to its effect. I took some comfort from the fact that I hadn't been selected for special treatment, it was directed at anyone in her path. From the time Nanny had assumed real power over her own life, probably the moment when she threw Pop out of her home, the pattern was set. Many of us had been thrown out of that house: John, me, Jackie, Stanley and even Michael. We walked out, never to return, until the next time. The list may have even included her sisters.

No matter, Nanny was the aunt, it turned out, with whom I chose to spend the most time. The obvious reason was that she lived longer than her sisters. By spending time with Nanny, I was as near to my mother as I could be. Her sister, with the red hair. The wrong red, but red.

By the time she was in her eighties I had grown to love her, in a strange way, and I knew that she looked forward to my visits. She started talking as soon as I got there, and I sometimes suspected that she was still talking to the night sky long after I had left to go home.

Now, towards the end, she was talking about things that she hadn't disclosed before. She was probably still working things out for herself. She was, however inadvertently, passing on what may have been secrets until then. Things that maybe Nanny didn't want to take with her. I asked her if she talked to Michael about such past events, and she said no, that he wasn't interested.

She told me about Mimi and her plans to go to New Zealand and 'marry George'. This mystery, which I was only to clear up long after Nanny's death, preoccupied us both on several of the evenings we shared.

She told me stories of how and why she and her sisters had all been born in different houses, how they spent their childhood, who was the favourite child of their parents and how it had affected them. How Pop and Mimi were always at war and that the only time they were united was in 'getting John from your mother'.

She said that Jackie and I would have had a different life if 'your mother had lived'. Stating the obvious, I know, but to me it meant a lot. It was a near apology for our spurious status within the family. Only Mater had acknowledged this before, not long before she died. But, even then, Nanny couldn't resist another 'but you don't belong to this family'. I held my tongue.

A week or two later, I sat with Nanny in her bedroom late one evening and we had tea on the tray, by the gas fire. This room also looked out on the willow tree, right into its uppermost branches. It was winter again and we talked about how bare it was, how cold the weather, how dark the afternoons. I decided to take a photograph and, as the camera flashed, Nanny shouted, 'Did you see that? Did you see the lightning?' I laughed and told her I had taken a picture.

Suddenly, Nanny said, 'When is God coming for me?'

'When he's ready, Nanny.'

'Well, I'm ready now. Where *is* he?'

Days later she moved into hospital, and she died in December, peacefully. She was 85. The last of the Stanley sisters.

60: *Package for Yoko*

I had been thinking about the house in Liverpool. I realised that for me it had become a symbol of John's recognition of me and Jackie as our mother's children. It was a space awarded to us, by John, as his sisters. It was a physical space, given with spiritual awareness of our family relationship.

After one visit to Nanny, during those last weeks, Michael and I had talked in the car park. We had been talking about Nanny's house and I had then mentioned the house in Liverpool. He shouted, 'Can't you just forget about that house!' No, I said, I couldn't.

He had no idea of the importance of that house. It wasn't the money. It was the concept. It was about acceptance, not rejection, big brother looking after small sisters. Our family. The idea of the house was like an umbilical cord. It ran back to Mummy, through John. It was about love.

I explained to Michael that the house was the only thing that Jackie and I had. Everything else had passed us by. He asked who I thought was to blame for the fact that Jackie and I had been neglected when it came to the family? I replied 'Mimi', and he said that I was right. He was telling me nothing new. Everyone knew it, but who defended us?

In the New Year of 1998 I started thinking about how to resolve the matter of the house, for good. I wanted to deal with it and put it away. Michael had a point. I had to get over it and let go. But I couldn't give up without a fight. Although the house had been given away I felt that Jackie and I should have been given its value, as an alternative. I decided to approach Yoko one more time.

I rang Cynthia, and she wrote me a letter of support, confirming that she and John had discussed our well-being and intended the house for me and Jackie, as a nest-egg, after our father's death.

I also rang my cousin Stan. He wrote a letter, confirming that he had been present when John said the house was for Jackie and me. Stan also gave me a copy of another letter, one written by John to Stan's mother, Mater. In this letter, written in July 1975, John was absolutely clear about his intention concerning the house. He said: 'As for Norman . . . he rang saying he would like to come and see me . . . I always thought of the house he's in as my contribution towards looking after Julia and Jackie. So I find it strange to hear that they were seldom in the place . . . and that Norman is living there alone . . . I would prefer the girls to use it.'

In addition I wrote a long letter of my own to Yoko explaining the history of the house. I sent it to her in a package containing copies of the other letters, plus a copy of the letter her lawyers had sent Uncle Norman in 1986 and copies of the correspondence from the Salvation Army. I felt that she had to know why the house was there. The package was the 'proof' that she had demanded during our phone call. I sent it on 24 February, by registered post, and asked her to write or phone.

Naïvely, I started to look for the postman after the first ten days and expected to hear Yoko on my answering machine. Nothing. The silence continued for a month, and I thought that the package might have gone astray.

I sent an identical set of copies on 6 April. And waited again. I sent the third and final set of copies on 13 May. I had realised by now, of course, that I was hoping for a response, rather than expecting one. This time I said that I was disappointed by the lack of response and that the matter was very important to me and to Jackie, and asked her once more to get in touch.

I came home from work late one evening very shortly after

that third package had been posted, and Roger said that Yoko's lawyer had telephoned from New York and would be ringing back. The lawyer told me that the house was Yoko's to do with as she pleased, and that she had done just that. If, however, Jackie and I needed help, Yoko might be prepared to help us out. I replied that I wasn't asking Yoko for her money. I just wanted the value of the house, as it was a symbol. I heard nothing more.

That was the end of the matter. Having done all I could, I felt it really was time to let it go. Knowing that the house had been intended for us, and that John had wanted to look after us – and having at last been able to demonstrate it was what mattered most.

Jackie and I are still on the high road to recovery, as many people are from some part of their lives. We are learning to accept and absorb the history of years gone by and to weave the threads into our present lives, filling gaps and enhancing the frame. We have grown in strength and resolve and we continue to expand into new horizons from the basis of mother-love that Julia gave us. We are adventurers who meditate. My partner, Roger, and I have seen some of the wonders of the world, and I have three beautiful children, who have been an endless source of joy. Jackie also has a son who has made her very proud.

I have my links with John too, which bring me real pleasure. Most recently I have become a director of the Cavern Club in Liverpool. It is not only the site of John's early success and the heady excitement of the Beatles' birth, but it also gives me a wonderful link into the new, energetic and effervescent Liverpool scene.

Past into Present into Future.

Postscript

I still feel John's presence in Liverpool, because it is still there. I feel the presence of my mother and father too. Perhaps that's why ultimately, I have not been able to tear myself away from the area, as many of the family have done. I need to walk those streets, to see those houses, to meet those people. I need to have the beautiful Welsh mountains and the sea within easy reach, where I can touch my reality. I often walk my childhood walk, from Woolton to Allerton, along Blackgates Lane and wander across the golf course where John and I collected stray balls all those years ago, dragging my past into my present.

Liverpool has become my umbilical cord.

I have always talked about Mummy with my children, she has always been a reality in our lives. I told them about what she said and did, how she looked, what she wore, how she laughed and how we played 'I spy with my big brown eye' in bed in the mornings. I am now Mummy and I have the big brown eye. They all know how she would have loved them. Once I had children of my own, it was an absolute release for me to be able to involve Mummy in our lives openly. Just to be able to talk about her, with great sadness and with great love. I wanted them to know and love her, as far as was possible.

Not attending her funeral has had the most profound and inexplicable consequences for me and Jackie. We had no chance to say goodbye, to acknowledge what everyone else knew but we didn't – that we had lost her. Because of this the sense of loss has stayed with us, powerful and tangible. People had invested so much energy in denying the truth that when it was eventually fully revealed to me, it felt unreal.

Some years ago my cousin David mentioned 'your mother's funeral'. So, there had been a funeral. It was true. My mother had really gone. Really. Unreally.

It was a shock. I told him that I had no idea that he had been to her funeral. David, who was only ten at the time and hardly knew her, was at my mother's funeral, when I couldn't be. David is not demonstrative, but he hugged me.

Jackie and I both tried to find our mother's grave, back in our teenage years. We thought about it a lot and each of us made separate, desperate journeys to try to understand. We were still living in a world where we believed we might meet her in the street. Her death just wasn't real. As neither of us understood that she wasn't listed as Julia Dykins, the name she'd taken when she moved in with our father, as we had grown up believing, we never found her grave. My daughter found it later, on her own journey, and she told me that it was listed under Mummy's married name. Julia Lennon. It had never occurred to us.

Jackie was fifty in October 1999. Her birthday usually falls at half-term, and I have always tried to spend it with her, wherever we've happened to be at the time. That year, however, my old dog died on Jackie's birthday. So I couldn't go to London, where Jackie was living. I decided that I was going to go to Liverpool, to the cemetery. I went there two days later, determined not to leave until I had found my mother's grave.

It was pouring with rain, and after walking mindlessly around the lines of memorial stones I had to ask in the office for help. They took me to the far end of the cemetery, where we found it. There was no headstone, but someone had put a stone cat there as a marker.

I don't think that anyone from my mother's family, apart from my eldest cousin Stan, who I knew had actually visited this neglected space since the funeral, for all kinds of reasons. I sat on the ground next to the cat and wept. Then I pulled my coat over my head and wrote Jackie a letter of love from Mummy and me.

A few days later I received a warm and loving reply from Jackie, which touched my heart.

Since that day I have been back, and Jackie and I have decided to commemorate our mother's grave in some way, from our father Bobby and from both of us and John. And Victoria/Ingrid, if she would like. All our mother's children.

My mother was a beautiful, vibrant and loving woman. And she was wronged.

'They've taken my son. They've taken him from me. They won't let me have him. I have to get him back.' My mother's heartbroken words.

She has him now.

Index